Teaching and Monitoring Education

TEACHING AND MONITORING EDUCATION

B.M. SHARMA

AKANSHA PUBLISHING HOUSE
NEW DELHI-110059 (INDIA)

AKANSHA PUBLISHING HOUSE
R 37-B, Vani Vihar, Uttam Nagar
New Delhi-110059
Email: ektabooks@yahoo.com
Ph. : 9212065579 / 9811582579

Showroom
4649/21B, Ansari Road
Darya Ganj
New Delhi - 110 002

Teaching and Monitoring Education

First Edition 2004

ISBN 81–87606–68-1

[The responsibility for the facts stated, conclusions reached etc. is entirely that of the Author. The publisher is not responsible for them, whatsoever.]

PRINTED IN INDIA

Published by M.P. Misra for Akansha Publishing House, New Delhi and Printed at Tarun Offset Press, Delhi.

Preface

In many countries there is a growing sense that education is the key to the future, and that the challenges and jobs of tomorrow will require an education of better quality than that which most students receive today. Increasingly, educational quality and relevance are defined by reference to students learning outcomes.

The current widespread concern for educational quality and relevance has complex origins and many nuances depending on the particular experiences of individual countries over the past quarter of a century. It has taken the form of a growing interest among national policy-makers in the monitoring, measurement and evaluation of educational processes and outcomes.

Teachers have a pivot role in making education effective. Effective teachers lead communities and nations in their march towards better and higher quality of life. To improve the quality of education teachers have to adopt new and innovative teaching strategies.

The present book provides an in-depth analysis of the effective teaching strategies. The importance of monitoring and evaluation of education in developing educational quality and relevance is strongly emphasized. The work will be highly beneficial to all the concerned.

Editor

Contents

Preface *v*

1. Expanding Educational Opportunities 1
2. Teaching Strategies 72
3. Challenges of Teacher Development 111
4. Assessment, Monitoring and Evaluation of Education 144
5. Effective Education : Concerns of the Future 216

Index 307

1

Expanding Educational Opportunities

Whereas the Universal Declaration of Human Rights proclaims that 'Everyone has the right to education', that elementary and fundamental education shall be 'free' and that 'Elementary education shall be compulsory', the Declaration adopted by the World Conference on Education for All proclaims that 'Every person —child, youth and adult – shall be able to benefit from educational opportunities designed to meet their basic learning needs'.

The Universal Declaration of Human Rights does not mention 'learners' or 'learning needs', and the World Declaration on Education for All does not mention 'elementary', 'fundamental', 'free' or 'compulsory' education. The twin notions of 'elementary and fundamental education' have been overtaken by the notion of 'basic education', while at the same time there has been a shift of emphasis from 'education' to 'learning': from what society should supply, so to speak, i.e. education that is 'free', 'compulsory' and 'directed towards', to what members of society are said to demand. Historically, the changes occurred in three phases or stages.

In the first phase, lasting from the late 1940s up until the early 1960s, international concern over the provision of 'fundamental education' came to focus particularly on the eradication of illiteracy, while at the same time pressures built up for the expansion of elementary education, especially in the newly independent developing countries.

In the second phase, lasting from the mid-1960s up until the late 1970s, the focus on illiteracy broadened to encompass 'functional illiteracy', while at the same time a vast expansion of elementary education got under way.

In the third phase, lasting from the early 1980s up until the present, 'functional literacy' came to be regarded as a particular aspect of 'learning needs', while at the same time 'elementary education' came to be regarded as forming part of 'basic education' designed to meet 'basic learning needs'.

Fundamental Education

The term 'fundamental education' has largely gone out of use today, at least in international debate and discussion about education, but at the time when the Universal Declaration of Human Rights was drawn up, it was more in vogue. It was included in the Declaration specifically in order to recognize the right to education for illiterate adults and others who had not had the opportunity when they were young to receive a full elementary education.

The term first came into use internationally when it was adopted by the Preparatory Commission of UNESCO in 1946. This Commission, composed of representatives from the various countries involved in establishing UNESCO, was charged with drawing up a proposed plan of work for the

Organization to be submitted to UNESCO's first General Conference in November-December 1946. Among other things, the Commission's proposals included provision for work in the field of 'Fundamental Education', which was put forward as one of UNESCO's primary fields of interest. In the words of Julian Huxley, the Executive Secretary of the Preparatory Commission and UNESCO's first Director-General:

Where half the people of the world are denied the elementary freedom which consists in the ability to read and write, there lacks something of the basic unity and basic justice which the United Nations are pledged together to further. Fundamental Education is only part of the wider and fuller human understanding to which UNESCO is dedicated, but it is an essential part.

While the whole range of human activity provides the subject matter of fundamental education, each particular programme should give first attention to the most pressing needs and problems of the community concerned. The content, therefore, varies widely with circumstances; but in the long run it should include:

— Skills of thinking and communicating (reading and writing, speaking, listening and calculation);

— Vocational skills (such as agriculture and husbandry, building, weaving and other useful crafts, and simple technical and commercial skills necessary for economic progress);

— Domestic skills (such as the preparation of food and the care of children and of the sick);

— Skills used in self-expression in the arts and crafts;

— Education for health through personal and community hygiene;

— Knowledge and understanding of the physical environment and of natural processes (for example simple and practical science);

— Knowledge and understanding of the human environment (economic and social organization, law and government);

— Knowledge of other parts of the world and the people who live in them;

— The development of qualities to fit men to live in the modern world, such as personal judgment and initiative, freedom from fear and superstition. sympathy and understanding for different points of view;

— Spiritual and moral development; belief in ethical ideals, and the habit of acting upon them; with the duty to examine traditional standards of behaviour and to modify them to suit new conditions.

The very difficulty of the task of fundamental education brings with it a sense of urgency. If the measures taken are to be effective, they must produce widespread and lasting results. Full use should be made of all possible educational agencies, and the latest techniques for the teaching of adults should be tried.

Corresponding to the diverse human needs, several forms of activity have been developed in fundamental education programmes: adult literacy campaigns, agricultural and health training and extension services, cooperatives, organizing of community groups for cultural ends. An expanded and improved primary schooling can provide one firm institutional basis for fundamental education: community centres, with library and museum techniques, may play a similar part. All these activities require teaching methods which include but go beyond the direct teacher-pupil relationship – hence the importance of the media of mass communications: the printed word, the film and the radio.

Fundamental education is concerned with the community as a whole, and should lead to social action. The methods must therefore be chosen with this end in view: to help people to help themselves.

There was some uncertainty at that time over what exactly was meant by 'fundamental education', especially as this term did not correspond to any of the terms then in use in most countries to describe a particular level or part of their education systems, but there was general agreement that it meant an education that would provide for the acquisition of literacy and the other essential skills, knowledge and values needed for full participation in society. It was preferred to other cognate terms which were circulating then, such as 'Mass Education', 'Popular Education' and 'Basic Education'. 'Mass Education' for example, was specifically rejected because it 'evoked unpleasing connotations of educational methods which paid insufficient attention to individual differences'.

The content at least of 'fundamental education' was conceived not very differently from that of 'basic education' half a century later, the main differences being the emphasis of 'fundamental education' on the 'pressing needs and problems of the community', and that of 'basic education' on preparation for 'lifelong learning'. The latter notion was not current in the 1940s. 'Fundamental education' was regarded as a kind of 'minimum' or 'basic amount' of education that each community or society needed to provide for everyone; the question of access to, or preparation for education beyond this 'minimum' was mostly left to one side.

From an operational standpoint, in terms of 'means and methods' of implementation, 'fundamental education' was broadly interpreted as community education (adult literacy programmes, agricultural and health education, and so on). In some formulations of the community education approach, it was suggested that primary schooling could serve as 'one firm institutional basis for fundamental education', along with community centres. This later developed into the idea of 'community education centres' providing primary schooling as well as adult literacy and other non-formal adult education programmes.

At that time, some experience of the community education approach had been accumulated in certain countries such as Brazil, India and Mexico, but there was little real understanding internationally of how to go about implementing this approach on a scale that could seriously respond to the 'fundamental education' needs of the vast rural populations of Africa, Asia and Latin America which had never experienced any formal education.

At the grassroots level, the approach presupposed a certain degree of community initiative and responsibility, as well as the capacity of communities to mobilize the necessary material and human resources for education, whether for formal education such as primary schools, or for non-formal education such as agricultural extension and health education. In much of Africa and Asia in the 1940s and 1950s, and also to a large extent in Latin America, significant advances in the provision of 'fundamental education' at the community level could hardly be made without the injection of substantial financial and/or material and human resources from outside the community, and this was not a major priority for most governments at that time.

Still, those who drew up the Universal Declaration of Human Rights were arguably less concerned with the precise form that 'fundamental education' should take than with the problem it was intended to address, namely, the millions of illiterate adults and others in the world who had not previously had an opportunity for modern education, whether formal or non-formal. How this problem could best be tackled was essentially a practical and not a theoretical matter: it would depend on the efforts undertaken – and the experience thus gained – by individual countries, whatever the label these efforts went under.

The notion of 'fundamental education' remained current internationally for only a decade or so, while its concern with literacy was absorbed into an expanded concept of 'adult education'. At first, 'fundamental education' and 'adult education' were regarded as two different aspects of 'popular education'. In the majority of countries then Member States of UNESCO, 'adult education' was an older and more well-established concept than 'fundamental education', but it was mainly concerned with the learning needs of adults who had already received an elementary education and wanted 'further' or 'continuing' education.

Thus, at the first International Conference on Adult Education it was agreed that illiteracy should be treated 'as part of the fundamental education field, closely related to but distinguishable from adult education'. However, this narrow interpretation of 'adult education' could hardly be sustained in those parts of the world where a majority of adults were illiterate. Thus, in the following years, the international focus of adult education gradually widened to include literacy and the learning needs of adults who had not previously received any formal education. As a result, little room was left for a separate concept of 'fundamental education'.

In 1960 the Second International Conference on Adult Education, held in Montreal, Canada, proposed that regional seminars be organized for countries in Latin America, Asia and Africa 'having common problems in regard to Adult Education in general, and illiteracy in particular'. In 1972 the Third International Conference on Adult Education, which was convened in Tokyo, Japan, went even further, declaring flatly that 'Literacy is a cornerstone of adult education'.

More than any other factor, the advent of a large number of countries to independence in the late 1950s and early 1960s was probably decisive in shifting international concern away from the notion of 'fundamental education', in its broad 'community education' sense, to what was coming to be considered as the key problem that 'fundamental education' (and 'adult education') needed to address: the eradication of illiteracy. Since literacy is quintessentially something that is gained (or not) by the learner, this shift was the earliest sign of that larger shift of emphasis from 'education' to 'learning' which eventually culminated, many years later, in international consensus on the priority of 'meeting basic learning needs'.

Pressures for international action to help eradicate illiteracy built up soon after the Universal Declaration of Human Rights was proclaimed. The United Nations was particularly concerned over the situation in colonial territories. In 1950, the General Assembly called upon UNESCO 'to communicate... full information on measures for suppressing illiteracy which could be applied with satisfactory results in Non-Self-Governing Territories, and to communicate annually to the United Nations an account of these measures'. In the course of the 1950s, illiteracy acquired preeminent status among indicators of the denial of the right to education.

By the early 1960s, its eradication had become a national priority in probably a majority of the newly independent and other developing countries. The challenge was to translate this priority into effective action. At that time, international understanding of the various factors that needed to be taken into account in devising effective approaches to the promotion of literacy was still limited.

Certain countries had carried out large-scale literacy campaigns before the Second World War, and there had been community education campaigns in a number of colonial territories after the war, but aside from these, a comprehensive body of international experience that could be drawn upon simply did not exist.

A critical uncertainty was whether the ease of acquiring literacy varied from one language to another. In order to throw some light on this question, UNESCO's 'fundamental education' programme had included, among other activities, an international study of the teaching of reading and writing, the conclusions of which greatly influenced subsequent international action for the promotion of literacy. Two conclusions in particular were especially influential:

(1) that 'the basic attitudes and skills involved in reading are the same in all languages', and

(2) that the only meaningful standard of literacy is a functional one.

The first of these conclusions helped to pave the way for increased international cooperation in promoting literacy, although the study's concentration on reading and writing in the mother tongue left a significant gap that was not fully appreciated at the time: literacy in a second language. This has since come to be recognized as a key problem in much of Africa and in many parts of Latin America and Asia, where, in the absence of sufficient learning materials in the mother tongue, literacy in a second language is often the only literacy that learners can realistically aspire to.

The second conclusion eventually led to the adoption, in the following decade, of a 'functional literacy' approach in the design of literacy programmes and projects. It also called into question the continued usefulness of the then international standard definition of a 'literate' person as someone 'who can with understanding both read and write a short simple statement on his everyday life'.

Worldwide Illiteracy

The earliest statistical estimates of the worldwide extent of illiteracy were published by UNESCO in 1957. These estimates were based on an extensive review of national censuses and other surveys going back in some cases to the beginning of the century. The countries with the higher illiteracy rates in 1950 generally still had the highest such rates in 1990. An important finding of the comparative analysis of national censuses was the great variety of questions utilized in the questionnaires to identify persons who were either 'literate' or 'illiterate'.

Table 1
Percentage of illiterates in the population aged 15 years and over as reported in censuses in selected countries around 1950 and 1990

	1950			1990		
	MF	M	F	MF	M	F
Algeria	82	79	86	50	37	64
Argentina	14	12	15	4	4	4
Bolivia	68	58	77	20	12	28
Brazil	51	45	56	20	20	20
Chile	20	18	22	6	5	6
Ecuador	44	38	50	12	10	14
Egypt	80	69	91	56	43	69
El Salvador	61	56	65	26	23	29
Greece	26	12	39	5	2	7
Guatemala	71	66	76	36	28	43
India	81	71	92	48	36	61
Mexico	43	40	47	12	10	15
Paraguay	34	25	43	10	8	11
Philippines	40	36	44	6	7	6
Portugal	44	35	52	12	8	15
Puerto Rico	27	23	30	10	11	10
Romania	23	15	31	3	2	5
Spain	18	12	23	4	2	5
Thailand	48	31	64	7	4	9
Trinidad and Tobago	26	22	31	3	2	4
Turkey	68	52	83	21	10	32
Venezuela	48	43	53	10	9	11

In some countries, for example Italy, the question was simply whether the person could read, whereas in others (the majority) it was whether the person could both read and write. Some countries specified a level or standard of reading and/or writing, for example India, and Turkey. Canada carefully formulated its census instructions so as to allow for the special situation of blind persons. There still are differences between countries today in the questions utilized by national censuses to identify literacy/ illiteracy, but a comprehensive analysis of current international practices is lacking.

This early work by UNESCO on world literacy data contributed greatly to international appreciation of the sheer scale of the challenge to eradicate illiteracy. Taking 'ability to read and write' as the criterion of literacy, and after making as much allowance as possible for differences between countries in their census definitions, it emerged that in around half the countries in the world in 1950, half or more of the adult population (persons aged 15 years and over) were estimated to be illiterate.

The great majority of such countries were located in Africa and Asia. In Africa, only in Lesotho and Mauritius were more than half the adults estimated to be literate. In Asia, among the larger countries or territories, only in Hong Kong, Israel, Japan, Myanmar, Philippines, Sri Lanka and Thailand were more than half the adults estimated to be literate. In Latin America the situation was somewhat better with more than half the adult population estimated to be literate in Argentina, Chile, Colombia, Cuba, Ecuador, Mexico, Paraguay, Puerto Rico, Uruguay and Venezuela.

An important finding of the historical analysis was that the world's illiterate population appeared to be steadily increasing even as the illiteracy rate was decreasing, which broadly indicated that the expansion of educational opportunities was not keeping up with population growth. This phenomenon had been suspected at the time, but had not up to then been clearly demonstrated statistically at the global level, although it was known to be the case in certain countries.

In Brazil, for example, the 1950 census showed an illiterate population of 15.3 million persons aged 15 years old and over, amounting to 51 per cent of the total population in that age-group, whereas in the previous census (1940) the corresponding figures were 13.3 million and 56 per cent. Other countries with good historical census data where the same phenomenon could be observed included Egypt, India, Mexico, Portugal, Sri Lanka, Turkey and Venezuela. Looking forward, it would not be until the late 1980s that the world's illiterate population would eventually peak. Thus, for forty years after the Universal Declaration of Human Rights was proclaimed, the absolute number of persons in the world with no meaningful experience of the right to education was actually to increase.

Two general conclusions for educational policy were drawn from the findings above. The first was the need to step up national efforts to reach out to the increasing number of illiterate adults, and the second was the need to accelerate access to elementary education for the younger generation so as to 'cut off the problem at its base', as was stated at the time.

Many countries expanded their literacy activities in the 1960s. Internationally, two competing views emerged concerning the appropriate strategy. One view, based largely on the prewar experience of the former USSR, stressed the 'national campaign' approach. However, national political, economic, social and cultural circumstances varied so much that this type of approach could not easily be replicated.

In any case, critics charged that this approach too often resulted in people just acquiring a superficial level of literacy that could contribute little to the society's overall development. Putting 'the struggle against illiteracy' on a 'war footing', they argued, could not dispense with the need for a sound methodology based on a thorough understanding of what would induce illiterate persons to make the effort to learn to read and write.

Thus, there emerged by the mid-1960s the idea of the 'selective approach' closely linked to the notion of 'functional literacy'. People are not 'made' literate, proponents of this approach contended, but make themselves literate when they have the motivation and incentives to do so. In other words, they learn when literacy meets their 'learning needs', although this term was not widely used at the time.

Next, it was argued that in place of the 'national campaign', efforts to promote literacy should be focused intensively on organized sections of society where motivation for literacy is strongest and where opportunities exist for using education to raise the level of living and accelerate development. This was taken to mean that literacy programmes needed to be closely integrated with socioeconomic development programmes, while literacy instruction needed to be combined with the provision of relevant information and vocational training tailored to the learner's specific socioeconomic situation within the broader development context. The term 'work-oriented adult literacy training' was used at the time to describe this approach.

These ideas came to the fore internationally at the World Congress of Ministers of Education on the Eradication of Illiteracy held in Teheran in September 1965, and they provided the basic rationale for what was to become the largest ever internationally-sponsored programme specifically focused on eradicating adult illiteracy: the Experimental World Literacy Programme (EWLP) launched in 1966 by UNESCO and the United Nations Development Programme (UNDP).

World Literacy Programme

This programme was to be a watershed in international co-operation for the eradication of illiteracy. EWLP was 'experimental' in the sense that it embraced a number of national pilot projects aiming to try out the 'selective approach' focused on 'functional' literacy, and in particular to test and demonstrate literacy's economic and social 'returns'. The hopes and expectations originally associated with EWLP were high. The 1960s marked the United Nations' first 'Development Decade', and EWLP was widely regarded at the time as a breakthrough in international recognition of the role of education in development.

Among other things, EWLP was expected to provide valuable information on the relationship of literacy to social and economic development, produce a considerable impact on economic development in the countries where projects were to be conducted and prepare the way for an eventual World Campaign for the Eradication of Mass Illiteracy. Altogether, eleven countries participated directly in EWLP before the programme was phased out in the mid-1970s: Algeria, Ecuador, Ethiopia, Guinea, India, Iran, Madagascar, Mali, Sudan, the Syrian Arab Republic and the United Republic of Tanzania. A number of other countries adopted similar approaches to those of EWLP.

By virtue of its sheer size and complexity, as much as by the ideas associated with it, EWLP attracted worldwide interest. At the time of the programme's full operation, around 1971, a total of nearly a quarter of a million adults were enrolled in the various national EWLP projects, and a vast amount of original instructional materials were developed. In contributing directly to expanding the capabilities of large numbers of relatively poor people, EWLP was highly successful.

However, the ambitious hopes of achieving a methodological 'breakthrough' that could justify the launching of a World Campaign were never realized. The differences between the various projects in organization, target populations, pedagogical objectives and methods were more pronounced that the similarities, and a well-defined model 'work-oriented' adult literacy methodology that could be applied on a global scale never emerged.

Promoted mainly as a technical solution to problems of 'socioeconomic development' rather than simply as a transfer of resources to help implement a human right, EWLP was fated to disappoint almost as soon as it started. From the outset, due to the very nature of literacy work – compared, say, to the construction of a new road or power station – it was never really possible for EWLP to demonstrate the social and economic 'returns' that would satisfy orthodox investment criteria. Thus, the whole idea of a World Campaign to eradicate illiteracy fizzled out and has never since been revived.

The international discussion and debate over the purposes and means of promoting literacy that flourished in the aftermath of EWLP maintained a broad consensus in favour of the concept of 'functional literacy', but this concept became increasingly accepted as relevant to a wider range of activities than just work and employment. Moreover, notwithstanding the international interest surrounding EWLP, many countries continued to mount mass campaigns for the eradication of illiteracy throughout the 1970s, e.g Algeria, Brazil, Burma (now Myanmar), Cameroon, China, Colombia,

Ethiopia, Guatemala, Guinea, Indonesia, Jamaica, Mexico, Peru, Somalia, Thailand, United Republic of Tanzania and Zambia, among others. The success of many of these campaigns and the diversity of approaches followed, further challenged the idea of a single 'model' approach as originally envisaged by EWLP.

In the aftermath of EWLP, that the Brazilian educator Paulo Freire's ideas concerning literacy became influential internationally. For Freire, the process of acquiring literacy, i.e. learning to read and write, was necessarily accompanied by the learner's increasing consciousness of his/her existential situation and of the possibility of acting independently to change it, a process which he termed 'conscientization', and which today would more likely be called 'empowerment'. In that perspective, literacy programmes necessarily had a 'political', and not merely technical-pedagogic, dimension.

Freire's ideas were influential in opening the way to an appreciation of the many uses of literacy beyond those relating to work and employment which had been given so much emphasis in EWLP: uses ranging from the exercise of civil and political rights to the upbringing of children, from reading for pleasure and enjoyment to reading for self-instruction or spiritual enlightenment. Learning to read and write, many advocates urged, was a crucial step in the process of learning to learn. Thus, the notion of 'functional literacy' was gradually pointed towards a more inclusive concept, that of 'learning needs', under which literacy could be accommodated both on its own account and as a necessary condition for satisfying many other 'learning needs'.

By the mid-1980s, the idea of illiterate adults and others who lacked formal education having a 'right to learn' had entered international discussion and debate. The Fourth International Conference on Adult Education, for example, felt moved to declare that 'recognition of the right to learn is now more than ever a major challenge for humanity'. At this time, elementary education, whether formal or non-formal, was increasingly coming to be regarded as a process that should be designed to meet 'basic learning needs'.

Throughout the 1970s and 1980s the earliest decades for which UNESCO has continuous time series estimates – illiteracy rates in the world's less developed regions steadily declined. This trend continued into the 1990s. In a growing number of countries, illiteracy as such, at least by the traditional measure of being unable to read and write a short simple statement about one's everyday life, was no longer the characteristic educational condition of the majority of the adult population. Thus, whereas half the countries in the world had estimated adult illiteracy rates of over 50 per cent in 1950, only twentythree countries are estimated to have such high rates today. A majority of countries in the world today have estimated illiteracy rates of below 10 per cent; in these countries and many others with low illiteracy rates, implementation of the right to education for adults represents a more complex challenge than was the case fifty years ago.

Nevertheless, illiteracy is still the characteristic educational condition of large numbers of adults in the world's less developed regions, and the numbers are estimated to be increasing in most of these regions, although at progressively slower rates. In Eastern Asia/Oceania, a long-standing national literacy campaign in China appears to have been decisive in bringing the number down. In the other regions, the expansion of elementary education, which has mainly been responsible for bringing down the overall rates of illiteracy, has not so far managed to stem the flow of 'new recruits' to the existing population of illiterate adults.

Moreover, despite the progress made over the past few decades in reducing world literacy inequalities, whether these refer to differences in literacy rates between males and females or between the major regions of the world, the majority of illiterate adults in the less developed regions of the world still are females and there still are region where the majority of adult females themselves are estimated to be illiterate. In every region with the exception of Latin America and the Caribbean, females account for a growing percentage of all illiterate adults. The percentage will continue to grow if girls are not given equal access to primary schooling. Besides its growing concentration among women, world illiteracy is also increasingly concentrated geographically in Southern Asia and the least developed countries in sub-Saharan Africa.

Of the twentythree countries with estimated adult illiteracy rates higher than 50 per cent today, fifteen are located in sub-Saharan Africa and five in Southern Asia. The three large Southern Asia countries, Bangladesh, India and Pakistan, are together estimated to account for nearly half of the world's illiterate adults today, compared to around one-third in 1970.

Yet, notwithstanding that there is still a vast number of illiterate adults in the world, growing numbers of the world's adults have received some formal education and have acquired some simple literacy skills. Even in those countries with the largest numbers of illiterate adults, that today account for nearly three-quarters of the world's illiterate adults, the estimated increase in the number of literate adults over the past thirty years has far exceeded the increase in the estimated number of illiterate adults. In the world as a whole, over the same period, the increase in the number of literate adults is estimated at 1,926 million, compared to an estimated increase of 17 million in the number of illiterate adults.

Undoubtedly many of the 'literate' adults to which these statistics refer have acquired only rudimentary literacy skills. Most will have received only primary education, often of dubious quality, and some will have dropped out of school before completing their primary school studies. Thus it is uncertain what percentage of the world's adults can be classified as functionally literate in their respective societies.

Recent surveys carried out in some of the Organisation for Economic Cooperation and Development (OECD) countries suggest that up to 20 per cent of adults in these countries can be regarded as functionally illiterate. In the less developed regions of the world, the figure is unlikely to be lower.

In a global perspective, therefore, implementation of the right to education for adults has become less a question of literacy in the traditional sense – although this indicator is still useful for the purposes of identifying the most flagrant instances of denial of the right to education – than a question of access to relevant 'learning opportunities', i.e. opportunities for the world's adults to satisfy their 'basic learning needs'. In so far as such 'learning opportunities' are embraced by the original notion of 'fundamental education', they arguably should be provided 'free' to all adults who wish to profit from them.

Elementary Education

Elementary education had a relatively clear interpretation in most countries at the time when the Universal Declaration of Human Rights was proclaimed. At least, it could be understood in practice to refer to the first stage or level of formal education. Most countries already had primary schools of one kind or another, and probably in the majority of the fifty or so countries which were then Member States of the United Nations there existed constitutional requirements and/or legislation providing for some measure of free and compulsory education.

In some countries at that time, the duration of compulsory education already extended beyond the primary stage or level. For those who drew up and adopted the Declaration, the principle of free and compulsory elementary education would not have appeared at the time to be an especially difficult principle to implement in the rest of the world, if there were the necessary political will and determination.

However, when interpreting subsequent progress towards the implementation of this principle, it should be borne in mind that the notion of 'elementary education' as utilized in the Declaration was not intended to refer to any particular stage or level in the systems of formal education that were then in existence. It broadly meant an education that would give all children a good start in life.

Extract from the 'Delhi Declaration' of the Heads of State of Nine High-Population Countries, 1993 is given below,

1. We, the leaders of nine High-Population developing nations of the world, hereby reaffirm our commitment

to pursue with utmost zeal and determination the goals set in 1990 by the World Conference on Education for All and the World Summit on Children, to meet the basic learning needs of all our people by making primary education universal and expanding learning opportunities for children, youth and adults. We do so in full awareness that our countries contain more than half of the world's people and that the success of our efforts is crucial to the achievement of the global goal of education for all.

2. We recognize that:

2.1 the aspirations and development goals of our countries can be fulfilled only by assuring education to all our people, a right promised both in the Universal Declaration of Human Rights and in the constitutions and law of each of our countries;

2.2 education is the preeminent means for promoting universal human values, the quality of human resources, and respect for cultural diversity;

2.3 the education systems in our countries have made great strides in offering education to substantial numbers, and yet have not fully succeeded in providing quality education to all of our people, indicating the need for developing creative approaches, both within and outside the formal systems;

2.4 the content and methods of education must be developed to serve the basic learning needs of individuals and societies, to empower them to address their most pressing problems – combating poverty, raising productivity, improving living conditions, and protecting the environment – and to enable them to play their rightful role in building democratic societies and enriching cultural heritage;

2.5 successful education programmes require complementary and convergent actions on adequate nutrition, effective health care and appropriate care and development of the young child, in the context of the role of the family and the community;

2.6 the education and empowerment of girls and women are important goals in themselves and are key factors in contributing to social development, wellbeing and education of present and future generations, and the expansion of the choices available to women for the development of their full potential;

2.7 the pressure of population growth has seriously strained the capacity of education systems and impeded needed reforms and improvements; moreover, given the age structure of the populations in our countries, it will continue to do so throughout the coming decade; and

2.8 education is, and must be, a societal responsibility, encompassing governments, families, communities and non-governmental organizations alike; it requires the commitment and participation of all, in a grand alliance that transcends diverse opinions and political positions.

The scope of the challenge to provide free and compulsory elementary education for all children in the world was not fully appreciated internationally until a decade or so after the Universal Declaration of Human Rights was proclaimed. By that time, UNESCO had managed to assemble the first statistical estimates of the numbers of children in the world who were in and out of school, and national educational policymakers in the less developed regions of the world had begun to implement initial strategies for expansion of their primary school systems.

UNESCO's earliest statistical estimates concluded that somewhat less than half of the world's children aged 5–14 years were enrolled in any kind of primary or secondary school in 1952. In half of the 201 countries and territories covered by these estimates, barely one quarter of the children aged 5–14 years were estimated to be enrolled.

Nevertheless, by the mid-1950s a considerable momentum of expansion of school enrolments had begun in most parts of the world. Behind this momentum two forces were at work. In those countries where compulsory education was already well-established, there were pressures to lengthen its duration.

Measures to that effect were taken, for example, in Belgium, parts of Canada, Finland, the then-Federal Republic of Germany, Switzerland and the former USSR. In cases where the duration of compulsory education already was longer than the first stage or level of formal education, this meant extending the duration further into post-primary or secondary education.

However, in other cases, where the duration of compulsory education covered only part of the full primary cycle, and/or where the duration of this cycle was considered to be too short, measures were taken to extend compulsory education to cover the full cycle and/or to lengthen the cycle, as for example in the then-Federation of Malaya, the Philippines and Thailand. In those countries where compulsory education was not already established, or where it largely existed in name only, as was then the case in many countries in Latin America, there were pressures both for wider access to primary schooling as such and for better opportunities to complete it. However, the existing model of primary schooling in many countries was unsuitable for general application and needed to be reconsidered, especially with regard to the needs of rural populations which had not hitherto had access to formal education. The contents of textbooks especially were a problem in many of the newly independent developing countries because so many of the textbooks were originally designed for use in the schools of the former colonial power. In any case, whatever school model was adopted, it could hardly be made compulsory unless it was first made generally available.

Most of the newly independent governments in Africa and Asia in the 1950s and 1960s were much more ready to give increased priority to education in the allocation of national resources than the previous colonial administrations had been. The 1950s and 1960s, therefore, witnessed a tremendous and historically unprecedented – expansion of primary enrolments in the less developed regions of the world.

Table 2

Primary enrolments (millions) by continent

	1950– 1997					
	1950	1960	1970	1980	1990	1997
World total	*206*	*342*	*411*	*542*	597	668
Africa	919	33	62	81	100	
Asia/Oceania	84	183	253	339	367	410
Europe	75	79	55	52	49	46
Latin America/Caribbean	15	27	44	65	76	85
Northern America	24	34	26	23	25	27

Between 1950 and 1970 – barely the space of one generation –primary enrolments nearly quadrupled in Africa and trebled in Asia/Oceania and Latin America/ Caribbean. In absolute terms, total primary enrolment in the three continents taken together increased from just over 100 million (half the world total) in 1950 to over 300 million (three-quarters of the world total) in 1970.

The driving forces behind this expansion were the huge, pent-up social demands in all regions for increased access to formal education combined with the commitments of most governments to provide increased access to and resources for education. If free and compulsory elementary education represented the ultimate goal, most governments approached the matter pragmatically. This was evident, for example, in the positions adopted at a series of regional conferences on Free and Compulsory Education organized by UNESCO during the 1950s: South Asia and the Pacific, Arab Countries of the Middle East and Latin America. The Bombay conference, for example, while recommending that 'the duration of compulsory education should be no less than seven years', nevertheless conceded that 'States could begin with a shorter duration, considering it as a provisional measure until such time as they could afford a longer period of compulsory education'.

The Cairo conference, which recommended a minimum duration of six years, also conceded that some States could not immediately afford it. The Lima conference, in also recommending a minimum duration of six years, noted that many Latin American countries had already established an official duration of six years but did not apply this in rural areas, where there typically existed a duration of only three years and 'a few centrally located 6-year primary schools'. The Lima conference also observed that the existing legislation in some Latin American countries put the onus of implementing compulsory education on parents, which was unfair: 'Just as school legislation imposes upon the parent the duty of sending his children to school, States should accept the obligation of providing enough schools to educate all children'. In all three conferences, it was implicitly recognized that schooling could not realistically be made compulsory unless schools were made generally available and were essentially 'free'.

The question of 'free' education, like that of compulsory education, was also approached pragmatically. In most countries at that time, 'free' education was generally taken to mean at least the absence of fees charged for attendance, but it could also be taken to mean in addition the provision of free textbooks.

Nevertheless, in all of the less developed regions of the world at that time there was wide acceptance of the idea that local communities themselves, especially in rural areas, would contribute more or less to the construction and maintenance of primary school premises, which often led to demands on parents for ad hoc contributions in cash or in kind.

The concept of 'elementary education' itself was broadly understood in most countries to mean primary schooling. While the duration and contents of this stage or level of education varied a great deal among countries, normally the aim was to provide for more than just the mere acquisition of literacy and numeracy. By the early 1960s, primary and secondary schooling were coming to be considered as 'successive phases of a continuing process' that should be made available to all children, but this was not yet a realistic possibility for most children in the less developed regions of the world. Of more immediate concern was equality of opportunity.

The vast expansion of educaticnal opportunities initiated in the 1950s and 1960s was accompanied by pressures from social groups everywhere for equal treatment and nondiscrimination in education. Although these principles were implicit in the Universal Declaration of Human Rights, by virtue of the Declaration's Article 2, they were not spelled out specifically with reference to education until an international Convention to that effect was adopted in 1960.

The expansion of the 1950s and 1960s was accompanied by increased emphasis in educational policymaking on economic questions, as a consequence of both the growing demands of education on public budgetary resources and the increasing international awareness of the role of education in economic development.

A corollary of this awareness became the movement in many countries towards national education planning and related efforts to integrate such planning with economic development planning. Regional indicative plans for the development of education in Asia and Africa – the so called 'Karachi' and 'Addis Ababa' plans – were adopted by conferences of States convened by UNESCO in Karachi (1960) and by UNESCO jointly with the United Nations Economic Commission for Africa in Addis Ababa (1961). Both the 'Karachi' and 'Addis Ababa' plans aimed broadly at achieving universal primary education in their respective regions by 1980.

Throughout the world, over the past two decades in particular, the view has been increasingly accepted that education is a continuing process from childhood to adulthood, and that schooling should not be conceived of as comprising two radically different kinds of educational process, one primary and one secondary, for two different kinds of children, whether these different kinds of children be separated one from the other on socioeconomic grounds or on the basis of their abilities and aptitudes.

The terms 'primary schooling' and 'secondary schooling' are coming more and more to be considered as no longer referring to different entities, but rather to successive phases of a continuing process that cannot be sharply distinguished except arbitrarily and by doing violence to the real continuity of growth and education. In so far as school systems and scholastic methods do break the continuity of growth they are coming to be regarded as imperfect instruments of education.

Along with the growing acceptance of this integral view of education which leads to the abolition of the former sharp distinctions, is a growing acceptance also of the belief that all young people should receive as complete an education as it is possible for their communities to provide.

The first stage in the acceptance of this belief is reached when it is realized that a nation loses much of its potential talent if it denies educational opportunity to the able young people of the poorer classes of the community; the final stage is reached when it is realized that a community is neglecting its human resources unless it gives to even its least able members the chance to continue to grow and develop as long as growth is possible. The corollary to such views is that communities try to develop a system of education that will be always available to all their members.

Non-formal Education

The primary school model was eventually questioned. Despite the best intentions in regard to planning, the expansion of enrolments in the 1950s and 1960s was not without problems. There were widespread shortages of qualified teachers, not to speak of textbooks and other learning materials. In many countries, there were fears for the quality of education.

In response to the social demand for increased access to education, the temptation was to provide the form of education, i.e. school places, but without meaningful substance, which just resulted in ineffective learning achievement and increased student dropout rates.

The planning ideal was to tailor the output of the education system, in terms of the numbers of graduates from the different levels of the system, so as to match the economy's estimated 'manpower needs', but the economists could not always get their figures right and were not always listened to anyway.

In many countries, especially in Africa, there were signs of what was called, at the time, 'the primary school leavers problem': young people who had graduated from primary school flocking to urban areas in search of white collar jobs that were not available, their education having failed to provide them with skills that could be useful elsewhere.

By the beginning of the 1970s, there were widespread doubts concerning the direction being taken by educational policies. The International Commission on the Development of Education in 1972 considered that most policies were guided by a principle of 'linear expansion' of the existing costly and ineffective school system. Some radical critics at that time called for the 'de-schooling' of society altogether.

While 'de-schooling' was clearly impractical, it nevertheless contained the germ of an idea that would have a lasting influence on educational policies worldwide: that of the 'learning society', as opposed to a 'schooling' one. According to this idea, education could not be equated with schooling, but should be equated broadly with learning, or at least with whatever could meet people's 'learning needs'. This 'learning-centred' view of education led naturally to an appreciation of the importance of other forms of education besides formal schooling, particularly since many young people at that time, especially in rural areas, either were not being reached by the expansion of primary schooling then under way, or had been reached but had received only limited benefits in terms of meeting their 'learning needs'.

From an examination of national educational strategies applied in the course of the 1960s, especially in countries where school enrolment has made comparatively little progress, it emerges that their guiding principle was linear expansion of systems and the numbers of people involved. This method is now out of date. No mechanical extrapolation can now yield valid forecasts of developments in such a dynamic and living enterprise as education.

This old system programmed educational needs as a direct function of the probable evolution of student flows and of the potential for expansion of the different elements of the school system: teaching staff, equipment, buildings, classrooms, etc. Objectives were established in the light of these various forecasts.

These exclusively quantitative methods are now only valid for a stable education system making normal, regular progress. But when a system organized to handle a specific quantity of children has to take in far more, extrapolation becomes unsatisfactory. Applying the method we are criticizing has, of course, led to undeniable quantitative progress. But status reports on the past decade make it clear that growth conceived and expressed in terms of global indicators conceals both the appearance and the exacerbation of a certain number of defects and points of imbalance.

Many countries have found that quantitative expansion of their educational systems did not go hand in hand with efficient educational action. Enormous financial and human resources were laid out to develop costly school models, the results of which often fell far short of expectations.

Linear expansion strategies can no longer be justified, either from the point of view of results obtained or their methodology. When an education system has to absorb a huge number of children, strategies must be modified, must move from the quantitative to the qualitative, from imitation and reproduction to a search for innovations, from a uniform procedure to diverse alternatives.

There was only a short step from a 'learning-centred' view of education to the idea of 'basic learning needs'. Internationally, this step was first prompted by a report presented to the United Nations Children's Fund (UNICEF) in 1973 by a non-governmental organization, the International Council for Educational Development (ICED), which had been commissioned to undertake a study of non-formal education for out-of-school children, adolescents and youth in rural areas of developing countries.

ICED came up with the concept of 'minimum-essential learning needs', which it argued gave 'practical meaning' to the child's 'right' to education. This 'right', ICED claimed, 'must be translated into terms of some "minimum package" of attitudes, skills and knowledge that every young person in a given society requires for an effective and satisfying adulthood'. The analogy was made with 'minimum nutritional needs'.

The idea of a 'minimum' was controversial, since it seemed to imply limits to the right to education. Given that the original problem as stated by ICED was 'to size up the educational requirements of children and youth in any rural area and to plan provisions for meeting them', there was a need to identify a 'package' but not necessarily a 'minimum' one. Why not a maximum one? For these reasons, the less restrictive term 'basic learning needs', which evoked the idea of a 'foundation' rather than a 'minimum', came to be preferred internationally in the course of the 1970s and 1980s.

It was eventually adopted by the World Conference on Education for All, together with its correlate 'basic education'. Since then, the notion of 'basic education', whether for children, youth cr adults, has generally been understood to overlap with the notions of 'elementary' and 'fundamental education' as utilized in the Universal Declaration of Human Rights, but there does not exist an internationally agreed text that actually says so. In so far as there is such an overlap, it can plausibly be argued that the spirit of the Declaration requires that basic education too 'shall be free', just like 'elementary and fundamental education'.

In contrast to the view that equates education with schooling and measures it by years of exposure, ICED [the

International Council for Educational Development] adopted from the outset a concept of education that equates it broadly with learning regardless of where, when or how the learning occurs.

This learning-centred view of education obliges us to start our analysis with the clients and their needs before moving on to consider alternative means for meeting them. It obliges us also to recognize that education by its very nature is a continuing process, starting from earliest infancy through adulthood, that necessarily entails a variety of methods and sources of learning.

We have found it useful to group these learning methods into the following three categories, recognizing that there is overlap and a high degree of interaction between them. By informal education we mean the truly lifelong process whereby every individual acquires attitudes, values, skills and knowledge from daily experience and the educative influences and resources in his or her environment – from family and neighbours, from work and play, from the marketplace, the library and the mass media. For the most part, this process is relatively unorganized and unsystematic. Yet it unquestionably accounts for a very high proportion of all that any person – even a highly-schooled one –accumulates in a lifetime.

By formal education we refer, of course, to the hierarchically structured, chronologically graded 'educational system', running from primary school through the university and including, in addition to general academic studies, a variety of specialized programmes and institutions for full-time technical and professional training.

For purposes of this study we define Non-formal education as any organized educational activity outside the established formal system – whether operating separately or as an important feature of some broader activity – that is intended to serve identifiable learning clienteles and learning objectives.

Examples applicable to children and youth would be: preschool daycare centres and nurseries; school equivalency programmes to provide a second chance for those who are missing schooling or dropped out early; adolescent and adult literacy classes; school-based extracurricular activities such as boy and girl scouts, young farmers' clubs, sports and recreational groups; and occupational training for adolescents in agriculture, construction, etc., carried on outside the formal school structure.

Many of the programmes defined as non-formal education, it should be added, were not originally conceived as 'educational'. Except for the few that bear a close resemblance to formal schooling – such as literacy classes, correspondence courses and vocational training programmes – they originally came under such rubrics as social and health services, community development and animation rurale, sports and recreation, agricultural extension and cooperatives. In other words, non-formal education embraces educational components of programmes designed to serve broad development goals, as well as more academic objectives.

Formal and non-formal education are alike in that both have been organized by societies to augment and improve upon the informal learning process – in other words, to promote and facilitate certain valued types of learning that individuals cannot as readily or as quickly acquire through exposure to the environment. They differ mainly in their institutional arrangements and procedures and to a considerable extent in their subject matter and learning clienteles. Occasionally their differences merge in 'hybrid' programmes combining significant features of both, which are of great importance for the future.

In the broad conceptual framework of a 'lifelong educational system' – a system which should ultimately provide every individual with a flexible and diversified range of useful learning options throughout his or her lifetime – formal, non-formal and informal education are clearly complementary and mutually reinforcing elements.

The increased willingness of policymakers in many countries in the 1970s to recognize that non-formal education could help to meet the learning needs of social groups that were not being reached by the formal school system did not imply a lessening of efforts to expand the coverage of the formal system.

Primary enrolment ratios in most of the world's less developed regions continued their upward trends into the 1970s, and the numbers of out-of-school children levelled off or even declined. These trends continued into the 1980s except in sub-Saharan Africa where enrolment ratios stagnated or declined and the numbers of out-of-school primary-age children rose.

The goal of universal primary education in Africa by 1980, defined in broad terms by the Addis Ababa Plan as a gross enrolment ratio of 100 per cent, was not attained despite the impressive growth of enrolment up until then. The same goal for Asia, set by the Karachi Plan, was attained in Eastern Asia/Oceania but not in Southern Asia.

The World Conference on Education for All reset the goal of universal primary education to the year 2000, as a result of which the decline in enrolment ratios that began in sub-Saharan Africa in the 1980s appears to have been halted or even reversed. Still, the overall gross enrolment ratio for this region does not appear to have recovered to the level it had already reached in 1980.

The prospect of faster progress in the decade ahead is uncertain. UNESCO's most recent revised (and still provisional) projections, based on trends up to 1997, foresee little change in the large number of out-of-school primary-age children in sub-Saharan Africa by the year 2010, whereas the number is predicted to decline in Southern Asia. These two regions together account for most (78 million) of the estimated 88 million out-of-school children in the world today. In both regions, a majority of the out-of-school children are girls.

While these broad trends represent significant aspects of the evolving pattern of progress towards universal free and compulsory elementary education, none of the currently available international statistical indicators showing access to and participation in education is by itself fully satisfactory for monitoring progress towards this goal.

A range of measures, such as those foreseen under the on-going Education for All 2000 Assessment, is needed. The two most commonly utilized indicators, the gross and the net enrolment ratios, can be readily estimated but present significant limitations.

Thus, the gross enrolment ratio, in essence the measure adopted when the Addis Ababa and Karachi Plans for universal primary education were drawn up, is basically an indicator only of the current overall capacity of the system to cope with the number of children who should be enrolled.

Defined as the ratio of enrolment at a given level of education (e.g. the primary level) to the total population in the official age-range for that level, the gross enrolment ratio is inflated in many countries by large numbers of over-age (and some under-age) children, many of whom are repeating their grades, while at the same time there remain significant numbers of children within the official age-range who are not enrolled at all, either because they have dropped out before completing the course or because they never entered school in the first place. This is the situation today in both the Latin America/ Caribbean and Eastern Asia/Oceania regions where the gross enrolment ratios are somewhat higher than 100 per cent.

This situation is less obvious when the gross enrolment ratio is lower than 100 per cent, although in sub-Saharan Africa, where the ratio is well below 100 per cent, the problems of repeating and dropout are actually much worse: in many countries in this region over a quarter of the children enrolled in primary education are repeating their grades, yet are occupying seats that in principle at least could be taken by children who are not in school.

Despite the repeating — or maybe because of it – up to a third or more of the children drop out before reaching the fifth grade. In these countries, where the primary education system seems almost to be designed both to produce 'failures' and to keep children out of school, the gross enrolment ratios signify the system's ineffectiveness almost as much they signify progress towards implementation of the right to education.

On the other hand, the net enrolment ratio, defined as the ratio of the number of children within the official age-range for a given level of education actually enrolled to the total population in the official age-range for that level, does not indicate the capacity of the system, since it does not take into account the presence of over-age children.

The obverse of the net enrolment ratio, i.e. the percentage of the population within the official age-range not enrolled in school, is clearly a useful indicator of the size of the remaining challenge to achieve universal enrolment, but the additional capacity that will need to be provided will also depend on the incidence of repetition.

Other indicators that could be relevant to the measurement of progress towards the goal of universal free and compulsory elementary education are less readily available. In regard to 'free' education, while it is doubtful that any country formally imposes fees for attendance as such in its public primary schools, actual practice as regards payments demanded of students and their families at the level of individual schools is another matter.

However, systematic data relating to fees and other 'user charges' in education have never been collected at the international level; such data are not normally collected on a regular basis at the national level.

In regard to 'compulsory education', data concerning duration are collected by UNESCO through the Organization's regular annual education statistics questionnaires, but in many countries the reported duration is to be understood more as a goal to be attained than as a reality, since large numbers of children are not actually in school for this duration.

In general, more data and indicators are available, both nationally and internationally, for the functioning of education systems and the characteristics of those who have access to education than there are for the characteristics of the population that for one reason or another is excluded or does not have equal access to education.

Thus, UNESCO from time to time has collected information from Member States on policies relating to access to education, in connection with the Organization's periodic monitoring of the implementation of the Convention against Discrimination in Education. However, fewer than half the States which have ratified this Convention normally reply to the questionnaires, and most States that do reply understandably tend to emphasize their positive achievements in this area, rather than the difficulties that need to be overcome.

Household sample surveys, which are carried out today in many countries for different purposes, are potentially an effective means of gathering information on obstacles to the implementation of universal free and compulsory elementary education, in so far as they could help to identify the problems facing social groups that are not being reached by the education system, in particular the constraints (fees, distance from school, language of instruction, irrelevant curricula, jobs to be done at home, etc.) that are of concern to families whose children are not participating in the system.

Many informal community-level surveys of this nature have been carried out by non-governmental organizations and individual researchers in recent years. If education generally, and basic education in particular, is to be regarded as a process of 'meeting learning needs', then national education policies need to be based on much more systematic information than is now typically available on how such 'needs' are perceived at the household level, for otherwise 'needs' will just tend to be decided in a 'topdown' manner. In committing itself to 'meeting the basic learning needs of all', the international community has opened up the whole question of how such 'needs' are to be determined.

Fulfilling Basic Learning Needs

The diversity, complexity, and changing nature of basic learning needs of children, youth and adults necessitates broadening and constantly redefining the scope of basic education to include the following components:

- Learning begins at birth. This calls for early childhood care and initial education. These can be provided through arrangements involving families, communities, or institutional programmes, as appropriate.
- The main delivery system for the basic education of children outside the family is primary schooling. Primary education must be universal, ensure that the basic learning needs of all children are satisfied, and take into account the culture, needs, and opportunities of the community. Supplementary alternative programmes can help meet the basic learning needs of children with limited or no access to formal schooling, provided that they share the same standards of learning applied to schools, and are adequately supported.
- The basic learning needs of youth and adults are diverse and should be met through a variety of delivery systems. Literacy programmes are indispensable because literacy

is a necessary skill in itself and the foundation of other life skills. Literacy in the mother-tongue strengthens cultural identity and heritage. Other needs can be served by: skills training, apprenticeships, and formal and non-formal education programmes in health, nutrition, population, agricultural techniques, the environment, science, technology, family life, including fertility awareness, and other societal issues.

— All available instruments and channels of information, communications, and social action could be used to help convey essential knowledge and inform and educate people on social issues. In addition to the traditional means, libraries, television, radio and other media can be mobilized to realize their potential towards meeting basic education needs of all.

These components should constitute an integrated system – complementary, mutually reinforcing, and of comparable standards, and they should contribute to creating and developing possibilities for lifelong learning.

'The Salamanca Statement' on Special Needs Education states that :

1. We, the delegates of the World Conference on Special Needs Education representing ninety-two governments and twentyfive international organizations hereby reaffirm our commitment to Education for All, recognizing the necessity and urgency of providing education for children, youth and adults with special educational needs within the regular education system, and further hereby endorse the Framework for Action on Special Needs Education, that governments and organizations may be guided by the Spirit of its provisions and recommendations.

2. We believe and proclaim that:

   — every child has a fundamental right to education, and must be given the opportunity to achieve and maintain an acceptable level of learning,

   — every child has unique characteristics, interests, abilities and learning needs,

   — education systems should be designed and educational programmes implemented to take into account the wide diversity of these characteristics and needs,

   — those with special educational needs must have access to regular schools which should accommodate them within a child-centred pedagogy capable of meeting these needs, regular schools with this inclusive orientation are the most effective means of combating discriminatory attitudes, creating welcoming communities, building an inclusive society and achieving education for all; moreover, they provide an effective education to the majority of children and improve the efficiency and ultimately the cost-effectiveness of the entire system.

Since the Jomtien Conference, the scope of 'basic education' has been widely understood to include, among other things, 'early childhood care and initial education', i.e. activities designed to meet the 'basic learning needs' of young children before they reach school-going age. There is growing recognition too of the need to remove artificial barriers within basic education, particularly with a view to the inclusion of children with special educational needs in regular schools.

Unlike 'elementary education' and 'fundamental education', 'early childhood care and initial education' is not specifically mentioned in the Universal Declaration of Human Rights, nor, indeed, is it mentioned in any of the international human rights conventions that have been adopted since 1948. It has always been recognized as an area that very much involves the family.

Indeed, the possibility that compulsory elementary education might impinge on the family and provide scope for abuse by the State was one of the considerations evoked. at the time when the Universal Declaration of Human Rights was being drawn up, in favour of including the third paragraph ('Parents have a prior right to choose the kind of education that shall be given to their children') in the Declaration's Article 26.

The Convention on the Rights of the Child, which defines 'a child' as a person 'below the age of eighteen years unless, under the law applicable to the child, majority is attained earlier' (Article 1), refers to education only at the primary, secondary and higher levels. However, under Article 18 of this Convention, it is agreed that 'States Parties shall take all appropriate measures to ensure that the children of working parents have the right to benefit from child care services and facilities for which they are eligible'. The protection accorded to parents and their children by the third paragraph of Article 26 of the Universal Declaration of Human Rights, as well as paragraph 3 of Article 13 of the International Covenant, remains.

The worldwide development of pre-primary education in recent decades, therefore, has been more a reflection of changing social practices · especially the increasing employment of women outside the home – than a response to internationally agreed commitments to implement a particular aspect of the right to education. International recognition of the importance of early childhood for the later development of the child is not a recent phenomenon.

The Faure Commission, mentioned earlier, was one of the earliest advocates of the importance of preschool education, stressing that: The importance of early childhood in the later development of aptitudes and personality is beyond doubt, as modern psycho-physiology and ordinary observation testify.

None the less current educational systems very frequently operate as if this phase of life were of no concern to them. Their shortcomings in this respect may obviously be explained in many countries by the inadequacy of resources available to meet the demand for education, but they do also result from a failure to recognize the importance to individual development of educational conditions in early childhood.

Since then, enrolments in organized preprimary education have grown considerably in most countries, although the overall rates of participation (gross enrolment ratios) are still low in the world's less developed regions, especially sub-Saharan Africa, Southern Asia and the Arab States. In every region, there is considerable variation in rates of participation among individual countries.

The setback during the 1990s in the countries of Eastern Europe and the former Soviet Union has recently been the subject of a special study by UNICEF's International Child Development Centre. In this region, much of the financing of organized preprimary education was traditionally provided by industrial enterprises for the families of their employees, and has thus been hard hit by the difficulties faced by many enterprises in the region's current economic restructuring.

The scope of 'basic education' in the other direction, beyond primary schooling, is a more complex matter. In prescribing that 'Elementary education shall be compulsory', it was arguably the original intent of the Universal Declaration of Human Rights that all young people should complete an education that would satisfy what today are called their 'basic learning needs', and not just an education that might happen to be called 'elementary'.

Lifelong Education

Adoption of 'lifelong education' and 'lifelong learning' as guiding principles of educational policy, both in countries that are currently able to provide extensive education and learning opportunities, and in those that are still struggling to eradicate illiteracy and get all children into primary school, represents a commitment to the democratization of education that is limited only by the resources available for its implementation.

The world's population is getting older, thus in principle reducing the burden on the adult population of ensuring the provision of basic education for the younger age groups while at the same time providing scope for increasing educational opportunities at the secondary and tertiary levels, including opportunities at these levels for the continuing education of adults themselves. In the growing number of countries in the more developed regions of the world where a majority of young people today can participate in formal education up until their early twenties, the educational boundaries between youth and adults are dissolving.

Although the ideas of 'lifelong education' and 'lifelong learning' have old philosophical roots and can be traced back historically to the earliest efforts to promote universal education, it is unlikely that they would have achieved their current status in educational policies if recent trends and developments in the wider political, economic, social and cultural context had not also been favourable. Both 'lifelong education' and 'lifelong learning' have come to represent in different ways the expectations that societies now have of education and of the scope that should be provided for every individual to develop his or her potential.

International interest in the concept of 'lifelong education' was first aroused in the 1960s by discussion and debate within UNESCO concerning the future development of adult education. International cooperation in adult education at that time was complicated by the fact that the challenges facing adult education varied so greatly among countries: in many of the newly independent countries the majority of adults were illiterate, which was not within the recent experience of countries where adult education programmes had long been established.

Moreover, among the latter there were many different approaches to adult education, ranging from the Folk High Schools of the Scandinavian countries to 'workers' education' in the former USSR, 'further education' in the United Kingdom, 'continuing education' in the United States and Canada, and education populaire in France. Other than the adult target group itself, there did not exist at that time a unifying principle or concept of adult education that could provide adult educators working in different national circumstances and traditions with a common ideal or purpose, nor one that could settle the question of adult education's status vis-à-vis the regular mainstream education system, to which in most countries adult education was usually regarded as an appendage and very much as a 'poor relation'.

Prompted in part by the Second World Conference on Adult Education, which recommended, among other things, that governments should 'regard adult education not as an addition, but as an integral part of their national systems of education', UNESCO's General Conference at its 12th Session two years later took up the matter and went one step further, inviting Member States 'to regard the various forms of out-of-school and adult education as an integral part of any educational system, so that all men and women, throughout their lives, may have the opportunities for pursuing education conducive alike to their individual advancement and to their active participation in civic life and in the social and economic development of their country'.

At the international level, this invitation was the genesis of the idea of 'lifelong education', for it was soon realized, as one of the leading protagonists recalled later, that the design of any coherent overall strategy for the development of out-of-school and adult education would need to consider education as a whole, as well as the succession and interrelation of its various stages over the life-cycle. The discussion and debate that ensued both within UNESCO and in the wider intellectual community was eventually absorbed later in the decade into a broader international discussion and debate over the future of education generally, culminating in the setting up in 1971 of the International Commission on the Development of Education. The Commission's report brought the idea of 'lifelong education' to the attention of a wide international audience.

The Commission put forward a vision of what it called 'the Learning Society', and recommended as the 'Guiding principle for educational policies' that 'Every individual must be in a position to keep learning throughout his [or her] life'. It added: 'The idea of lifelong education is the keystone of the learning society'. In the Commission's vision:

> The lifelong concept covers all aspects of education, embracing everything in it, with the whole being more than the sum of its parts. There is no such thing as a separate 'permanent' part of education which is not lifelong. In other words, lifelong education is not an educational system but the principle on which the overall organization of a system is founded, and which should accordingly underlie the development of each of its component parts.

For the Commission, therefore, 'learning throughout . . . life' and 'lifelong education' were complementary concepts, the latter being essentially a precondition ('the keystone') for the realization of the former. However, the Commission did not specifically attempt to situate its vision in the context of the Universal Declaration of Human Rights, apart from taking note of the fact that the application of the right to education 'continues to be hampered in many places by conditions similar to those prevailing at the time it was first expressed'.

Meeting shortly after the Faure Commission's report was published, the Third World Conference on Adult Education specifically evoked the Universal Declaration of Human Rights in declaring its belief that 'the right of individuals to education, their right to learn and to go on learning, is to be considered on the same basis as their other fundamental rights, such as the right to health and to hygiene, the right to security, the right to all forms of civil liberty, etc.' This was the first time that the idea of a 'right to learn and to go on learning' was expressed by an international conference, although it was formulated as synonymous with 'the right of individuals to education', not as an additional, separate right.

In fact, in the years immediately following the publication of the Faure Commission's report, 'lifelong education' and 'lifelong learning' were usually considered together as a single overall concept, as for example in the Recommendation on the Development of Adult Education adopted by the General Conference of UNESCO in 1976. In the Recommendation:

— the term 'adult education' denotes the entire body of organized educational processes, whatever the content, level and method, whether formal or otherwise, whether they prolong or replace initial education in schools, colleges and universities as well as in apprenticeship, whereby persons regarded as adult by the society to which they belong develop their abilities, enrich their knowledge, improve their technical or professional qualifications or turn them in a new direction and bring about changes in their attitudes or behaviour in the twofold perspective of full personal development and participation in balanced and independent social, and cultural development;

— adult education, however, must not be considered as an entity in itself; it is a subdivision, and an integral part of, a global scheme for lifelong education and learning;

— the term 'lifelong education and learning', for its part, denotes an overall scheme aimed both at restructuring the existing education system and at developing the entire educational potential outside the education system;

— in such a scheme men and women are the agents of their own education, through continual interaction between their thoughts and actions;

— education and learning, far from being limited to the period of attendance at school, should extend throughout life, include all skills and branches of knowledge, use all possible means, and give the opportunity to all people for full development of the personality;

— the educational and learning processes in which children, young people and adults of all ages are involved in the course of their lives, in whatever form, should be considered as a whole.

By the end of the 1980s, the idea of a 'right to learn' distinct from that of the 'right to education' had gained ground, with the Fourth International Conference on Adult Education, for example, adopting a Declaration on the 'right to learn' that did not actually mention the 'right to education' at all. However, the balance was restored at the Fifth International Conference on Adult Education, with the Conference declaring that 'The recognition of the right to education and the right to learn throughout life is more than ever a necessity'.

Since the early 1990s, the trend in educational policies towards a learning-centred view of education generally, and of adult education in particular, has been especially marked in some OECD countries. As far back as the early 1970s, policy-makers in these countries had shared the doubts of the Faure Commission concerning the viability of continued 'linear expansion' of the formal system of full-time education, and in addition were skeptical towards the possibility of further expansion being fully financed by governments.

By the end of the 1990s, the idea of public financing of educational opportunities beyond the period of compulsory education had given way in these countries to the idea of shared responsibility or 'partnership' between government, employers and learners themselves. In France, to take one example, the financing of participants in 'recurrent' or continuing education (formation continue) programmes provided in higher education establishments under the control of the Ministry of National Education in 1996 was accounted for to the extent of 40 per cent from public funds, 40 per cent by employers and 20 per cent by the participants themselves.

With different percentages according to national circumstances, this tripartite distribution of responsibility for the financing of 'lifelong education' has increasingly become the norm in the industrial countries. In these countries, therefore, the 'right to lifelong learning' has run into the quite basic question of 'Who should pay?' In regard to regular mainstream secondary and higher education at least, this is answered by Article 13, paragraph 2 of the International Covenant on Economic, Social and Cultural Rights, which requires 'the progressive introduction of free education'.

The 'introduction of free education' in respect to secondary education is also mentioned in Article 28 paragraph 1(b) of the Convention on the Rights of the Child. However, in regard to continuing education for adults at the secondary and tertiary levels, the position with respect to the international treaties is not as straightforward. This kind of education was not anticipated in the Universal Declaration of Human Rights or in any of the international treaties, and States apparently do not feel under an obligation to ensure that such education shall be provided 'free'.

In so far as the 'right to lifelong learning' is understood to include a 'right' to continuing education, it would seem in practice to amount to little more than the 'right' of any citizen to participate, at his or her own expense, in the market for goods and services generally, with more or less encouragement from public funds depending on the situation in individual countries. Yet, this was once pretty much the position everywhere in regard to initial education at the secondary and higher levels; it did not last.

The readiness of most countries, both rich and poor, to commit public funds for the expansion of educational opportunities beyond the 'elementary and fundamental stages' was to be largely responsible for the worldwide development of secondary and tertiary education that is considered broadly in the sections which follow.

Secondary Education

Secondary education is not actually mentioned in Article 26 of the Universal Declaration of Human Rights. In those days, the broad view of society's educational needs that prevailed even in the more highly developed countries was that the great majority of the population should receive an 'elementary education' while a selected minority could also proceed to secondary and higher education. Secondary education at that time was largely oriented towards preparing students for entry to university or equivalent level education. It was probably for these reasons that there was a tendency during the drafting of the Declaration to refer broadly to education above the 'elementary and fundamental stages' as 'higher education'.

The first treaty to mention 'secondary education' was the Convention against Discrimination in Education: 'The

States Parties [undertake to] make secondary education in its different forms generally available and accessible to all. The International Covenant adopted the same wording, but added the words 'including technical and vocational secondary education' after the word 'forms'. The Convention on the Rights of the Child uses slightly different wording: 'including general and vocational education'.

Opportunities for secondary-level education increased dramatically in every region of the world (though from different starting points) in the years after the adoption of the Declaration, with world total enrolment doubling in each of the following two decades.

Table 3
Secondary enrolments (millions) by continent, 1950– 1997

	1950	*1960*	*1970*	*1980*	*1990*	*1997*
World total	40	79	169	264	315	398
Africa	1	2	5	14	24	34
Asia/Oceania	15	37	84	146	184	241
Europe	16	25	47	63	63	70
Latin America /Caribbean	2	4	11	17	22	29
Northern America	7	11	22	24	22	25

At first, the expansion was based mainly on existing institutional structures, but in the many countries where there existed different forms of post-elementary education, the type of education to provide soon became an issue. In the 1940s and 1950s, the concept or model of a 'comprehensive' secondary school 'open to all' existed only in North America, the ex-USSR and a handful of other countries.

In Europe, Latin America and much of the rest of the world, the post-elementary model was one of 'differentiated' schooling: different kinds of schools mainly with a vocational orientation alongside a traditional academic secondary school that was not intended for mass participation. Since much of the social demand was for increased access to the traditional secondary school, the opening up of increased opportunities for secondary level education constituted a major challenge for the 'aims and purposes', indeed, the 'very conception of secondary schooling'.

The situation in the Netherlands in the early 1950s is a good example of the nature of this challenge: around 10 per cent of primary school leavers entered the traditional academic secondary schools, around 20 per cent continued for two or three years in what was then known as 'advanced' or 'upper' primary education with a prevocational orientation, around 25 per cent entered vocational/technical schools (also including a small number of agricultural/horticultural schools), and 45 per cent left school altogether.

So long as there were only a limited number of places available in post-elementary education generally, and hence a need to ration the overall demand for places, pressures for reform of post elementary education structures could largely be resisted. However, once the commitment had been adopted to open up opportunities in those countries like the Netherlands that adhered to the 'differentiated' schooling model, the question of which kinds of secondary/post-elementary education to expand could not be avoided, especially since the practice of sorting students into different kinds of schools was arguably at variance with the democratic impulse that was ultimately behind the opening up of opportunities in the first place.

In much of the world, therefore, the decades that have passed since the original commitments were adopted to make 'secondary education in its different forms generally available and accessible to all' have been marked by a continuing process of adjustment of secondary education structures to accommodate ever-increasing cohorts of students.

This process has now virtually run its course in the industrial countries and countries in transition, where the secondary gross enrolment ratios are close to, or above 100 per cent, but it is still under way in the majority of countries in the other regions of the world. Sub-Saharan Africa, according to UNESCO's most recent (and still provisional) estimates of net enrolment ratios, is the only region where the absolute number of secondary-school-age youth who are out of school is still growing.

At the risk of oversimplifying the record of what has in fact been a very complex process in most countries from the 1950s onwards, the challenge to make 'secondary education in its different forms generally available and accessible to all' has essentially been met by extending the common trunk of formal schooling from primary education through to the first or lower stage of secondary education and then, depending on national circumstances, eventually making the whole trunk compulsory.

In the process, lower secondary education has come to be reconceptualized, in terms of content, as a general education for all, while purely academic and vocational/ technical education have gradually been displaced towards the post-compulsory and/or upper stage of secondary education. Nevertheless, many countries which started with the 'differentiated' schooling model have adopted a 'comprehensive' type model for both lower and upper secondary schooling while at the same time retaining some provision for separate vocational/ technical schools at the post-compulsory and/or upper stage of secondary education.

In those countries where the 'comprehensive' model already existed, the admission of larger cohorts of students had implications for reform of curricula so as to take into account the wider range of abilities and interests as well as social backgrounds of the students coming into the schools.

There were some notable 'holdouts' against the overall trend above towards general secondary education, chiefly the countries of East and Central Europe where secondary-level education at both the lower and upper stages was strongly vocational and technical up until the early 1990s.

Moreover, in countries which are still struggling to achieve universal primary education, and which can provide only limited opportunities for secondary level education, a certain amount of provision continues to be made for post-primary vocational education. Even so, there is broad acceptance of the idea of eventually moving towards the provision of a common lower secondary education for all when resources permit.

In a global perspective, the 'comprehensive' model predominates, especially in North America, Asia, the Arab States and sub-Saharan Africa, where the percentages of students enrolled in 'general' secondary schools as opposed to 'vocational/ technical' schools are substantially higher than in Western Europe and the countries in transition, and somewhat higher than in Latin America and the Caribbean.

In recent years there has been a shift away from predominantly 'vocational/technical' secondary education in the countries of East and Central Europe. In both the latter region and Western Europe, vocational/ technical programmes are provided today mainly at the upper secondary stage: the average percentage of upper secondary students enrolled in vocational/technical programmes in the fifteen countries of the European Union, for example, is around 60 per cent, although there is variation among individual countries.

Table 4
Percentage distribution of secondary school enrolment by type of education in each region, 1970 and 1997

	1970			1997		
	General	*Vocational*	*Teacher training*	*General*	*Vocational*	*Teacher training*
More developed regions:						
Northern America	100	0	0	100	0	0
Asia/Oceania	83	16	1	75	25	0
Europe	74	25	1	69	31	0
Transition countries	67	33	1	81	18	0
Less developed regions:						
Sub-Saharan Africa	88	9	3	95	5	1
Arab States	87	10	3	92	8	0
Latin America/ Caribbean	81	15	4	84	16	0
Eastern Asia/ Oceania	85	10	5	91	8	1
Southern Asia	97	2	1	100	0	0

The corresponding percentage for upper and lower secondary students taken together, is somewhat lower because lower secondary education is predominantly 'general'. In all regions, secondary-level teacher-training programmes have now mostly been phased out in favour of programmes at the post-secondary/ tertiary level.

A complete picture of developments in regard to technical and vocational education at the secondary level would require more systematic information on the position of technical and vocational components in the curricula of 'general secondary' schools than is currently available internationally. UNESCO's enrolment data have long been based on the distinction between 'general secondary' and 'vocational/technical' schools rather than programmes. This, however, gives only part of the picture. The Convention on Technical and Vocational Education, which was drawn up principally with a view to stimulating 'the exchange of information and experiences' and 'strengthening international cooperation in this field', defines technical and vocational education as follows:

> . . . all forms and levels of the educational process involving, in addition to general knowledge, the study of technologies and related sciences and the acquisition of practical skills, know-how, attitudes and understanding relating to occupations in the various sectors of economic and social life.

It is in this perspective that technical and vocational education have in recent years come to be more clearly recognized as having an essential role to play in 'lifelong learning'

According to the Second International Congress on Technical and Vocational Education:

— Lifelong learning is a journey with many pathways and technical and vocational education (TVE) is an integral part of the voyage. Therefore TVE systems should be designed as developmental life experiences with cultural and environmental aspects in addition to their economic dimensions.

— TVE systems need to be open, flexible and learner-oriented. They must provide the learner with knowledge and skills for specific jobs. They must also prepare individuals more generally for life and the world of work. TVE is for personal, social and economic benefit.

— TVE needs to be based on a learning culture shared by individuals, industry, different economic sectors and government in which individuals are empowered to take progressively more responsibility for their own knowledge-management and independent learning while public and private providers ensure programmes that facilitate access to and through the pathways of lifelong learning.

— TVE has an important role to play in reducing levels of anxiety in the midst of constant uncertainty by providing information and knowledge, skills and competencies, entrepreneurial capacity and the development of the human personality.

— TVE should develop close interfaces with all other education sectors, particularly schools and universities, to facilitate seamless pathways for learners. The emphasis must be on articulation, accreditation and recognition of prior learning to enhance their learning opportunities.

— Perhaps the biggest challenge which faces TVE is to coordinate the needs of a general and a vocational education through curriculum, pedagogy and delivery.

— TVE should inspire in young people a positive attitude to innovation, enable them to help shape change and prepare them for self-reliance and citizenship.

— TVE is particularly important in ensuring a seamless transition from the school to the workplace. To achieve this it needs a holistic approach which captures the dichotomies of the academic and the vocational, the theory and the applied, knowing and doing, the use of the head and the hand. This requires effective partnerships with schools and with industry and other economic sectors which embrace shared values, shared curricula, shared resources, and shared outcomes.

— The informal economic sector is often excluded in the spectrum of lifelong learning. TVE has a vital role to play in reaching out to this sector in every way possible to ensure that the less privileged have access to the pathways of continuous learning.

— To achieve all of these aspirations for Technical and Vocational Education a number of urgent considerations must be addressed:

  — The status and prestige of TVE must be enhanced in the eyes of the community and the media. This includes raising the status of teachers in TVE.

  — The sectors of education must achieve more effective interrelationships to facilitate more seamless pathways for learners.

  — There must be flexibility in programme administration and curriculum design to facilitate a smooth passage through lifelong learning.

  — Career guidance and counselling is of the utmost importance for all clients of education systems.

  — All stakeholders, particularly industry and educationalists, must be involved in new TVE partnerships.

  — The high cost of many TVE programmes must be addressed.

  — The lifelong learning continuum will be best sustained if there is a diversity of funding, a diversity of providers, and a diversity of delivery mechanisms.

— Quality assurance is essential to ensure a new higher status for TVE.

— We need to understand more about the critical moments of choice on the journey of lifelong learning.

The principle of 'equal opportunity' has been central to the question of what kinds of education to provide at the secondary level, because of the range of student abilities and interests that need to be catered for. If ideally 'secondary education should be the time when the most varied talents are revealed and flourish', this was hardly possible so long as a majority of young people did not have access to it, which in any case is still the situation in half the countries in the world today.

The first mention of 'equal opportunity' in an international treaty dealing with education was in the Preamble of UNESCO's Constitution ('the States Parties to this Constitution, believing in full and equal opportunities for education for all. . .'). Article 26 of the Universal Declaration of Human Rights proclaims something analogous (but with a slightly different meaning), namely, that 'higher education shall be equally accessible to all on the basis of merit'. This expression, in the light of the discussion that took place during the drafting of the Declaration, essentially meant 'equally accessible to all on the basis of individual capacity', as came to be spelled out later by the UNESCO Convention against Discrimination in Education. The International Covenant and the Convention on the Rights of the Child adopted the wording: 'on the basis of capacity'.

Both the Convention against Discrimination in Education and later the Convention on the Rights of the Child refer to the general principle of 'equal opportunity' in education. In fact, the Convention against Discrimination in Education was designed in part to promote this principle and specifically included Article 4 to that effect. The Convention on the Rights of the Child adopts the principle of 'equal opportunity' as the basis of action to be taken by States Parties with a view to achieving the right of the child to education, but implicitly assumes that the various dimensions of this principle are known, presumably because they had already been spelled out earlier in the Convention against Discrimination in Education.

Thus, the Convention on the Rights of the Child does not include any wording corresponding to Article 4(b) of the Convention against Discrimination in Education: 'to ensure that the standards of education are equivalent in all public educational institutions of the same level, and that the conditions relating to the quality of education provided are also equivalent'.

While the provision of 'equal opportunity' for 'varied talents' to 'flourish' has been as much of a challenge for elementary or primary as for secondary education over the past fifty years, it has generally been a matter of intense concern in secondary education because of the differences in the rewards that societies typically accord to the different types or forms of education at this level.

The methods of selection (tests and examinations) utilized in assigning students to different types of secondary education have therefore been the subject of controversy in most countries at one time or another ever since the worldwide expansion of opportunities for secondary level education got under way.

In the many countries which inherited the 'differentiated' schooling model in secondary/ post-elementary education, the critical factor in generating resistance to further expansion of this model was probably evidence that prevailing selection methods tended to favour the access of children from socially and economically better-off families to the academic secondary schooling that led to higher education, while children from poorer families were channelled towards vocational schooling that was essentially terminal.

Educational and economic arguments also were brought to bear: in the former case by demonstrating the uncertainty (if not injustice) inherent in trying to identify children's abilities and interests –and hence life-chances – at too early an age, and in the latter case by demonstrating the uncertainty inherent in trying to predict the economy's future needs for different categories of skills and competencies.

If these reservations have been gradually overcome by the trend in recent decades towards the provision of a general ('basic') education for all at the lower secondary level, it has been because the whole issue of 'equal opportunity' in selection for different types of education has largely been displaced to the upper secondary and tertiary levels.

Thus, the policy challenge that existed earlier with respect to opportunities for 12–14 year-old primary school leavers has in more and more countries become one of education/learning opportunities for secondary school leavers who are 16–18 years old or even older.

In those countries that have retained the 'differentiated schooling' model in post-compulsory education at the upper secondary level, chiefly in Europe and to a lesser extent in Latin America and other regions of the world, educational opportunities at this level have essentially been partitioned into schools giving academic programmes that lead directly to higher education, and schools giving vocational/technical programmes that are designed primarily to prepare young people for employment.

In those countries that have adopted the 'comprehensive' model of secondary schooling, as in North America and much of the rest of the world outside Europe, a similar partitioning can exist within individual schools but is attenuated by the fact that the vocational/technical programmes of these schools normally do not preclude later access to higher education, for which the basic prerequisite is usually the successful completion of secondary education as such. The two models are linked to differing conceptions of higher education: in the former case a highly differentiated conception, and in the latter case a relatively broad one. Which of the two models is more consistent with the principle of equal educational opportunity is difficult to assess, since this depends in part on how well each of them prepares young people for a successful transition to adult life and subsequent personal development. If the history of 'differentiated schooling' at the secondary level is any guide to the future, there is likely to be continuing pressure from within societies for the removal of boundaries at the tertiary level between educational programmes that foreclose future opportunities for 'lifelong learning' and those that keep such opportunities open.

Tertiary Education

Whereas the various treaties all refer to making secondary education in its different forms both 'available' and 'accessible' (to 'all' or to 'every child'), in the case of higher education they refer only to making it 'accessible to all' ('on the basis of capacity', or of 'individual capacity'). The International Covenant adds: 'by every appropriate means, and in particular by the progressive introduction of free education'. The Convention on the Rights of the Child adds simply: 'by every appropriate means'.

Table 5
Tertiary enrolments (millions) by continent 1950– 1997

	1950	*1960*	*1970*	*1980*	*1990*	*1997*
World total	*6.5*	*12.1*	*28.1*	*51.0*	*68.6*	*88.2*
Africa	0.1	0.2	0.5	1.5	2.9	4.8
Asia/Oceania	1.2	3.2	7.4	14.6	23.9	36.1
Europe	2.5	4.5	9.0	16.4	18.9	21.8
Latin America/Caribbean	0.3	0.6	1.6	4.9	7.3	9.4
Northern America	2.4	3.7	9.5	13.5	15.6	16.0

Enrolments at the tertiary or higher education level have increased even more dramatically than at the secondary level in the decades since the Universal Declaration of Human Rights was adopted, in part because many countries were basically starting from scratch. At the end of the 1940s, more than half the countries in the world had fewer than 1,000 students enrolled at this level, and probably a quarter had no tertiary level institutions at all; only nine countries (China, ex-Federal Republic of Germany, France, India, Italy, Japan, ex-USSR, the United Kingdom and the United States) had more than 100,000 students enrolled.

By the end of the 1990s virtually all countries had at least one tertiary level institution, sixty-eight countries had more than 100,000 students enrolled at this level, and twenty-one countries had more than 1 million such students enrolled. This development was hardly foreseen at the time when the

Universal Declaration of Human Rights was drawn up. In those days, mass access to higher education as achieved in some countries today would have seemed to be almost a contradiction in terms. Indeed, neither the Declaration nor any of the international treaties concerning education adopted since then affirm that higher education shall be made 'generally available' or 'available . . . to every child', as for example they do in respect to secondary education.

Although the Universal Declaration of Human Rights did not directly call for the worldwide expansion of higher education, it nevertheless affirmed a principle – 'equally accessible to all on the basis of merit' (or 'individual capacity') – that inevitably would facilitate access to this level of education for social groups that had hitherto been under-represented or excluded. In this connection it should be noted that the notion of 'merit', as originally included in Article 26 of the Universal Declaration of Human Rights, was intended to provide protection against discrimination in access to higher education on grounds such as 'race, colour, sex, language, religion, political or other opinion, national or social origin, property, birth, or other status'.

Perhaps even more so than at the secondary level, since secondary education was traditionally considered to be mainly a preparation for higher studies, the expansion of enrolments at the tertiary level has represented a decisive step in the democratization of the world's education. Half a century ago, access to this level of education was regarded in most parts of the world as a privilege to which children of ordinary families could not aspire. If it is still beyond their reach in much of the world today, it has at least come to be recognized as a right that only their countries' want of the necessary resources can deny them.

In the early years following the adoption of the Declaration, the expansion of higher education was accompanied in many countries by a good deal of debate over the question of equity in admission procedures. A wide-ranging and definitive international study of these procedures, carried out jointly by UNESCO and the International Association of Universities, highlighted the difficulty of applying the principle of 'equally accessible to all on the basis of merit': that even where agreement could be reached on what constituted 'merit' (or 'individual capacity'), 'admission to higher education is not a single act but a process covering all the years of education'.

In that perspective, the study concluded, it was imperative to supplement admission procedures by measures designed to ensure that social and especially financial hardship would not prevent good students from being admitted. In those days, as was noted earlier, official opinion at the intergovernmental level favoured 'the progressive introduction of free education' in higher education, and wrote this into the International Covenant.

However, opinion has probably shifted since then. At least, 'free' higher education was not reaffirmed in the Convention on the Rights of the Child, which simply says 'make higher education accessible to all on the basis of individual capacity and by every appropriate means'; and many countries today have policies in favour of student loans and 'cost recovery' in higher education.

The reason could be the sheer scale of expansion of higher education in recent years, especially in the industrial countries, and associated fears concerning the possible consequences of 'free' higher education for public expenditure. The equity consequences of increasing 'cost recovery' are obscured by the very expansion of student enrolments, but in a number of countries there is evidence of a growing problem of student indebtedness.

Cutting back on 'free' higher education with the aim of diverting funds towards basic education has become a feature of 'Structural Adjustment Programmes' in developing countries in recent years, but evidence on whether this aim has been successfully achieved is currently lacking.

In the 1950s and 1960s there were fears that the development of higher education could lead to the emergence of a 'meritocracy'. These fears have not been realized. In opening up to progressively larger intakes of students at a time of accelerating change in the wider economy and society, higher education systems have been challenged both internally and externally to open up structures, courses and programmes to an increasingly diverse array of abilities and interests that cannot be ordered hierarchically under a single unidimensional conception of 'merit' (or 'individual capacity').

In fact, with over half the age-cohort in the industrial countries now participating full-time in some form of tertiary level education, and a third enrolled in universities, the opposite problem has arisen: the emergence in these countries of a minority 'underclass' of young people in precarious employment outside the formal education system, lacking the skills and competencies needed for full participation in the modern economy. It is difficult to trace the structural changes in higher education with a great deal of precision at the global level because of differences between countries, for historical or other reasons, in the interpretation of the concept of the 'university', and in the criteria for assessing whether other institutions provide an 'equivalent' education.

With that reservation to one side, it appears nevertheless that the increased tertiary enrolments worldwide have mostly been accommodated in universities and institutions that are considered by countries to be 'equivalent' to universities, although other post-secondary/tertiary programmes (including distance education programmes), often with a mainly vocational orientation, account for nearly half of tertiary enrolments in parts of Asia and a third of such enrolments in some industrial countries and a number of countries in sub-Saharan Africa.

The different fields of study are grouped broadly into Humanities (education, arts, humanities, social sciences and law) and Science (natural sciences, engineering, medicine and agriculture). The figures shown in the table are the unweighted averages of the individual country percentages in each region. Countries for which the relevant data are available for both dates. The number of such countries in each region is shown in parentheses.

Table 6

Percentage distribution of tertiary enrolments broad field of study, by region, 1970 and 1996

	1970		1996	
	Humanities	Science	Humanities	Science
More developed regions:				
Asia /Oceania	69	31	66	34
Europe	63	37	64	36
Countries in transition	47	53	63	37
Less developed regions:				
sub-Saharan Africa	50	50	69	31
Arab States	73	27	67	33
Latin America /Caribbean	56	44	61	39
Eastern Asia/Oceania	63	37	66	34
Southern Asia	73	27	68	32

Although the larger higher education systems in the more developed regions of the world certainly provide a more diversified range of courses and study programmes – often of a much higher quality – than is provided by the smaller systems in the less developed regions, it does not appear from the data available to UNESCO that there are fundamental differences between the various systems in the distribution of student enrolments by broad fields of study.

In fact, higher education systems appear to have converged in recent decades towards a common global pattern, with around two-thirds of total enrolment studying in the 'humanities' fields and around one-third studying in the 'science' fields. In other words, there is not a greater tendency – as is sometimes thought – for the less developed regions of the world to concentrate on the less costly 'humanities' fields than there is for the more developed regions. The reasons for the pattern observed above are not fully understood, but they probably reflect the convergence of highly educated human resources in different countries towards a common overall skill profile rooted in standard fields of study.

The significant differences between countries and regions in their higher education, as in the case of primary and secondary education, relate to the quality of the education provided and the general problem, faced by all countries, of how to balance the demand for access with the resources available. Internationally, there exists a broad measure of agreement on the 'core missions' of higher education, including that of providing 'opportunities for higher learning and learning throughout 'life.

2

Teaching Strategies

Good teaching, in whatever form it takes, is ultimately derived from an academic's own thinking and uniquely creative response to three sorts of question. These are: questions about the scope and nature of the disciplinary knowledge that is being taught; questions about the potential in different kinds of teaching contact with students; and questions about students' learning needs, including the need for social interaction.

Good teaching process is a unique series of transactions, deriving their particularity from students' and tutors' own knowledge and experience, their capacities to learn from and to inform the other, and the nature and quality of the relationship that they enjoy.

It is impossible to reduce to simple formulae the knowledge, understanding, and creative academic judgement that results in good teaching. Educational research can, however, help us to understand the student experience of learning, and supply fresh opportunity for reflection on the principles that underpin our approaches to teaching.

Effectve Teaching Strategies

The teachers have to deal with children studying in different classes. Under such a set-up when teachers have to cope with teaching across the classes, it is important to examine how the teacher utilises effectively the time and space available for instruction.

Creating and a healthy Classroom Environment

The teacher should have knowledge about the likes and dislikes of the pupils and thorough knowledge about the psychology of children. The psychological environment of the school can be improved by respecting children's individuality, being sensitive to their needs, being warm and positive to them, giving a patient hearing whenever children need it, winning their confidence, encouraging them, etc. Imagine how you might feel if you, are required to spend daily five to six hours a day sitting quietly in a bare room on a mat or on the floor listening to someone performing repetitive tasks and subjected to petty discipline. You cannot talk freely, you cannot laugh, you are totally at the mercy of someone who may or may not respect you as an individual. You are constantly told that you have to perform meaningless tasks because it is for your good to equip you for your later life. Write down what you think children like best in the school and what they dislike most, then ask children what they like best in the school and what they dislike most about school. Compare the two sets of responses. Children generally respond to a warm, pleasant teacher who is positive in approach. Children like to be called by their names and not by the generic term 'child'.

For creating a proper psychological environment in the school, the following suggestions may be tried out:

— Get to know the names of every individual child in the class. Address the child by his/ her name.

— Greet the children everyday with a smile. Give the children a special word of welcome when they come to school for the first time; come after a long holiday; come after a long period of absence due to sickness.

— Praise children when they do something which is desirable. Make it a point to show children that we are happy with their good behaviour.

— Physical punishment causes fear and shame in children. It causes more harm than good to them. It is, therefore, better to avoid physical punishment.

— Children have different abilities. Build on children's assets rather than harp on their limitations. Do not put children to shame.

— Every teacher sets a role model to his/her children. Do not expect children to do tasks which we ourselves do not do.

A healthy physical environment is essential for children. The physical en ment includes a properly swept. clean school. walls displaying children's work, an open playground with play equipments such as ropes, ladders, swings with old tyres or a sand pit, clean mats for children to sit on, etc. Many of us do not realise that at times schools can be alarmingly rude places. Children are continually ticked off for not learning or for bad manners but very seldom praised for desirable behaviour. Children also like clean, bright surroundings. We at times think that without adequate financial input, it is not possible to maintain an attractive school. This is not always correct. List five inexpensive activities that you can do to brighten up the school/class. Discuss how you can get your pupils to participate brightening up in the school. For an effective physical environment the following suggestions may be tried out:

— Get children to clean up the school premises.

— Encourage children to use the wastepaper basket. They can make one for themselves in the work experience period.

— Select children to form cleanliness committee, drinking water committee, garden committee, display board committee, etc. Children may be encouraged to choose their membership according to their interests.

— Each committee then works out its plan. The garden committee will think of ways and means to start a school garden. The display board committee will decide how it will make display facilities, what it will display, how frequently the display will be changed, etc.

Management of Time

Effective management of time is essential for a healthy learning environment. Most of our schools have a duration of five to six hours. The national curriculum framework gives the guidelines on how this time is to be proportioned. These guidelines need not be followed on a day-to-day basis but it gives an overall idea of the required weightage of subjects 30 per cent for language, 15 per cent for mathematics, 20 per cent for work experience, 15 per cent for environmental studies and 10 per cent each for health and physical education, and art education. The school time-table needs to be, therefore, drawn on this basis. However, if yours is two-teacher school and if you have to teach more than one class, you require certain adjustments. For example, between the two teachers, you may like to decide who will teach the young children of classes I-II and who will work with older children of classes III-V. After having selected the classes, then the question arises as to how to go about it. One way of doing it is to conduct certain activities such as creative arts, physical and health education, work experience, parts of environmental studies such as observation, classification, discussion, etc., and parts of language education such as development of listening and speaking skills in large groups. But when it comes to developing competencies of reading, writing and mathematics, it may be better to do it in smaller groups. This arrangement gives the teacher an opportunity to observe if all children are mastering the competencies. Even in the small groups, care may be taken to see that children of different ability levels are grouped together. This will enable children to learn from each other. Child-to-child approach is often found to be effective in helping children learn. You may probably wonder why 20 per cent of time is allotted to work experience. This is because children at this stage learn primarily by doing.

Many of the motor skills such as eye-hand coordination and finger dexterity, and cognitive skills like observation, reasoning and problem solving, and social skills like working together, sharing and cooperating are learnt by children through activities involving work experience. Moreover, these activities interest children and they derive a good deal of enjoyment out of it. Draw up a weekly time-table indicating small group and large group learning activities for each area of learning. By and large, most of our schools now have at least two rooms. In such a case, both the groups, the older and the younger children, may have a class each for themselves. For small group-learning activities, we may keep one class with us while the other class may have activities such as art activities, work experience, etc., which may be done either in the verandah or outdoor if weather permits. It may also be good to set apart a little space for a science corner or a reading corner. Children may be encouraged to collect samples of plants, rocks, birds' nests, etc., which may be used for discussion. Draw a plan for your school.

Time management enables the teacher to fully engage pupils in activities. To plan time schedule, the following points are suggested.

— Weekly planning helps more than the day-to-day planning.

— It is not desirable to draw one standard from daily routine.

— The environment of the school should be such as to create a learning climate and to avoid distraction.

— Collective teaching should be planned for the whole year.

— Both indoor and outdoor activities should be planned in the time-table.

— Teaching for the same subject should be planned at the same time for all grades.

Teachers can also refer to the curriculum of his/her state about the weightage and make changes, if any. The schedule should be drawn in a way that even with a full work load of 40 hours per week in one teacher school, about 18 hours per week should be devoted to classes I and II exclusively, and about 22 hours per week for classes III to V activities. The remaining nine hours could be for collective teaching and so on.

Space Management

There are constraints in space, time and resources affecting teaching learning interactions. For example, when the teacher is teaching pupils of one class, the pupils of other classes get disturbed. One way to minimise distractions is to try seating arrangements in the same class.

In multigrade schools, use of walls could be planned in teaching-learning process. The more the writing space, the more will be pupils' participation. Writing space should be all around so that children can learn through rotational teaching, monitorial assistance, self-study and collective activities.

Teaching Methodologies

The following methodologies will help to spread teacher's available time to engage the students.

— Direct teaching

— Monitorial assistance

— Peer tutoring

— Peer group work

— Self-study

— Field trips

— Extended teaching periods

— Supplementary readings

— Making use of community resources

— Collective teaching work.

Direct teaching: In multigrade teaching system, the teacher cannot afford full time for a single grade. He/she has to plan his/her time according to the work-load. Only a part of time could be available for direct teaching. The time for direct teaching is of great significance. Direct teaching should be preceded and followed up by monitorial assistance, peer group work, supervised study, self-study by the pupils. Use of different types of materials, audiovisual aids and sometimes software quite helps in enhancing the quality of direct teaching. Direct teaching should start with every new topic and lesson. An overview of the lesson/topic should be presented summarily. Explaining the different sub-activities of the lesson, arousing learner's curiosity, explaining the role of monitors and peers, assigning self-study exercises for reinforcement, all these may be done along with direct teaching. The teacher should again take to direct teaching for formative evaluation and remedial measures.

Monitorial assistance: Monitorial assistance is a must in multigrade teaching. The monitor facilitates the teacher in sharing his/her work. The monitor fills up the gap while the teacher is engaged with other grades. The monitor assistance helps:

— to facilitate the teacher on miscellaneous counts;

— to coordinate and organise peer group and, individual learning activities;

— to prepare learners for direct teaching;

— to demonstrate the material to the learners;

— to lead the learners in outdoor activities;

— to conduct drills;

— to supervise self-study and work sessions;

— to report to teacher about such pupils who have accomplished the task;

— to maintain discipline and minimise interruption.

There should be different monitors for different subjects and also for different ability groups. They should be changed according to the situations, watching the degree of receptivity they command. As far as possible monitors should be taken from the same class and not from the senior classes. A monitor should have:

— the ability to grasp the topics

— the ability of making the peer learners understand the content

— the readiness in seeking concept clarification from the teacher without any hesitation or shyness

— the ability to control group/class

— the ability to prepare the class for learning situations

— the skills for demonstrative teaching

— the temperamental qualities of perseverance, diligence, sympathy, cooperation, leadership, etc.

Peer tutoring: Peer tutoring helps in lessening the work load of the teacher and also in facilitating the individual learner in his/her learning. A peer tutor could help his classmates with devotion and attention, as he being the co-learner. Peer tutoring is of several types. Two learners may help each other. In a group, a learner who is high achiever in one subject leads others and thus seeks help from others in the subject of his own deficiency. Sometimes, a peer tutor may be self-appointed to his/her co-learners. For example, if learners are transcribing a particular paragraph in language, and one of the learners faces difficulty in writing a particular word, he/she finds that his/her colearner is writing it. So he/she seeks help on his/her own.

Peer group work: Peer groups are formed by bringing together bright, average and weak pupils. They help each other. Since they are of the same age level, they constitute a cohesive group. One learner activates the other. The peer group leader is chosen by the pupils themselves. Anyone who is considered the best in a particular field becomes the leader of the peer group for activities in that field. The peer group strategy helps in sustaining the interest of the learners. Peer tutoring helps in increasing individual attention of the learners. As tutoring is done in small groups, there is close contact within the group. It helps the learners to progress at their own pace and seek immediate guidance, whenever required. Peer tutors can provide assistance to teachers on:

— bringing the weak and average learners' up to the level of minimum competencies.

— diagnosing the learning difficulties of the learners and reporting these to the teacher for remedial work

— developing a sense of cooperation amongst the learners to help each other in learning.

— explaining duties and school routine to the peer, wherever essential.

— giving drill exercise to reinforce certain concepts.

— helping recitation.

— activating the rate of learner participation.

— demonstrating for effective learning.

Self-study: Self-study is best suited in the use of self-learning materials. Self-learning materials may be used right from class I. Children may be given play materials such as toys of different colours and sizes. Different pupils may be given different activities to perform. For example, while some of the pupils match the colours, others collect toys of particular shapes and sizes, while some learn counting. Tracing pictures by using pencil and paper is being done by some others. Arranging pictures on flannel-board to make patterns or a short story can be another activity. Revision for comprehension, drill in language skills, use of assignment cards, etc., are some other self-study activities. Study of books from the library and silent reading is yet another form of self-study.

Field trips: Field trips help children to understand their surroundings. These are of help to the teacher in initiating several new activities. Small groups of pupils are made in pursuance of an activity. In field trip activities, pupils are to be guided to how to observe, explore, understand and react to the environment. In such activities, pupils may be led to:

— observe and record facts and phenomena;

— compare notes;

— examine pros and cons of opinion;

— infer rules, relationships and laws; and

— draw generalisations.

The knowledge gained by the pupils may be systematised in House activities by involving children of several classes in debates.

Extended teaching period: Some children have to help their families in domestic and other economic activities. Doing routine homework is a problem to such children. Such children may have to stay back for about an hour after the school timings to do the homework. During this time, pupils of senior classes may help the children of lower classes. This is best done by vertical grouping, taking due care of ability levels. During the same time, the teacher may provide guidance to peer group leaders for the next day's work.

Supplementary reading material: Supplementary reading material helps to reinforce pupils' learning. It creates reading interests, introduces variety in reading habits and develops learning habits. The teacher also gets an off from classroom teaching and can attend to non-academic work while children are engaged in supplementary readings.

Use of community resources: Community participation can be used in different ways. In a rural environment the help of some retired persons, social workers, educated parents in the teaching work can be sought to supplement teachers' efforts. The cooperation of some old students can also be sought. Local expertise in craftsmanship such as a carpenter, blacksmith, weaver, *gramsevak*, etc., could also be utilised. Doctors and other health workers from the primary health centre could be invited to conduct health check-up. Evening games for school children can be arranged with the help of some educated young people of the village.

Collective teaching : A teacher uses a variety of activities to engage his students. In normal schools the same strategy of teaching and learning is followed for the whole class. But the multigrade schools have different characteristics than the normal schools. The same teacher engages different grades with different strategies, but for the same subject.

Minimum Level of Learning (MLL)

The achievement standards of primary school children are rather low all over the country. There is a need for laying down the minimum levels of learning below which no school should be allowed to fall. There has always been a gap between what our majority of learners achieve and what is expected of them to achieve. Despite that investment of the huge amount of money, time and efforts, our schools, in general, have not moved towards the goal of increased learning for all learners. Substantial achievements have been made with regard to providing primary schools/ non-formal education centres within walking distance of the child and also increasing enrolment. But children achievement continue to reflect not only low levels of achievement but also achievement gaps amongst the children. These levels of achievement and achievement gaps which vary from school to school make it crystal clear that educational opportunity in terms of infrastructural facilities alone is not good enough to do the job.

What is more important is the laying down of standards of learning (quality) which must be ensured to be achieved by all the learners (equity). This brings in the idea of 'quality coupled with equity' which means that each and every child should have access to education of a satisfactory quality. In fact, this idea of 'quality coupled with equity' underlies the attempt at laying down of Minimum Levels of Learning (MLLs) at the primary stage. Students are expected to achieve certain predetermined standards of learning in each area of school subject. With this end in view you may be working hard with your students so as to help them achieve the expected standards of learning. But very often you find that the majority of your students do not reach the standards expected of them. Studies in this area have revealed that achievement levels of the majority of primary school children are very low. For exarnple, in language it is reported that majority of the students cannot read/write correctly all the letters of the alphabet even at the end of Class III. Similarly, they cannot read/write correctly many familiar words or simple sentences. Listening and reading compre-hension is also reported to be very poor. In the area of mathematics, students often cannot count, recognise or write correctly numbers from 1 to 100 even at the end of class II. Achievement is pretty low in four basic arithmetical skills of addition, subtraction, multiplication and division even at the end of class IV or V. These findings may, therefore, be very similar to your own experiences.

The teacher must be concerned about the low level of achievement of your students. In fact, parents, educational administrators and planners and knowledgeable members of the community are must concerned about the low achievement of our primary school students. Recently, the concern for improving the quality of achievement of all students at the primary stage has been attracting the attention of educational policymakers and practitioners. In this context, the National Policy on Education (NPE) 1986, recommended that minimum levels of learning be laid down for each stage of school education and that steps be undertaken to ensure that students achieve these minimum levels of learning.

The urgency for ensuring minimum levels of learning of all students has again been re-emphasised in the revised-policy formulation and programme of action 1992. As a follow-up of the directive of NPE 1986, a committee to lay down minimum levels of learning at the primary stage was set up in 1990 by the Ministry of Human Resource Development, Department of Education, Government of India. In 1991, this committee, submitted its report entitled Minimum Levels of Learning (MLL) at primary stage. The report has laid down minimum levels of learning for classes I-V in language, mathematics and environmental studies. The minimum levels for each subject has been stated in terms of competencies. These specified levels of learning set a standard which all students should achieve at the end of each grade. The school system has to ensure that all students achieve these levels of learning as they progress from class I to V. This would help achieve the goal of increased learning for all learners, and, this would lead to improvement in the quality of education.

The concept of MLL includes three aspects, namely 'minimum', 'levels' and' learning'. Of them, the words 'minimum' and 'levels' are two qualifiers for learning. The word 'learning' means desirable and durable change in the learner's knowledge, understanding the values. attitudes and motor skills. In the educational context this learning takes place through curricular experiences in or outside the school premises. The word 'levels' refers to standards or levels of performance. In fact, each level consists of a statement of competencies and every competency requires a particular learning which in turn becomes levels of learning. The word 'minimum' refers to the quantum of competencies which ought to be acquired by each and every learner having undergone a stipulated time-frame of learning. There is an important thing which we must know about 'minimum' and that is that 'minimum' is not necessarily optimum. This minimum does not mean that it sets the upper limit of learning for all children. There will be children who can learn beyond the minimum levels specified in the report. Such fast learners should be encouraged to achieve more than what is contained in the MLL's report.

In the MLLs report the concept of minimum levels of learning has been stated in the form of competencies. In the context of MLLs, competencies are learning objectives. When a competency has been developed in a student he/she would be able to perform a specific task related to that competency. For example, according to the language competency under writing skill for class I, the student should be able to write simple familiar words and simple sentences. Again, in mathematics under the area 'understanding whole numbers and numerals', there is a competency for class II, wherein the students should be able to state the place value of digits within a two digit numerals. Similarly, in environmental studies for class III, there is a competency wherein the student should be able to interpret important road symbols. The minimum levels of learning will help a teacher in the following ways:

— It sets clear goals for the teacher and thus provides direction to his/her work. The effort of the teacher will now be directed at helping all the students achieve the competencies to reach the levels which have been laid down. Covering merely the syllabus or completing the content of the textbooks will not be the only aim of his/her teaching.

— It helps the teacher choose an appropriate teaching-learning strategy. It provides clarity about the choice of methodology and subject-matter to be used for developing the competencies.

— It helps the teacher choose appropriate method of evaluating pupil achievement. It provides direction to the teacher so as to make him/her know about what, when and how to evaluate.

Some important features of MLL's approach in the teaching-learning process, include:

— mastery learning,

— competency-based teaching, and

— competency-based comprehensive and continuous evaluation.

Mastery learning: Competencies for each subject and for each grade have been arranged from simple to more complex. Each competency must be learnt thoroughly which then provides the basis for learning the next competency, and so on. If a student is not able to learn thoroughly a given competency, then it would be difficult for him/her to learn the next competency. It is necessary to ensure that each competency is learnt thoroughly. When a competency is learnt thoroughly we say that the competency has been mastered. Thus, the minimum levels of learning approach implies that each competency should be developed at the mastery level.

In our context, mastery learning means that all the competencies or almost all the competencies are to be mastered by all the children or almost all the children. Suppose there are 20 competencies to be learnt by a group of 20 children in the class. If all these 20 competencies are thoroughly learnt by all the 20 children, we may say that these competencies have been fully mastered by the class. This is often expressed as 100 × 100. If 80 per cent of the competencies are mastered by 80 per cent of the children (80 × 80), this may also be considered as acceptable. However, there are certain competencies which must be mastered by all the learners, for example, 'recognises common letters of alphabet in combination and singly' (language), and 'recognises numerals and matches numbers to numerals from 1-100 (mathematics). Mastery learning is the key aspect of the MLL's approach. In day-a-day teaching-learning situation ensuring mastery of competencies by the learners is the target for the teacher.

Competency-based teaching: In MLLs approach, development of the competencies until the mastery level is the major concern. For this purpose, a competency serves as a basis for selecting and arranging appropriate teaching-learning activities with a view to meeting learning needs of learners. This calls for child-centred and activity-oriented competency-based teaching. Teaching-learning activities have to be organised in such a manner so as to suit the needs of the individual learner. As a teacher you should be clear about the competency/competencies to be developed amongst your students. This will help you decide:

— suitable content

— appropriate teaching methodology

— suitable teaching aid

— appropriate evaluation techniques

— necessary remedial measures for those facing learning difficulties.

Comprehensive and Continuous Evaluation (CCE) : In order to assess whether or not a learner has mastered the competencies, it is necessary to evaluate his/her achievement on a regular basis. A learner can acquire the next competency only if he/she has mastered the earlier related competency. Therefore, it becomes necessary to adopt a scheme of evaluation which helps the teacher confirm regularly whether or not the competencies have been mastered by the learner competencies. This means that the scheme of evaluation has to be continuous. But very often the tests that are used for evaluating learners' achievement measure only the knowledge of content. Not much attention is paid to evaluate the achievement of competencies. It has also been observed that evaluation is done only in the cognitive areas of learning such as knowledge, understanding and mental skills. Evaluation of non-cognitive areas of learning such as attitudes. personality, qualities, values, and psychomoter skills is seldomly carried out.

The report on 'minimum levels of learning at the primary stage' has specified certain personality qualities which need to be developed in schools. Effective evaluation procedures need to be employed so as to measure both cognitive and non- cognitive learning outcomes. Such a procedure of evaluation which adequately measures both cognitive and non-cognitive learning outcomes is commonly known as comprehensive evaluation.

The process of evaluation should start with pretesting. Pretesting should be carried out right in the beginning of the academic session. This will help you know whether or not the learners are prepared to acquire the related competencies to be developed in the new class. This will help you identify those children who are not ready to learn competencies of the new class. For them, you may have to organise a suitable remedial programme. For a teacher, organising teaching-learning activities is a regular process in which the learner's evaluation has also to move side by side. That is, evaluation has to be continuous. This continuity in evaluation has to be viewed in two ways. They are:

— The teacher while developing a competency simultaneously tries to assess the development of the competency amongst his/her learners.

— The teacher may assess periodically the development of the cluster of interrelated competencies which may be termed as a periodical test, such a periodical test could be held six to seven times in an academic year. Besides, the teacher may like to conduct an annual test which is often called as end of course or summative test.

Evaluation primary school students is to be developmental in nature instead of summative because at this stage child is in a formative stage of learning. Emphasis at this stage laid should not be on the measurement of the students' learning but on improvement of their achievement. If a child is weak in his/her studies, diagnostic evaluation and remediation for effective learning should be adopted by you. The purpose of this module is to provide you practical suggestions as to how you can use the concept of comprehensive continuous evaluation at the primary stage. Emphasis on the following aspects of teaching, learning approach at the primary stage has been laid:

— Learner-centred

— Competency-based minimum levels of learning

— Use of Operation Blackboard (OB) material

— Continuous and comprehensive evaluation of learning experiences.

In learner-centred approach the child is exposed to posing problems, asking questions, collecting information, finding solutions to problems and answering questions through his/her effort/activity. At this stage the teacher has to encourage the child's participation in the above process through activities.

The whole process of teaching-learning is geared to the development of the learner's creativity and thinking. Competency-based minimum teaming has been already dealt with elsewhere here. Use of OB material supplied to your school is emphasised while you are teaching. Your class has to make relevant, effective and realistic effort. You can use your own immediate environment in addition to your OB material. The concept, use and practice of comprehensive continuous evaluation includes three words: 'comprehensive', 'continuous' and 'evaluation'. 'Evaluation' in short means information gathering, information processing, judgement forming and decision-making. These above four components relate to the achievement/performance of a learner in his/her teaching-learning process under the given schooling conditions.

Learning at the primary stage has to be evaluated on a formative/developmental pattern, hence it is to be evaluated on a continuum, i.e., in a continuous and sequential integrated form. Concepts are learnt in a hierarchical form which appear from simple to complex in sequential learning. For example, you teach the competency of recognising and writing numerals from 1 to 100 in class I. The following competencies are involved:

— Concept of numerals

— Recognition of numerals

— Writing of numerals

— Sequential order of writing of these numerals.

These above competencies are to be mastered in a sequential, graded and integrated form. Teaching in this sequential form has to be done and once this is done then evaluation has to be done so that you ensure that your pupils have mastered these four steps while gaining competency.

Under the NPE, 1986, the scheme of evaluation has to cover all learning experiences—curricular subjects and non-cognitive areas. Hence, evaluation in the scheme is comprehensive in character.A policy of automatic promotion is followed in all or initial classes of the primary education. But with this, a sound procedure of evaluation on a continuous basis is to be followed. But evaluation aimed at content improvement of learning is either neglected or paid inadequate attention, as a result of which the weakness of basic skills of reading, writing and computation goes on accumulating. It has been recommended that formal examination at least in the first two classes of the primary stage should be avoided. But it is also necessary to devise 'oral mechanism' of evaluation for these two classes so that the children gain competencies of the basic skills which are expected to be mastered in these classes. The MLL's approach implies a calculated effort to include those minimum essential and common competencies that all children must master. Oral questioning has all along been a part of the classroom activity. At this stage the teacher can use the following mechanism:

— Quiz contest

— Single question put to individuals in a group while the lesson is being taught.

Oral mechanism can help to test the ability to speak with correct articulation and intonation, the ability to speak grammatically correct language, vocabulary and its usage and communication skills. The general techniques for oral examination are:

— reading aloud picture story card

— prepared questions

— conversation on prepared topics

— questions on pictures and role playing, etc.

The teacher should prepare sample oral questions on cards of different varieties and depth such as:

— Recall type (objective type questions)

— Understanding type (very short-answer type)

— Application level (expression type).

Operation Blackboard Scheme (OB)

The Operation Blackboard (OB) scheme was initiated in 1987 as part of the implementation of the resolutions of National Policy on Education (NPE), 1986. All the existing primary schools in the country were targeted to be covered by the end of Seventh Five Year Plan but due to various factors the targets could not be achieved during that period. By March 1992, 4.14 lakh (77 per cent) schools in 5, 385 (84 per cent) community development blocks and 1, 142 (29 per cent) municipal areas had been covered under the scheme. Meeting the basic learning needs and enhancing the achievement level of primary school children are global concern today.

India's efforts towards the achievement of this objective had started as early as early the fifties when the Constitution was adopted and provision of universal elementary education to all children of the age group 6-14 years was accepted as the constitutional obligation through Article 45 under the directive principles of state policy. Since then substantial progress has been made in providing primary schooling facilities within walking distance from the home of every child and relating the curriculum to the daily life needs of the child and needs of the local community aiming at their social and economic upliftment. But the targets of keeping all enrolled children in school till they complete the age of 14 years and helping them to attain the identified standards have still been not achieved. Some of the major factors responsible for this state of affairs have been:

— non-availability of adequate/suitable physical facilities including classrooms and other essential structures,

— non-availability of sufficient number of teachers in a large number of primary schools, and

— non-availability of essential teaching learning material for teachers and children.

Rising concern about these factors as great hindrances in reducing the dropout rates and raising the achievement level of children led to the conception of the OB scheme which was included as a significant policy formulation in the NPE. The major components of the scheme are:

— Provision of at least two reasonably large rooms that are usable in all weathers, with a deep verandah along with separate toilet facilities for boys and girls.

— Provision of at least two teachers, as far as possible one of them a woman in every primary school.

— Provision of essential teaching and learning material including blackboards, maps, charts, a small library, toys and games and some equipment for work experience.

Implementation of the scheme was reviewed by the ministry of Human Resource Development, Government of India in 1991-92. Some modifications have been made in the scheme as well as the mode of its implementation. The modified scheme as given in the Programme of Action (POA) 1992 has the following sub-schemes:

— Continuation of ongoing OB scheme to cover all the remaining primary schools, especially those in SC/ST areas.

— Expanding the scope of OB to provide three teachers and three rooms to primary schools, wherever enrolment warrants them.

— Expanding OB to upper primary schools.

The Operation Blackboard (OB) scheme has unique features that recommend well-defined steps for the improvement of facilities in a primary school aiming at making it a pleasant place for children and encouraging teachers to adopt child-centred, activity-based teaching-learning strategies. Some of the significant features are:

— It defines the concrete facilities, that are a must for any school to function effectively, in terms of building, teachers and teaching-learning material.

— The items identified as minimum aids for teaching-learning process take care of the requirements of the teachers and pupils for self-learning as well as teaching of various concepts in different subject areas included in the scheme of studies at the primary stage.

— Norms and specifications of each supply item have been laid down in order to maintain the quality of each item. Thus, the scheme provides opportunities not only of equal access to education but also creating conditions for equal participation and attainment of comparable levels by all children.

The print and non-print OB material has been developed by the NCERT in the context of utilisation of the material supplied under the scheme. The materials have been disseminated to all states and union territories.

Digital Technologies for Teaching

Today new information and communication technologies including compact discs and CD-ROMs, videodiscs, microcomputer-based laboratories, the Internet, local and wide area networks, instructional software, Macs, PCs, laptops, notebooks, educational television, voice mail, e-mail, satellite communication, VCRs, cable TV, interactive radio, etc. are available for education. With these tools, teachers should be able to evolve the components of the conventional model into the corresponding components of the new model. These six far-reaching implications pose a daunting challenge for the education strategist. Education will not be a location anymore, but an activity: a teaching/learning activity.

This is the ultimate raison d'être of ICTs for education. Imagine a highly interactive, synchronous and asynchronous, multimedia learning experience between distant locations over vast national and international networks, allowing learners to obtain simultaneous distance learning services from their geographically dispersed organizations, schools, and other colleagues. In this new paradigm, ICTs are not a substitute for schooling. They constitute one integral element of this education model-supplementing and enriching traditional institutions, delivery systems, and instructional materials. In this sense, ICTs contribute to the whole system of knowledge dissemination and learning. Policy makers and practitioners tend to refer to ICTs as one monolithic entity, in which case they question the potential of technology-in the singular. Such inquiry is unanswerable because technologies are very different in their potential and use. The potential of different technologies depends on what we use them for.

There are at least five hierarchical levels at which technologies may be used: presentation, demonstration, drill and practice, interaction, and collaboration. If technology is to be used for representation and demonstration only, investment in computers and connectivity may not be justifiable. On the other hand, the potential for interactive and collaborative learning can best be achieved by networked computers and connectivity to the World Wide Web. Therefore, technology should not be equated with computers and Internet. There is still an important place for other technologies, such as interactive radio, broadcast TV, and correspondence courses.

Different ICTs have the potential to contribute to different facets of educational development and effective learning: expanding access, promoting efficiency, improving the quality of learning, enhancing the quality of teaching, and improving management systems. ICTs also offer possibilities in lifelong learning, adult training, and e-training for the workplace. Planning for effective use of ICTs in education necessitates an understanding of the potential of technologies to meet different educational objectives and, consequently, to decide which of these objectives will be pursued.

The potential of ICTs to reach large audiences was tapped initially in the late 1800s, when correspondence courses became an alternative means to provide education for individuals who could not attend regular schools due to geographical, social, or cultural barriers. Experiments with radio broadcast started in the early 1900s, and, in 1924, the British Broadcast Corporation (BBC) began to air educational programmes. Since then, radio has been instrumental in reaching scattered and rural populations. Although experiments with televised broadcast began in the 1930s, it took another 20 years for television to become popular.

Computer-related technologies began to make inroads 30 years ago and are changing the concept of time and space rapidly. There are now virtual high schools, virtual universities, and virtual programs provided by campus-based universities. About 60% of U.S. universities provide virtual education programs. In addition, open universities expand opportunities to populations that traditionally have been excluded from education due to geographic, cultural, and social barriers: minorities, girls, rural populations, and the elderly.

The personal contact with peers and with teachers in a good on-site institution is incomparable in its richness. Libraries, possibly obsolete in a not-too distant future, still serve as an unmatched resource for investigation and learning. Distance learning, on the other hand, provides opportunities for those who could not attend courses on campus because of cost and time constraints.

Distance learning increasingly provides rapid and personal interaction; it can provide more reliable learning materials than inferior institutions; it is generally far lower in terms of cost to the student; and it often offers more for lower capital and recurrent costs. ICTs promote efficiency of delivery of educational services by supplementing conventional delivery mechanisms, for example: Technology's capacity to reach learners in any place and at any time has the potential to promote revolutionary changes in the educational paradigm. Such capacity eliminates the premise that learning time equals classroom time.

To avoid overcrowded classrooms, a school may adopt a dual-shift system without cutting actual study time for its students. The students attend school for half a day and spend the other half involved in independent technology-enhanced education activities at home, in a library, at work, or in another unconventional setting. For places with low population density, multigrade schools become viable alternatives with the injection of high-quality programs prepared by the best teachers, miles away, and transmitted or transferred electronically to these schools. Another illustration of efficiencies is the domain of virtual labs. All school systems want to provide labs because science is empirical. But few schools have them, fewer have furnished them with equipment and supplies, and fewer yet are willing to risk using them. Technology allows for video and digital demonstrations as well as digital simulation of lab activities in a very real manner, but without the risks and costs associated with lab experiments. Simulations will not replace hands-on activities completely; rather, they prepare the learner to conduct real-life experiments-in the same manner flight simulations prepare the student-pilot for test flying. Multimedia modules, the product of few instructional designers and master teachers, may be shared with many schools.

Since expertise in instructional design and multimedia materials development is scarce, technological networking allows for economies of expertise. Concerns about costs are always raised in discussions related to technology. Depending on the technology used, start-up costs can be high, but economies of scale are significant. That is, the more the technology is used, the lower the unit costs will be. The unit costs of producing a video or writing an educational contentware decrease as more students use the product. In addition, trade-offs must be considered as well when evaluating technology's initial costs. For instance, the costs of simulation software offset the costs of constructing, maintaining, and replenishing school laboratories. Unlike labs, the costs do not increase with the number of schools adopting such software. In many schools, teachers are not well qualified to translate the curriculum into teaching/learning activities or to be the chief mediators between knowledge and learners.

Their initial training, often the only one they have received, generally does not include the preparation of teaching materials or the use of contemporary technologies for teaching. Most teachers are reluctant to invest substantial amounts of their own time and resources in bringing their knowledge and competencies up to date in these areas, and few school systems provide time or incentives for this to take place. But, teachers can be empowered with high-quality educational videos and software. Teachers are no longer the sole providers of information but facilitators of the learning process. Second, most educational software comes with a teacher's guide and tutorials, and support can be found on the Internet.

E-mail and Internet-related collaborative environments provide teachers with individualized and immediate help. regardless of their geographical location. At the same time. ICTs can contribute significantly to the teacher professional development continuum:

First, ICTs and properly developed multimedia materials can enhance initial preparation by providing good training materials, facilitating simulations, capturing and analyzing practice teaching, bringing world experience into the training institution, familiarizing trainees with sources of materials and support, and training potential teachers in the use of technologies for teaching/learning.

Second, ICTs open a whole world of lifelong upgrading and professional development by providing courses at a distance, asynchronous learning, and training on demand.

ICTs can be revised easily and they can introduce new courses in response to emerging demands.

Third, ICTs break the professional isolation many teachers suffer from. With ICTs, they become part of a network with colleagues and mentors, with universities and centers of expertise, and with sources of teaching materials.

Equally important, research and experience have shown that ICTs, used well in classrooms, enhance the learning process, in many ways. For example, they have the potential to:

— allow materials to be presented in multiple media for multichannel learning;

— motivate and engage students in the learning process;

— bring abstract concepts to life;

— enhance critical thinking and other higher levels of cognitive skills and processes;

— provide opportunities for students to practice basic skills on their own time and at their own pace;

— allow students to use the information acquired to solve problems, formulate new problems, and explain the world around them: provide for access to worldwide information resources;

— be the most cost-effective (and in some cases the only) means for bringing the world into the classroom; and

— offer (via the Internet) teachers and students a platform through which they can communicate with colleagues from distant places, exchange work, develop research, and function as if there were no geographical boundaries.

They are flexible, unconstrained by time and place, can be used on demand, and provide just-in-time education. They have the potential to offer synchronous as well as asynchronous learning opportunities. But, above all, if well prepared, they can pack a wealth of expertise and experience in efficient packages that can be modified and updated all the time in response to feedback, new demands and varied contexts. Possibilities fall in a wide range of technologies, including videos, correspondence, Internet, and e-learning superstructure. This may be the first time in the history of the human race when lifelong learning is not only desirable and urgent, but feasible as well.

However, successful exploitation of technology for lifelong learning for all is dependent on a number of factors:

— Adults need to have a minimum level of basic education, including literacy. Technology should not blind us to the fact that there are still millions of adults who cannot read or write, and, because of that, they cannot use educational programs offered through information technologies, or even through classical correspondence.

— Schools should equip individuals with the necessary cognitive and technical skills to pursue and manage their own continuous learning-how to search, assimilate, define problems, apply knowledge to problem solving, etc.

— Technology literacy-the ability to use technology hardware and software-should be part of basic education and a prerequisite for adults to make good use of ICTs.

Traditional training programs cannot address new realities adequately; they are costly in terms of travel and lost time on the job, disruptive, slow to be modified, and incapable of responding to new needs and provisions in a timely fashion. Network technologies have the potential to deliver timely and appropriate knowledge and skills to the right people, at a suitable time, in a convenient place. This is what e-training is about. It allows for personalized, just-in-time, up-to-date, and user-centered educational activities.

E-training has been most popular (and successful) in the corporate world, probably because of the culture of innovation and light bureaucracies, the feasibility of having limited and clear educational objectives, and quantifiable trade-offs. It also is used by consumers for informal skill formation and for professional training and upgrading in certain specializations. But corporate and consumer e-training modalities have opened new paths, raised new ideas, and generated new paradigms in the academic world, and the sector that responded most to e-training applications is the tertiary-level sector, worldwide. The education enterprise is huge and intricate. It involves educational institutions all over the country, teachers and administrators in large numbers, and students of every age, who can reach a total of up to 30% of the population.

Recent reforms within the education enterprise have resulted in observable successes in making educational opportunities more accessible and equitable and the teaching/learning process more effective. Expanding educational opportunities means more schools in isolated rural areas and more diversified modes of delivery. Aiming for education for all means including students from underserved populations who require special measures to reach and have special needs to meet. The accent on learning requires setting reliable and measurable standards, and attending to individual differences.

Decentralization and devolution of decisions to district and local levels require better information systems and management procedures.

Involvement of more stakeholders in the education process (parents, employers, unions, political parties, etc.) is resulting in more transparency and accountability. These developments demand a consistent flow of information and force the education enterprise to be managed better and more efficiently. Any business that is even a fraction of the size and complexity of a country's educational enterprise and uses the management techniques of most educational systems will go out of business in no time. Big businesses have discovered how important management is to keep their companies well run, efficient, and competitive. In so doing, they have used the potential of technology to restructure their procedures and overhaul their production, distribution, training, feedback, maintenance, and administration processes. However, education systems have been slow in exploiting the power of technology. Many educational institutions and systems have introduced simple management and statistical information systems; but this should be only the beginning. The same elements of computing and telecommunications equipment and services that made businesses more efficient and cost-effective can be applied to schools and school systems to enable principals and superintendents to streamline operations, monitor performance, and improve use of physical and human resources.

At the system-wide level, technologies provide critical support in domains such as school mapping; automated personnel and payroll systems; management information systems; communications; and information gathering, analysis, and use. Technology also can be powerful in driving and managing new approaches to learning that involve more student interaction, more connections among schools, more collaboration among teachers and students, and more involvement of teachers as facilitators. These needs are especially critical in self-study, distance education, and e-learning settings, and many platforms have been developed to meet such needs.

No ICT potential is realized automatically-not in education, in business, or in entertainment; many computerized businesses are managed badly and go bankrupt, and many movies are a complete failure. Placing a radio and TV in every school, putting a computer in every classroom, and wiring every building to the Internet will not solve the problem automatically. The problem is not strictly technological; it is educational and contextual; constraints must be alleviated and conditions met.

Technology is only a tool: no technology can fix a bad educational philosophy or compensate for bad practice. In fact, if we are going in the wrong direction, technology will get us there faster. Likewise, distance learning is not about distance, it is about learning. Just as we can have bad education face to face, we can have bad education at a distance. Therefore, educational choices have to be made first in terms of objectives, methodologies, and roles of teachers and students before decisions can be made about the appropriate technologies. For instance, if teaching is demonstrating and telling, and if learning is memorizing and reciting, using learning technologies and multimedia programs for this purpose will not have the desired impact. Also, if students are not asked to search and work collaboratively, and if teachers function independently, investment in connectivity will not be cost-effective.

The effectiveness of different levels of sophistication of use of ICTs depends to a large extent on the role of learners and teachers as practiced in the educational process. Unfortunately, however, much introduction of technology into the educational system comes not from a process of needs identification and analysis but in response to a perceived need to innovate or to pressure from outside groups (parents, manufacturers, employers). This is not necessarily a bad thing for triggering the process, but cannot be the only reason for investing in ICTs. Classrooms are constrained environments, and conventional instructional materials are static. If technology-enhanced education programs are taped classrooms, digital texts, and PowerPoint transparencies, then we are missing out on the tremendous potential of technologies that can animate, simulate, capture reality, add movement to static concepts, and extend our touch to the whole universe.

Movies and TV programs are not replicas of theater-packaged theaters; they tell the same story in a more dramatic and multifaceted manner. So should ICT-enhanced education. In October 2001, the OECD issued Learning to Change, the results of a study of how ICTs are being put to use in the most advanced countries. Essentially, according to the report, they are being used to do traditional things in different ways. Examples include "putting on screen what can be found on the page of a book," using material from the Internet to "support conventional teaching practices," and employing didactic software to rehearse basic skills. This merely replicates existing learning methods in technological form. If ICTs are to fulfil their potential, "innovation and change are called for at all levels of the school environment."

In advantaged communities, change is an upheaval for established authorities, systems, and capacities. In disadvantaged communities, the infrastructure must be put into place along with serious attention to pedagogy. There is also a basic difference between using technology as an add-on to make the current model of education more efficient, more equitable, and cheaper, on the one hand, and integrating technology into the entire education system to realize structural rethinking and reengineering, on the other. It is the difference between a marginal addition and a radical systemic change. It is in the second scenario that technology can provide the greatest impact.

Information technology is the fundamental underpinning of the science of structural re-engineering. It is the force that revolutionizes business, streamlines government and enables instant communications and the exchange of information among people and institutions around the world. But information technology has not made even its barest appearance in most public schools. Before we can get the education revolution rolling, we need to recognize that our public schools are low-tech institutions in a high-tech society.The same changes that have brought cataclysmic change to every facet of business can improve the way we teach students and teachers. And it can also improve the efficiency and effectiveness of how we run our schools. There is a temptation these days to equate technology with computers and the Internet.

There is still an important place for other technologies, depending on how they will be used. The application of each technology falls over a wide spectrum, from the simplest to the most sophisticated. It is important, therefore, to identify the most appropriate, cost-effective, and sustainable technology and level of application for the different educational objectives. Then the whole prerequisite hardware infrastructure needs to be in place with the supporting elements, such as electricity, maintenance, and technical services.

Different educational and institutional objectives are served by different configuration options: computers in classrooms, on wheels, in computer rooms or labs, or in libraries and teachers' rooms. Turning computers into powerful communication tools requires access to the Internet; however, getting a school online, particularly in a developing country, is not a straightforward task. First, schools need to figure out why they need to connect and to what. The next problem is communication infrastructure. In many areas, it is either nonexistent or expensive to use. Some forms of terrestrial wireless and satellite technologies are being introduced that do not require installation of wireline networks and are ideal for remote and isolated areas. Finally, schools need to find out whether they have the resources, beyond the initial investment, to cover connectivity's operating costs.

3

Challenges of Teacher Development

Educational policies worldwide are currently in a state of flux and common strands are difficult to identify except possibly at the regional and sub-regional levels. Student enrolments in the various regions of the world have been increasing at different speeds; at some levels of education in the more developed regions and countries in transition, they have even been decreasing. In consequence, teacher recruitment priorities have been constantly shifting, with 'knock-on' effects on other educational priorities and plans. However, educational policies have also evolved in response to broader political and economic trends and developments. In a global perspective, the two main strands of educational policies are the deepening commitment of most countries to the democratization of education and the tendency towards a more productivist view of educational quality and purposes. 'Assessment', 'adjustment', 'effectiveness', 'performance', 'outcomes', 'fiscal constraints' and of course 'human capital' are just some of the signs of how widely the productivistic view has permeated educational policies, compared, say, with thirty years ago. A third strand, 'accountability', is linked to the other two; sometimes it is mainly associated with policies designed to decentralize/democratize educational decision-making and at other times it is more closely associated with demands for improved educational 'effectiveness' and 'performance'.

There are, of course, many substrands and variations according to particular national circumstances, but it is becoming increasingly apparent that the two main orientations of educational policy do not sit quietly together. Teachers are aware of this. They are caught in the middle, regarded on the one hand as carriers of light into dark places, be it tolerance, international understanding or respect for human rights, and, on the other hand, as costly factors of production in an enterprise which absorbs a significant proportion of public budgets. If the latter is rarely stated as bluntly outside of professional economic journals, the consequences for teachers of current worldwide efforts to hold down public expenditures are nonetheless real enough.

During the 1990s, the double orientation of educational policies noted above has been evident in every region of the world, although there is of course great variation among countries and regions in the specific contents of policies. In the more developed regions, most countries have been engaged like Canada in a process of retrenchment and restructuring of public expenditure, including expenditure on education, while at the same time seeking to redefine accountability structures and continuing to democratize access to and participation in education, especially at the tertiary level, which is becoming increasingly diversified with respect to institutional forms and programmes, student populations and funding arrangements.

Retrenchment and restructuring of public expenditure have, of course, been key features of the economic and social transformation now under way in the transition countries of East and Central Europe and the Russian Federation, but the objective conditions have been much more difficult, and education budgets have suffered, impeding the educational reform process and causing considerable hardships for teachers notwithstanding the role they are called upon to play in helping to forge new political identities and cultures. A notable casualty of the economic dislocation in the transition countries has been pre-primary education, where enrolments have fallen sharply. This level of education was traditionally provided mainly by enterprises for the children of their employees, but the difficulties of adjustment to the market economy have forced most enterprises to cut back on their social services, including kindergartens and pre-school programmes, and many teachers in these programmes have lost their jobs.

In both the more developed regions and the transition countries, the ageing of the population has been an important (though little noticed) indirect contributory source of pressure on state education budgets, because of the competing demand it makes for funds to pay for social security and retirement benefits within the overall social sector budget envelope. In the less developed regions, where population pressures are still strong and student enrolment growth rates generally have been positive,

Education for All goals, including improvement in the quality of basic education, have been the main focus of educational policies, at least to the extent that political and economic conditions have allowed, since many of the same impulses towards public expenditure retrenchment and restructuring which have constrained educational policies in the more developed regions have also been at work. There have been differences of emphasis among the less developed regions in how these constraints have been handled, because of the differences between regions in the stages of development of their educational infrastructures and differences too in their systems of governance.

In the Latin American/Caribbean region, where broadly speaking the educational infrastructure is more highly developed than in the other regions, the 1990s have witnessed several major initiatives towards the decentralization of once- monolithic state education systems, e.g. Argentina, Brazil, Colombia and Mexico. In each case, this has entailed, among other things, complex and protracted discussions with teachers' unions, which traditionally had negotiated teachers salaries and conditions of service at the national level and were still wary of further erosion of their incomes coming after the experiences of inflation and structural adjustment policies in the 1980s. In the Eastern Asia/Oceania region, where economic growth has been strong, there has not been the same degree of emphasis on retrenchment and restructuring of public expenditure as in Latin America.

The overall pattern of educational development has also been different: that of the Republic of Korea, for example, has perhaps been paradigmatic. The region's figures for enrolment growth rates are heavily weighted by China, where there has been a marked decline in the birth rate. Nevertheless, it is generally the case in this region that universal access to primary education has virtually been achieved, that rapid progress is being made towards the universalisation of access to secondary education and that pressures are building up for expansion of tertiary level education. Given the region's favourable economic situation, there has been more scope for teachers incomes to rise, although in many countries there is evidence of widespread moon—lighting by teachers in second jobs. In fact, moon lighting by public school teachers to supplement their low official salaries has been an important source of supply of teachers for private schools throughout the region. The same phenomenon has also been evident in other regions, especially in Latin America.

In the sub-Saharan Africa, Arab States and Southern Asia regions, which include most of the least developed countries, educational policies have been very much hostage to economic and political circumstances although, as already noted, there has been a certain measure of success over the last decade and a half in responding to the great population pressures for increasing educational enrolments. That enrolments in tertiary level education in these regions have grown as fast as, or faster than, in primary and secondary level education is probably more a reflection of the low starting base of tertiary level enrolments (especially in sub-Saharan Africa) than of policy preferences in favour of tertiary level education as such.

Nevertheless, it has been a bone of contention with external financing agencies strongly influenced by interpretations of the educational foundations of the East Asian development miracle, in particular the idea that the universalization of primary and secondary education should precede any shift of emphasis to the expansion of higher education. In the large majority of countries in the sub-Saharan Africa, Arab States and Southern Asia regions which have been free of war and violent political conflict, economic conditions have improved since the beginning of the 1990s compared with the previous decade and many countries are beginning to make progress towards Education for All goals. Where violent internal political conflict has ocurred, the effects on education have been disastrous. In the less developed regions of the world generally, economic and social changes in recent years have reinforced the impulse towards the democratization of education, establishing a momentum of rapid growth in most education systems that tends continously to push up against existing limits placed on the public budgetary resources available for education. In consequence, the teaching force is constantly growing and mutating in a situation of severe resource constraints. These conditions are not favourable to improvements in the status of teachers. Even in countries which in recent years have experienced rapid economic growth and increasing prosperity, the status of teachers has hardly improved and may even have declined.

In other developing countries, the pursuit of Education for All goals is often still constrained by structural adjustment programmes. Although such programmes today are conceived with more consideration for the needs of the social sectors than was the case in the 1980s, some of the effects of the earlier programmes on the employment and conditions of service of teachers are still being felt, the most notorious probably being the encouragement given by these programmes to the hiring of contract teachers at lower rates of remuneration than the rates accorded to already employed teachers with similar qualifications.

Pressures of Student Enrolments

While the growth in the total number of teachers in the world's formal education systems can be basically regarded as a response to the pressure of increasing student enrolments, the global pattern of student enrolments by region and level of education has changed considerably over the last thirty years, and continues to evolve. Taking the size of the population in the 6-14 age-group as a broad indicator of the overall demand for education, recent decades have witnessed strong pressures on teacher demand-supply balances in Southern Asia, sub-Saharan Africa and the Arab States. In the other major regions, the pressures have levelled off or even declined, except in so far as there has been increasing demand from students already in the education system to continue their education to higher levels.

The teacher shortages of the 1960s and the 1970s, especially in the less developed regions of the world, were met to some extent by employing large numbers of unqualified, untrained teachers; in many cases they were simply primary-school graduates. A measure of the tremendous efforts exerted by countries in the less developed regions to provide teachers to meet the challenge of the explosive growth in their school-age populations is that they managed to achieve an improvement in their enrolment ratios, i.e., the percentages of the relevant age-groups enrolled at the various levels of education. Even so, sub-Saharan Africa was an exception: the gross enrolment ratio in primary education fell back between 1980 and 1995.

The special difficulties faced in recent years by the countries in transition in maintaining the growth momentum of previous decades in secondary and tertiary education are indicated by the stagnation and/or fall in the overall gross enrolment ratios for these levels between 1980 and 1995. In the more developed regions, the falling birth rates and declining population pressures on school enrolments and hence softening of the demand for teachers provided an opportunity for reducing student-teacher ratios and class sizes at the middle and lower levels of the education system, although this was offset by an increasing need for teachers to meet the expansion of enrolments at the upper and lower ends of the education system in higher education and pre-primary education respectively. Still, over time, as the outputs of the education systems in the less developed regions of the world increased and teacher-training capacities expanded, the levels of recruitment improved and growing numbers of qualified, trained teachers entered employment. The consequence of this trend, though, was that by the late 1970s and early 1980s, the primary-level teaching force in many countries was made up of groups of teachers with often very different educational and training backgrounds, ranging from teachers who in some cases had not received much more than a primary education themselves to others who had received a full secondary education and teacher training in addition.

The whole issue of the status of teachers was thus extremely complex, since in all these countries there was really no such body as a 'typical' primary-school teacher, at least in the same sense that this term could be applied in countries with a stable primary-level teaching force, most of whose members had received a similar education and training. The situation in respect to secondary-school teachers was not much different.

Initiatives to reform school curricula could not be followed up successfully in many countries without taking into account the very heterogenous composition of the teaching force which would have to implement the new curricula in the schools. One further aspect of the demographic background that needs to be noted with respect to global teacher demand-supply balances is the gradual ageing of the world's population.

Table 1
Early childhood, school-age and old-age dependency ratios (percentages), by region, 1995 and 2015

	1995			*2015*		
	0 –5	*6–14*	*65+*	*0 –5*	*6–14*	*65+*
World total	20.8	29.6	10.5	16.2	23.3	12.1
More developed regions	11.2	17.3	20.9	10.3	15.3	27.2
of which:						
North America	13.7	19.8	19.1	12.1	17.0	22.1
Asia /Oceania	9.5	15.8	19.8	9.9	15.8	34.5
Europe	10.0	15.9	22.8	8.9	13.6	28.9
Countries in transition	12.7	23.0	16.9	10.9	16.2	18.1
Less developed regions	23.6	32.8	7.7	17.5	25.1	9.4
of which:						
Sub-Saharan Africa	40.4	46.5	5.7	32.0	40.8	5.7
Arab States	30.8	41.2	6.2	22.0	31.4	7.0

Latin America /Caribbean	22.3	32.5	8.3	15.9	23.4	10.9
Eastern Asia /Oceania	17.4	25.8	8.5	12.5	18.1	11.2
of which: China	15.5	23.5	9.0	11.5	16.0	12.2
Southern Asia	26.1	36.9	7.2	17.1	26.3	8.5
of which: India	23.8	34.0	7.6	14.6	23.7	9.4
Least developed countries	36.8	46.1	5.8	29.2	38.1	5.8

In consequence, the educational 'burden' represented by the proportion of the adult population who must become teachers in order to provide education for any given percentage of young people is gradually diminishing, although more rapidly in the less developed than the more developed regions where it has almost levelled off. For example, in Latin America and the Caribbean the percentage ratio of young persons in the age-group 6 -14 to older persons in the age-group 15 - 64 is programmed to decline from 32.5 in 1995 to 23.4 in the year 2015, whereas in North America over the same period the ratio is projected to decline from 19.8 to 17.0. Two further aspects of the current demographic context may be noted. First, the percentage of the adult population aged 15 -64 who are teachers in the formal education system is smaller in the less developed regions (13 teachers per 1,000 adults) than in the more developed regions (23 teachers per 1,000 adults).

In the least developed countries there are only 8 teachers per 1,000 adults. On a comparative basis, therefore, the less developed regions would seem to have a substantial 'margin' of adult labour potentially available for expansion of their teaching forces to meet increases in student enrolments. However, the adult population in the less developed regions is less well educated and has a higher percentage of illiterates than the adult population in the more developed regions. Correspondingly, a higher percentage of the adult population is employed in traditional agriculture than is the case in the more developed regions. Thus the real pool of adults in the less developed regions who potentially could be teachers in the formal education system is smaller than is suggested above. In the more developed regions, now that a majority of young people in many countries can participate in formal education up until their early twenties, the adult population is running out of people to educate, so to speak, unless it starts educating itself. It could be partly for this reason that the idea of lifelong education is gaining ground so rapidly in the industrial countries.

Challenges to Employment

The status and profile of the world's teachers that emerges from the development of education over the last decade is highly differentiated with respect to countries and regions, in particular their overall development experience and the stages of development of their education systems. In a relatively small minority of countries, teachers have reasonably comfortable incomes and conditions of employment; most of them are higher education graduates and, in addition, they generally have been trained as teachers. In a minority of other countries, teachers can barely survive on their official salaries (when they are paid at all), have other jobs too and in many cases have not themselves received an education at a level much higher than the students they are required to teach. The majority of the world's teachers fall somewhere in between these two extremes. There are few signs that this situation is likely to change significantly in the near future. Although teaching is a 'growth' occupation in a majority of countries demographic pressures virtually guarantee continuing increases in student enrolments and hence the need for more teachers the economics of the education sector have not markedly favoured improvements in teachers incomes in the past when teachers have been in short supply; too often the educational authorities have simply lowered the standards of recruitment for new teachers.

In fact, the general feeling in most regions was that there had probably been a decline; likewise in the majority of the replies by national authorities to the questionnaire administered by the International Bureau of Education (IBE) in preparation of the Conference. Only in a handful of wealthy industrial countries with relatively stable teaching forces (e.g. Austria, Canada, Finland, Germany and Switzerland) and a few others was it claimed that the general standing and remuneration of teachers was not a cause for anxiety. The prospects of reversing the apparent decline in the status of teachers mainly depend on the readiness of countries to finance educational expenditure more generously than they have done in the past, on the ability of teachers to make their claims for improved incomes and status heard, and on the changing profile (age, sex, and education and training background) of teachers themselves.

Thus, it seems that in so far as the share of education in GNP has been increasing in recent years, this has probably been due mainly to the continuing expansion of education systems rather than to a fundamental shift in public expenditure priorities, let alone significant improvements in teachers' incomes. In no region of the world at present has the average share of educational expenditure in GNP yet reached the 6 per cent level recommended by the International Commission on Education for the Twenty-first Century, although a number of individual countries have reached this level. Moreover, external aid to education, after a jump at the end of the 1980s, appears to have levelled off. Global trends in teachers' incomes are very difficult to identify.

A certain amount of systematic information was assembled in the late 1980s/early 1990s in studies carried out by various international organizations, as well as by independent researchers, into the effects of the structural adjustment programmes. In general, most of these programmes froze (or even reduced) public sector salaries, especially in sub-Saharan Africa and Latin America. Still, in the more stable economic conditions of most regions in the 1990s, it is possible that the real incomes of teachers in many countries are rising again. Whether they are keeping up with average incomes generally is difficult to say; reliable evidence on movements in teachers' salaries relative to those of other major occupational groups in different countries is very scarce. The numerous studies of the effects of the structural adjustment programmes of the 1980s, for example, never clearly established whether teachers' incomes generally suffered more than those of other public sector employees.

More recently, OECD has assembled systematic data on primary and secondary teachers' salaries scales in its member countries, but these data refer only to a recent year and comparable data for other occupational groups are still lacking. However, even if such data were available, international comparisons of teachers' economic status are especially difficult to make because of differences between countries in the educational backgrounds and working conditions of teachers, as well as of other professional groups. Consider, for example, India and the United States. Data for the various Indian states on the starting level salaries of public primary-school teachers and other government employees with comparable educational backgrounds, India in its national studies to the 1996 International Conference on Education, show that the salaries of primary-school teachers tend to lie in the middle of the range, somewhat less than those of trained nurses but more than those of policemen. In the United States, where primary-school teachers in general have a college (university) degree, unlike in India, quite different occupations are usually chosen for comparison. Thus, the National Commission on Teaching and America's Future compared the average annual earnings of teachers with those of physicians, lawyers and judges, engineers, accountants and auditors, social workers and other occupations which normally require a college (university) degree and found that teachers lie at the bottom of the range.

The fact that the majority of teachers in most countries are not employed in the private but in the public sector, where the salary scales of the different categories of employees are typically linked together, offers a certain amount of protection against loss of economic status relative to other occupations, but this also depends in part on the viability and coherence of the public sector itself.

Where the latter has collapsed, as in the countries of the former Soviet Union, teachers along with other public servants have suffered dramatic erosions of their incomes. Teacher attrition, i.e., the percentage of teachers who leave the profession each year, excluding retirees, could be a useful indicator of the relative status of teachers compared to other occupational groups, but reliable, internationally comparable data on teacher attrition rates do not exist and even national data are very scarce.

In most countries, a certain amount of teacher attrition is accounted for by transfer and/or promotion to administrative and managerial positions within the education system itself; because of this, teacher attrition rates may tend to be higher in the less developed regions of the world, where education systems are rapidly expanding, than in the more developed regions with low birth rates and slowly growing student enrolments. In the 1960s and 1970s, ex-teachers could be found throughout the state administrations of most of the newly independent countries. However, in recent years, teacher attrition rates have probably been highest in East and Central Europe, and the countries of the former Soviet Union, partly because of the difficulties facing all categories of public sector employees in most of these countries, but also in part because many teachers found that they had skills (e.g. foreign languages, information technology) which have been in demand in the burgeoning private industrial and service sectors. In sum, it is hard to find, for any region of the world, clear evidence of an overall trend towards improvement in teachers' economic status. Probably there is no country even where it can be confidently asserted that such a trend has ocurred.

Finally, it may be that part of the difficulty for teachers in getting their claims for improved economic status heard is that there still are many countries in which teachers do not have well-established collective bargaining rights. This is itself partly due to education's position in the public sector. Where teachers are considered to be public servants, their collective bargaining rights are often restricted. Governments traditionally have been cautious in their readiness to recognize formally the collective bargaining rights of their own employees.

Despite their numbers, therefore, teachers in a majority of countries have not been in a strong position to resist the apparent erosion in their economic status in recent years. It remains now to consider whether the profile of the world's teachers has changed. In the less developed regions, this has probably facilitated the increasing educational enrolment of girls. In countries where female teachers are a majority, it has sometimes been argued that the fact that teaching is more of a woman's profession than most other professions has negative implications for the status of teachers. This could of course be true in so far as society accepts discrimination against women. While there probably are very few (if any) countries today where women teachers are paid on different salary scales from their male counterparts, at least in the public sector, it could be argued that the overall levels of teachers' salaries are kept below the levels which would prevail if teaching were a male profession, but this is speculation and very difficult to prove empirically. In probably a majority of countries, though, women still are under-represented in educational leadership and management positions. Conceivably, if progress continues to be made worldwide in eliminating discrimination against women generally, improvements in teachers incomes could encounter less resistance from employers.

In any case, in some of the countries where teaching is still mainly a male profession, survival on a teacher's salary is pretty difficult for both men and women. Secondly, the composition of the world's teaching force is also changing with respect to the age-profile of teachers. Teachers in the less developed regions of the world generally are younger than their counterparts in the more developed regions. Among other things, this implies a need for well-designed systems of professional guidance and supervision, but this need has not always been given the attention which it merits. It also implies a built-in pressure on education budgets as teachers grow older and move up their salary scales a process which probably has largely stabilized in the more developed regions.

The composition of the world's teaching force is changing with respect to the educational backgrounds of teachers. Most of the industrial countries have moved towards requiring all teachers in primary and secondary schools to have a university degree or its equivalent. While this undoubtedly represents the long-term trend for the world's education systems, the distance still to be travelled by countries in the less developed regions is considerable. The percentage of the world's teachers who have received at least a secondary education is almost certainly higher than thirty years ago, but there still are many countries where significant numbers of teachers have received less.

Table 2
Education and training backgrounds of primary- and secondary-school teachers, in selected countries, 1994

	Percentage of teachers with university or equivalent qualification		Percentage of teachers who have received educational pedagogical training	
	Primary	Secondary	Primary	Secondary
Argentina	17	39	90	59
Ecuador	1	1	86	58
Egypt	55	100	36	49
Ghana	...	...	69	72
Indonesia	5	62	91	84
Japan	79	93	...	...
Jordan	42	75	...	...
Kuwait	41	90	...	...
Lesotho	14	44	77	79
Nigeria	9	...	...	...
Panama	6	9	...	...
Poland	61	91	...	...
Qatar	74	98	55	44
Slovakia	78	69	...	...
Swaziland	1	47	90	87
Uganda	1	25	61	80
United Arab Emirates	32	96	...	...
Venezuela	...	...	78	84

The emerging profile of the world's teachers, aside from those employed in a relatively small number of industrial countries, and possibly a few others, has doubtfully strengthened their claims for improved status. Although they are better educated than thirty years ago, so is the general population who are not teachers. The fact that society still is willing to accept at all that people can be employed as teachers without having received any specific preparation for the job points to the difficulty for teachers in getting their claims heard. Probably no other aspect of teacher employment policies has done as much to retard progress towards recognition of teaching as a profession.

Most governments have been preoccupied by other aspects of education: while wanting continued progress towards the democratization of education and the expansion of educational opportunities, they have at the same time been concerned to hold down educational expenditure and to make education systems more 'accountable' for such expenditure. This policy environment has not been favourable to improvements in the status of teachers. Yet in the 1990s at least, there also have been signs of increasing concern over the quality of education. If this trend continues, teachers and teaching are likely to come more into focus than has been the case up to now. Therefore, consideration is given to what teachers are expected to do.

Technology and Teacher Professional Development

Information and communication technologies (ICTs) can improve preservice teacher training by providing access to more and better educational resources, offering multimedia simulations of good teaching practice, catalyzing teacher-to-trainee collaboration, and increasing productivity of noninstructional tasks. ICTs also can enable inservice teacher professional development at a distance, asynchronous learning, and individualized training opportunities. ICTs can overcome teachers' isolation, breaking down their classroom walls and connecting them to colleagues, mentors, curriculum experts, and the global teacher community.

Technology and teacher professional development in its use is best introduced in the context of broader educational reform, which embraces a shift away from teacher-centered, lecture-based instruction toward student-centered, interactive, constructivist learning. This has consequences for reform of curricula, examinations, provision of educational resources, and teachers' professional development. Indeed, one of the most exciting aspects of information and communication technology is its role as a catalyst for such educational reform.

Most teachers want to learn to use educational technology effectively, but they lack the conceptual framework, time, computer access, and support necessary to do so. A well-planned, ongoing professional development program, grounded in a theoretical model, linked to curricular objectives, incorporating formative evaluation activities, and sustained by sufficient financial and staff support is essential if teachers are to use technology effectively to improve student learning.When designing or implementing any teacher professional development program for technology, it is important to situate that program within the context of a theoretical framework for adult learning.

Teacher professional development in the use of technology should be designed and implemented to move teachers (and, eventually, students) toward the right-hand end of this continuum. This framework emphasizes the potential of Web-based instruction to contribute to pedagogical reform, rather than technology's rich multimedia features or its ability to access information resources around the world. Stated more simply, technology can promote effective instruction that is more student-centered, interdisciplinary, more closely related to real-life events and processes, and adaptive to individual learning styles.

Such instruction encourages development of higher-order thinking and information-reasoning skills (rather than memorization of facts) among students, and socially constructed (collaborative) learning, all of which are increasingly required in today's knowledge-based global economy. This potential of technology to improve instruction needs to be integrated into the design and delivery of teacher professional development programs in the use of technology.

Perhaps most important for the purpose of teachers' professional development, technology implies a shift in the teacher's role from being the sole source of knowledge and instruction to being a facilitator of students' learning, which is acquired from many sources. This is often referred to as a shift from being "the sage on the stage to the guide on the side." Again, teacher professional development for ICTs needs to incorporate and model this shift.

Failure to incorporate these 10 dimensions of interactive learning into teacher professional development programs in the use and integration of technology will cripple the potential of technology to improve teaching and learning. This implies that teacher professional development in the use of technology should embody and model the forms of pedagogy that teachers can use in their classrooms.

Teacher professional development in the use of technology needs to combine lecture/ presentation modalities with small-group and plenary discussion, individual and collaborative activities, and opportunities for teachers to reflect on their actual teaching practices and how they might do things differently with technology. Such an approach also means that learning materials need to be in several formats: print, CD-ROM, e-mail attachments, online (HTML and Java), and even DVD. It also implies a need to develop both synchronous and asynchronous modalities, so that teachers can take advantage of training opportunities when they have the time, which is not necessarily when the trainer is available.

Key to successful teacher professional development programs is a modular structure, corresponding to different levels of teacher experience and expertise using technology. Adapting materials to teachers' comfort level and starting points is essential. In this way, teachers new to technology can be exposed to the full series of professional development modules, while those further along on the learning curve can enter where their knowledge and skills stop, and help their less technology-savvy colleagues along.

Technology enables a collaborative approach and maximizes peer-to-peer sharing of the challenges, frustrations, advantages, and successes of using technology to teach and learn. Such an approach encourages use of illuminating failures in the use of technology in the classroom as well as examples of best practice. Finally, these principles imply the need to build ongoing community and systems of support from peers, mentors, and experts. Single, "one-shot" training events that leave teachers alone afterward should be avoided.

Professional Development Programmes

Designers of a teacher professional development program for use of technology need to determine current teacher competency levels in this area. The International Society for Technology in Education (ISTE) has produced a set of standards for teacher skills and knowledge in the use of technology, a useful guide for determining the content of teacher professional development programs. The "Professional Competency Continuum," can be used to determine the skill levels of individual teachers and their professional development needs.

European, Asian, and Latin American educational associations have developed similar sets of standards adapted to their educational contexts. No attempt is made here to resolve these ongoing discussions and divergent views regarding the content required for teacher professional development in the use of technology. Indeed, differing economic, social, cultural, educational, and technological realities require different approaches. That said, some minimum guidelines and suggestions for the content of teacher professional development in the use of technology are warranted.

Policy makers should assume as a bare minimum requirement at least 24 hours (three full days) of teacher training in the use of technology. This includes basic operating systems (turning computers on and off, opening and closing files, etc.), word processing, and spreadsheets (particularly useful for such noninstructional tasks as grading). Obviously, the more time allocated for this training, particularly hands-on time, the greater the mastery of these basic skills will be. Teachers should finish this basic course with at least the fundamentals necessary for them to practice and develop their skills further back in their schools. Adding another 16 hours of training and Internet access would enable teachers to access information on the Internet, do some basic lesson planning integrating technology, and exchange e-mail messages and files with colleagues and experts.

With this base of 40 hours of professional development, provided the methodology of the course incorporates some of the key interactive learning principles described above, teachers should be able to begin using technology in their classrooms. Experience of the World Links program suggests that at least 80 hours of professional development are required before teachers can really begin to integrate technology into their teaching.

Additional content would include linking curricular objectives to technology-based activities, development of lesson plans and evaluation strategies that incorporate technology, construction of educational Websites, and discussion of ethical issues related to technology and education. Ideally, this is provided in various stages, allowing time for teachers to experiment with and apply their new technological skills and knowledge in the classroom before moving on to move advanced applications.

This approach also allows teachers to reflect on and share their learning experience (both positive and negative) with their peers, thereby promoting the social construction of knowledge. World Links has been a pioneer in developing and delivering teacher professional development programs in the use of technology to improve teaching and learning in developing countries. It is by no means the "definitive" programme, nor is it the most easily replicated and scaled. The complete World Links Teacher Professional Development program includes 200 hours of training, equivalent to five 40-hour weeks. This takes teachers with no prior contact with computers to full competency over a two- to three-year period. In addition to content, professional development for technology should incorporate the fundamental components that research has found to be essential, including:

— Direct connection to student learning. The goal of teacher professional development is improved student achievement.

— Hands-on technology use. This requires development of core technology competencies and skills and actual application of skills in the classroom.

— Curriculum-specific applications. To the fullest extent possible, teachers need to see a direct link between technology and the curriculum for which they are responsible.

— New roles for teachers, as facilitators and guides, not simply as lecturers or instructors.

— Active participation of teachers and collegial learning.

— Professional development as an ongoing process.

Teachers generally are reluctant to change their teaching styles and habits; are cautious of time-consuming activities that may take away from other high-priority obligations (economic, familial, or educational); have difficulty seeing the potential payoff beforehand of this kind of training; and may feel so threatened by technology that they want to distance themselves from it rather than embrace it. Put simply, many teachers require additional motivation and incentives to participate actively in professional development activities.

A brief description of some incentives (extrinsic and intrinsic) that have been used successfully in the past follows.

— *Certification from Ministries of education* : Ministries of education should be more active in designing criteria for certifying technology-focused teacher professional development programs. They can begin by seeking examples of best practices/examples of professional development programs (domestic or international), relating training programmes to existing teacher knowledge and skill standards, and comparing programs to curricula. Then, departments of inservice training should certify the best teacher training programs and link teachers' progress in salary and grade scales to successful certification. This would send a clear message to teachers and school directors that such training is valued at the highest levels of the ministry, and that it increases teachers' incentive to actively participate.

— *Recognition and Time Allocation by Supervisors:* Teachers need to be encouraged by administrators, particularly their school directors, to participate in training activities. Administrators need to ensure that teachers have adequate time to participate, and do not have to sacrifice too much personal time to do so. From an administrative perspective, this should be viewed as an investment and a contribution to the capacity building of the country's teaching force. But, in addition to time allocation, supervisors should recognize publicly teachers who successfully complete professional development courses. This provides immediate personal reward to teachers, raises their status in the eyes of their peers, and encourages others to participate.

— *Reduced isolation and increased professional satisfaction:* Many teachers lead an isolated professional existence, with little input from or collaboration with their peers or supervisors. Alone in front of a class of 25-75 students, they teach according to what they learned (both content and pedagogy) several or more years ago in a preservice teacher training institute. Learning new technological skills, especially if they include Internet and e-mail, allows teachers to break down the walls of their classroom and share lesson plans, evaluation strategies, student assessments, and even just the joys and frustrations of teaching. In other words, technology reduced their isolation and made them more excited about teaching. Sharing that experience should serve to motivate other teachers to participate in similar professional development programs.

— *Enhanced Productivity:* Technology can speed up and increase the efficiency of a range of noninstructional teacher activities such as student attendance, grading, textbook distribution, and preparation of administrative reports. It also can enhance the productivity of basic instructional tasks. More advanced applications include fast identification of educational resources (online), use of CD-ROM materials. In fact, there is a nearly limitless range of opportunities for teachers who develop the necessary skills and knowledge in the effective use of technology in the classroom, and who have access to technology and Internet.

Teachers may be motivated to participate in professional development workshops in the use of technology because they see them as an opportunity to become a trainer/mentor for other teachers. In many cases, becoming a trainer brings additional financial and professional opportunities (travel, participation conferences, publications, etc.). If the training workshops come with some form of official certification for successful completion, motivation is enhanced further. School directors, finance officers, and other administrative personnel also need professional development in the use of technology for noninstructional purposes. Technology can improve significantly the productivity of activities related to financial management, class scheduling, personnel management, student tracking, administrative reporting, communicating with parents, etc. However, training of school directors should not be limited to noninstructional uses of technology.

It is vital that school directors understand and support teachers' efforts to integrate technology into the classroom. Far too often, school directors minimize the time and effort required for teachers to develop the skills and knowledge required to use technology effectively, and, in many cases, directors actively oppose teachers' efforts to use technology in innovative ways. For this reason, it is strongly recommended that all school directors participate in introductory professional development workshops in the pedagogical application of technology. If at all possible, this should be done in collaboration with teachers, so school directors understand that technology requires us to be both learners and facilitators of the learning of others.

School directors need to see the potential of technology to be a catalyst for more effective learning. They also need to understand (and empathize with) the process and the time required to tap this potential. If this happens, they will be far more likely to encourage their teachers to participate in training workshops, allow them needed release time, and encourage them to experiment with innovative teaching practices using technology. Parallel to, and in conjunction with, teacher professional development is the need to provide training for students in the use of technology. It is shared wisdom now that youth acquire technological skills far more quickly than adults, and they are far more likely to share their skills with their peers. Rather than seeing this as a threat to their authority, teachers should embrace this reality and use it to their advantage.

Technology training for students has a "viral" character to it in that it tends to replicate itself spontaneously and spread among other students, many of whom have extremely strong intrinsic motivation to learn new skills. This motivation is related to youth's natural affinity for new technologies, their desire to improve their academic performance for downstream educational and economic opportunities, and their understanding that these skills are increasingly demanded in their countries' labor markets. Such motivation is not often present among teachers. Technologically savvy students can help teachers use technology in the classroom in many ways, especially when collaborative, constructivist, and authentic learning strategies are used.

At a basic level, students can provide technical support in the classroom to their peers and even to the teacher in the use of software, Internet research, leadership of small groups, and even simple computer maintenance and troubleshooting of common glitches. At a more advanced level, students often have more time and desire than teachers to develop their technological skills further. Generating parent support for technology in schools is important if technology investments are to be sustained and/ or expanded. World Links' experience in more than 20 developing countries suggests that parents are often the primary source of recurrent financing for technology in schools and, actually, the most logical source from an economic perspective.

This is because universal access to technology simply is not possible now (even if the hardware and software were free, a huge proportion of schools in developing countries lack the electricity and phone lines needed to use them), and those schools that meet basic technical criteria usually are located in more urban and/or middle-class socioeconomic areas. In other words, technology can exacerbate inequity of educational and economic opportunities within a country. With their children as the direct beneficiaries of technology-enhanced learning, parents are the natural source of financial support to sustain technology at the school level.

Offering training for parents in the use of technology helps them to understand its potential for their children. Consequently, such training makes them more likely to bear a portion of the financial burden and encourage their children to take advantage of these new opportunities. In addition, trained parents can become invaluable "monitors" or aides in school computer labs, either paid or volunteer. This eliminates the need to assign teachers to the computer lab during nonteaching hours, encourages greater school-community integration, and provides opportunities for students and adults to share their skills and knowledge with one another. Once teachers have mastered the basics of ICTs—operating systems, word processing, and e-mail and Internet navigation—they can use the technology to access professional development opportunities. This enables anytime, anywhere learning and overcomes the conventional limitations of face-to-face training workshops (cost, travel, accommodations, and low numbers of participants).

Many different technologies have been used to support or provide teacher professional development. Often grouped under the vague heading, "distance learning," they include basic correspondence courses, broadcast television, interactive radio, and video. This section focuses on the potential of new digital technologies (the Internet, digital radio, CD-ROMs, DVDs) for teacher professional development. To begin, it is important to distinguish among different approaches or models for online professional development.

uture trends in teacher professional development in the use of technology will be shaped by two main factors: increasing demand for teacher training and new technologies/ methodologies to enable that training. The demand from ministries of education and teachers themselves for professional development in the use of technology is outpacing the capacity of conventional approaches, such as face-to-face training, to respond. There is a simple issue of scale as ministries of education implement nationwide educational technology programs, and the sheer numbers of teachers who need to be trained exceeds financial, human, and technical capacity to handle teacher training requirements. In addition, greater complexity and content of the training are required as the Internet and other new technologies are introduced.

At the societal level, what teachers are expected to know and do is increasing every year. Teachers not only have to know their subject matter and basic pedagogy, they also are expected to model higher-order thinking processes, work in interdisciplinary teams, and demonstrate leadership and communication skills. At the same time, they are supposed to deliver better student results on standardized tests, while addressing larger societal problems.

Traditional teacher training approaches simply are not equipped to deal with all of these new expectations. By contrast, ICTs can help teachers to meet these expectations, by providing productivity tools, access to information and colleagues, and collaboration opportunities. As teachers experience these external pressures, and realize the potential of technology to help them respond, their demand for training in the use of technology will grow. Scale and complexity exacerbate the issue of teacher motivation. Ministries of education around the world are struggling for techniques and incentives to get beyond the "champion teachers" and so called early adopters to reach the average teacher. Paradoxically, there is both excess teacher demand for training (relative to capacity to provide it) and insufficient teacher demand for training (relative to the physical distribution of computer hardware in the schools).

New teacher professional development methodologies are required to address this issue of motivation. In the future, ministries of education will issue new standards for teacher competencies in the use of technology, which will affect both preservice and inservice teacher training levels. These standards are likely to be linked to official certification requirements and processes, so that education ministries can track the proportion of teachers who have the necessary skills and knowledge, and so that teachers have an incentive to participate.

4

Assessment, Monitoring and Evaluation of Education

Since the beginning of the 1990s, national educational policies have been marked by an increasing concern for quality and relevance, especially in basic education. Education systems, it is widely felt, are not performing effectively, not doing what they should be doing to ensure that the young people passing through them learn well what they are supposed to learn, and are well prepared to assume their future adult roles and responsibilities in the family, the workplace, and the wider community and society.

In many countries there is a growing sense that education is the key to the future, and that the challenges and jobs of tomorrow will require an education of better quality than that which most students receive today. Increasingly, educational quality and relevance are defined by reference to students learning outcomes. For the International Commission on Education for the Twentyfirst

Century, the importance of the quality of teaching, and therefore of teachers, cannot be overemphasized'. This will require additional resources, as the Commission itself recognized. Yet the assumption underlying many educational policies in recent years, is that 'more can be achieved with less', in effect, that the quality and relevance of education in general, and learning outcomes in particular, can be improved in the context of existing resource constraints.

The changing contexts and pressures facing teachers in the light of both the increasing focus of national educational policies on students' learning outcomes and the continuing resource constraints facing a majority of the world's education systems.

Trends and developments in earlier decades, both within and outside education, contributed to the upsurge of concern for educational quality at the beginning of the present decade. In the less developed regions of the world, the dramatic expansion of educational enrolments in the 1960s and 1970s severely strained the qualitative foundations of many, if not most, education systems. The difficulties faced by many countries in tackling these problems were compounded by the economic circumstances and budgetary constraints of the 1980s. Growing numbers of school leavers and higher education graduates entered adulthood ill-prepared for the difficult futures that awaited them. In the more developed regions of the world, where the expansion of educational enrolments had been less dramatic, there too was a widespread feeling that standards of educational quality had declined.

Anxiety increased in the 1980s with the rapidity of changes in the world economy and the resulting pressures on countries to adjust to a more competitive global economic environment in which the educated intelligence of a countrys population 'human capital' was coming increasingly to be recognised as a strategic resource. If there has consequently been a tendency in some countries to consider the quality and relevance of education mainly in terms of educations contribution to the successful pursuit of economic goals and purposes, in other countries sweeping political and economic changes and developments have brought a broader range of objectives to the fore.

The current widespread concern for educational quality and relevance, therefore, has complex origins and many nuances depending on the particular experiences of individual countries over the past quarter of a century. It has taken the form of a growing interest among national policy-makers in the monitoring, measurement and evaluation of educational processes and outcomes.

Monitoring and evaluation of education are not in themselves new; educational research has largely been defined around them. What is new is both the interest of national policy-makers and the scope of their concerns, which extend to the entire education system or to entire sub-sectors of it such as basic education or higher education. Until very recently, most educational research had focused on small groups of pupils or students, often located in a single educational institution or handful of institutions; few studies aimed to consider the education system as a whole. At least, educational research has now taken root in many countries where ten or twenty years ago it was virtually unknown. Government financial support is still very modest; even in wealthy industrial countries the sums involved hardly compare to those allocated for research in other areas such as agriculture or health, let alone defence. Nevertheless, it is significant that even in countries where education budgets are very tight, some official support is given for educational research.

The World Conference on Education for All helped to bring to the fore the need for more research in the field of basic education in the world's less developed regions and the need too for increased support for co-operation among educational researchers in these regions. In response to the World Conference's call for countries to 'define acceptable levels of learning acquisition for educational programmes and to improve and apply systems of assessing learning achievement', UNESCO, in collaboration with UNICEF, has sought to strengthen national capacities in this field; a joint UNESCO-UNICEF Monitoring Learning Achievement programme involving five countries was launched in 1992. In addition, established networks of co-operation, such as the Information Network on Education for Latin American and the Caribbean (REDUC) and UNESCO's Asia and the Pacific Programme of Educational Innovation for Development (APEID) were given a fresh impetus, and new networks such as the recently formed Southern Africa Consortium for Monitoring Educational Quality (SACMEQ), involving Botswana, Kenya, Malawi, Mauritius, Namibia, Swaziland, the United Republic of Tanzania, Zambia and Zimbabwe, have emerged. Given the scarcity of funds available for educational research in the world's less developed regions, much of the research carried out in these regions necessarily is highly pragmatic and down-to-earth, focused on concrete obstacles or handicaps in the way of improving educational quality.

In Africa, for example, many studies concern different aspects of textbooks: their cost (e.g. a study of parents' purchasing power with respect to buying school textbooks in Mozambique), their distribution (e.g. a study of the distribution and modes of utilization of school textbooks in Guinea) and their contents (e.g. an evaluation of textbooks for Arabic, French, mathematics and 'awakening to science' for fourth grade pupils in Tunisia). The growth of educational activity in the less developed regions has begun to lay the foundations of systemwide mechanisms for the monitoring, measurement and evaluation of educational quality. A small but growing number of countries - up to now chiefly in Asia and Latin America - are beginning to set in place national systems of evaluation. In many countries, the poor state of national educational statistics has been a handicap.

It has been mainly among the OECD countries that the development of systemwide mechanisms has gone furthest. These countries have given a high priority to improving the coverage, reliability and policy relevance of their national educational statistics, as well as their international comparability, and have co-operated with UNESCO for that purpose; this has been an area of concern to the Organization since its earliest days. Much of the co-operation among the OECD countries has focused on the development of internationally comparable indicators of the various aspects of the quality and performance of their education systems: educational participation and attainment, education finance, students' learning outcomes, adult literacy, education and the labour market, the functioning of schools and school systems, and public attitudes towards education.

Assessment of Teaching and Learning

Teachers who approach management as a process of establishing an effective learning environment tend to be more successful than teachers who emphasize their roles as disciplinarians. Effective teachers do not need to spend much time responding to behaviour problems because they use management techniques that elicit students' co-operation and sustain their engagement in activities. Working within the positive classroom climate implied by the principle of a learning community, the teacher articulates clear expectations concerning classroom behaviour in general and participation in lessons and learning activities in particular, teaches procedures that foster productive engagement during activities and smooth transitions between them, and follows through with any needed cues or reminders.

Effective teachers allocate most of this time to lessons and learning activities rather than to non-academic pastimes that serve little or no curricular purpose. Their students spend many more hours each year on curriculum-related activities than do students of teachers who are less focused on instructional goals. Effective teachers convey a sense of the purposefulness of schooling and the importance of getting the most out of the available time. They begin and end lessons on time, keep transitions short, and teach their students how to get started quickly and maintain focus when working on assignments. Good planning and preparation enable them to proceed through lessons smoothly without having to stop to consult a manual or locate an item needed for display or demonstration. Their activities and assignments feature stimulating variety and optimal challenge, which help students to sustain their task engagement and minimize disruptions due to boredom or distraction.

Billions of dollars are spent each year for educational development, yet there is widespread dissatisfaction with our educational system among educators, parents, policymakers, and the business community. Efforts to reform and restructure schools have focused attention on the role of assessment in school improvement. After years of increases in the quantity of formalized testing and the consequences of poor test scores, many educators have begun to strongly criticize the measures used to monitor student performance and evaluate programs. They claim that traditional measures fail to assess significant learning outcomes and thereby undermine curriculum, instruction, and policy decisions.

The higher the stakes, the greater the pressure that is placed on teachers and administrators to devote more and more time to prepare students to do well on the tests. As a consequence, narrowly focused tests that emphasize recall have led to a similar narrowing of the curriculum and emphasis on rote memorization of facts with little opportunity to practice higher-order thinking skills. The timed nature of the tests and their format of one right answer has led teachers to give students practice in responding to artificially short texts and selecting the best answer rather than inventing their own questions or answers. When teachers teach to traditional tests by providing daily skill instruction in formats that closely resemble tests, their instructional practices are both ineffective and potentially detrimental due to their reliance on outmoded theories of learning and instruction.

Good assessment information provides accurate estimates of student performance and enables teachers or other decisionmakers to make appropriate decisions. The concept of test validity captures these essential characteristics and the extent that an assessment actually measures what it is intended to measure, and permits appropriate generalizations about students' skills and abilities. For example, a ten-item addition/subtraction test might be administered to a student who answers nine items correctly. If the test is valid, we can safely generalize that the student will likely do as well on similar items not included on the test.

The results of a good test or assessment, in short, represent something beyond how students perform on a certain task or a particular set of items; they represent how a student performs on the objective which those items were intended to assess. Measurement experts agree that test validity is tied to the purposes for which an assessment is used. Thus, a test might be valid for one purpose but inappropriate for other purposes. In the context of performance-based and open-ended assessment, inter-rater reliability also is essential; it requires that independent raters give the same scores to a given student response.

Following are the characteristics of good assessment for classroom purposes:

a) The content of the tests (the knowledge and skills assessed) should match the teacher's educational objectives and instructional emphases.

b) The test items should represent the full range of knowledge and skills that are the primary targets of instruction.

c) Expectations for student performance should be clear.

d) The assessment should be free of extraneous factors which unnecessarily confuse or inadvertently cue student responses.

In United States, researchers at the National Centre for Research on Evaluation, Standards, and Student Testing (CRESST) are developing an expanded set of validity criteria for performance-based, large-scale assessments. Multiple-choice measures have provided a reliable and easy-to-score means of assessing student outcomes. In addition, considerable test theory and statistical techniques were developed to support their development and use. Although there is now great excitement about performance-based assessment, we still know relatively little about methods for designing and validating such assessments. CRESST is one of many organizations and schools researching the promises and realities of such assessments. Methods of assessment are determined by our beliefs about learning.

According to early theories of learning, complex higher-order skills had to be acquired bit-by-bit by breaking learning down into a series of prerequisite skill, a building-blocks-of-knowledge approach. It was assumed incorrectly that after basic skills had been learned by rote, they could be assembled into complex understandings and insight. However, evidence from contemporary cognitive psychology indicates that all learning requires that the learner think and actively construct evolving mental models. From today's cognitive perspective, meaningful learning is reflective, constructive, and self-regulated.

People are seen not as mere recorders of factual information but as creators of their own unique knowledge structures. To know something is not just to have received information but to have interpreted it and related it to other knowledge one already has. In addition, we now recognize the importance of knowing not just how to perform, but also when to perform and how to adapt that performance to new situations. Thus, the presence or absence of discrete bits of information-which is typically the focus of traditional multiple-choice tests-is not of primary importance in the assessment of meaningful learning. Rather, what is important is how and whether students organize, structure, and use that information in context to solve complex problems.

Contrary to past views of learning, cognitive psychology suggests that learning is not linear, but that it proceeds in many directions at once and at an uneven pace. Conceptual learning is not something to be delayed until a particular age or until all the basic facts have been mastered. People of all ages and ability levels constantly use and refine concepts. Furthermore, there is tremendous variety in the modes and speed with which people acquire knowledge, in the attention and memory capabilities they can apply to knowledge acquisition and performance, and in the ways in which they can demonstrate the personal meaning they have created. Current evidence about the nature of learning makes it apparent that instruction which strongly emphasizes structured drill and practice on discrete, factual knowledge does students a major disservice.

Learning isolated facts and skills is more difficult without meaningful ways to organize the information and make it easy to remember. Also, applying those skills later to solve real-world problems becomes a separate and more difficult task. Because some students have had such trouble mastering decontextualized "basics," they are rarely given the opportunity to use and develop higher-order thinking skills. Recent studies of the integration of learning and motivation also have highlighted the importance of affective and metacognitive skills in learning. For example, recent research suggests that poor thinkers and problem solvers differ from good ones not so much in the particular skills they possess as in their failure to use them in certain tasks. Acquisition of knowledge skills is not sufficient to make one into a competent thinker or problem solver.

People also need to acquire the disposition to use the skills and strategies, as well as the knowledge of when and how to apply them. These are appropriate targets of assessment. The role of the social context of learning in shaping higher-order cognitive abilities and dispositions has also received attention over the past several years. It has been noted that real-life problems often require people to work together as a group in problem-solving situations, yet most traditional instruction and assessment have involved independent rather than small group work.

Now, however, it is postulated that groups facilitate learning in several ways: modelling effective thinking strategies, scaffolding complicated performances, providing mutual constructive feedback, and valuing the elements of critical thought. Group assessments, thus, can be important. Since the influence of testing on curriculum and instruction is now widely acknowledged, educators, policymakers, and others are turning to alternative assessment methods as a tool for educational reform.

The movement away from tradiuonal, multiple-choice tests to alternative assessments-variously called authentic assessment or performance assessment-has included a wide variety of strategies such as open-ended questions, exhibits, demonstrations, hands-on execution of experiments, computer simulations, writing in many disciplines, and portfolios of student work over time. These terms and assessment strategies have led the quest for more meaningful assessments which better capture the significant outcomes we want students to achieve and better match the kinds of tasks which they will need to accomplish in order to assure their future success. There is continuing faith in the value of assessment for stimulating and supporting school improvement and instructional reform at national, state, and local levels.

While the terms may be diverse, several common threads link alternative assessments:

a) Students are involved in setting goals and criteria for assessment.

b) Students perform, create, produce, or do something.

c) Tasks require students to use higher-level thinking and/ or problem solving skills.

d) Tasks often provide measures of metacognitive skills and attitudes, collaborative skills and intrapersonal skills as well as the more usual intellectual products.

e) Assessment tasks measure meaningful instructional activities.

f) Tasks often are contextualized in real-world applications.

h) Student responses are scored according to specified criteria, known in advance, which define standards for good performance.

While assessment has the potential to improve learning for all students, historically it has acted as a barrier rather than a bridge to educational opportunity. Assessments have been used to label students and put them in dead end tracks. Traditional tests have been soundly criticized as biased and unfair to minority students. And, the assessment of language minority students has been particularly problematic. What we know about performance-based assessment is limited and there are many issues yet to be resolved. We do know that approaches which encourage new assessment methods need the broad-based support of the community and school administration.

Like any change in schools, changes in assessment practices will require:

a) Strong leadership support

b) Staff development and training

c) Teacher ownership

d) Continuing follow-up and support for change through coaching and mentoring

e) Environments that support experimentation and risk-taking

As schools move toward more performance-based assessment, they also will need to come to some resolution on a number of issues, among them that performance-based assessments:

a) Require more time to develop

b) Cost more

c) May limit content coverage

d) Require a shift in teaching practices

e) Require substantial time for administration

f) Lack a network of colleagues for sharing and developing

g) Require new methods of aggregating and reporting data

h) Require new viewpoints about how to use for comparative purposes

Classroom Monitoring

Successful teachers are clear and consistent in articulating their expectations. At the beginning of the year they model or provide direct instruction in desired procedures if necessary, and subsequently they cue or remind their students when these procedures are needed. They monitor the classroom continually, which enables them to respond to emerging problems before they become disruptive. When possible, they intervene in ways that do not disrupt lesson momentum or distract students who are working on assignments. They teach students strategies and procedures for carrying out recurring activities such as participating in whole-class lessons, engaging in productive discourse with classmates, making smooth transitions between activities, collaborating in pairs or small groups, storing and handling equipment and personal belongings, managing learning and completing assignments on time, and knowing when and how to get help.

The teachers' emphasis is not on imposing situational control but on building students' capacity for managing their own learning, so that expectations are adjusted and cues, reminders and other managerial moves are faded out as the school year progresses. These teachers do not merely maximize 'time on task', but spend a great deal of time actively instructing by elaborating content for students and helping them to interpret and respond to it. Their classrooms feature more time spent in interactive discourse and less time spent in solitary seatwork. Most of their instruction occurs during interactive discourse with students rather than during extended lecture presentations.The educational policy-makers, textbook publishers and teachers often become so focused on content coverage or learning activities that they lose sight of the larger purposes and goals that are supposed to guide curriculum planning.

Teachers typically plan by concentrating on the content they intend to cover and the steps involved in the activities their students will carry out, without giving much thought to the goals or intended outcomes of the instruction. Textbook publishers, in response to pressure from special interest groups, tend to keep expanding their content coverage. Students taught using such textbooks may be asked to memorize parades of disconnected facts or to practise disconnected subskills in isolation instead of learning coherent networks of connected content structured around powerful ideas. These problems are often exacerbated by externally imposed assessment programmes that emphasize recognition of isolated bits of knowledge or performance of isolated subskills. Such problems can be minimized through goal-oriented curriculum development, in which curricular planning is guided by the overall purposes and goals of the instruction, not by miscellaneous content coverage pressures or test items.

All components of the curriculum are aligned to create a cohesive programme for accomplishing instructional purposes and goals. A curriculum is not an end in itself; it is a means of helping students to learn what is considered essential for preparing them to fulfil adult roles in society and realize their potential as individuals. Its goals are learner outcomes-the knowledge, skills, attitudes, values and dispositions to action that society wishes to develop in its citizens.

The goals are the reason for the existence of the curriculum, so that beliefs about what is needed to accomplish them should guide each step in curriculum planning and implementation. Goals are most likely to be attained if all of the curriculum's components are selected because they are believed to be needed as means of helping students to accomplish the overall purposes and goals. This involves planning curriculum and instruction to develop capabilities that students can use in their lives inside and outside school, both now and in the future. In this regard, it is important to emphasize goals of understanding, appreciation and life application.

Understanding means that students learn both the individual elements in a network of related content and the connections among them, so that they can explain the content in their own words and connect it to their prior knowledge. Appreciation means that students value what they are learning because they understand that there are good reasons for learning it. Life application means that students retain their learning in a form that makes it usable when needed in other contexts. Content developed with these goals in mind is likely to be retained as meaningful learning that is internally coherent, well connected with other meaningful learning and accessible for application. This is most likely to occur when the content itself is structured around powerful ideas and the development of this content through classroom lessons and learning activities focuses on these ideas and their connections.

The value of establishing a learning orientation by beginning lessons and activities with advance organizers or previews. These introductions facilitate students' learning by communicating the nature and purpose of the activity, connecting it to prior knowledge and cueing the kinds of student responses that the activity requires. This helps students to remain goal-oriented and strategic as they process information and respond to the questions or tasks embodied in the activity. Good lesson orientations also stimulate students' motivation to learn by communicating enthusiasm for the learning or helping students to appreciate its value or application potential.

Advance organizers orient students to what they will be learning before the instruction begins. They characterize the general nature of the activity and give students a structure within which to understand and connect the specifics that will be presented by the teacher or text. Such knowledge of the nature of the activity and the structure of its content helps students to focus on the main ideas and order their thoughts effectively. Therefore, before beginning any lesson or activity, the teacher should ensure that students know what they will be learning and why it is important for them to learn it. Other ways to help students learn with a sense of purpose and direction include calling attention to the activity's goals, overviewing main ideas or major steps to be elaborated, pretests that sensitize students to main points to learn, and pre-questions that stimulate their thinking about the topic.That networks of connected knowledge structured around powerful ideas can be learned with understanding and retained in forms that make them accessible for application. In contrast, disconnected bits of information are likely to be learned only through low-level processes such as rote memorizing, and most of these bits either are soon forgotten or are retained in ways that limit their accessibility.

Similarly, skills are likely to be learned and used effectively if taught as strategies adapted to particular purposes and situations, with attention to when and how to apply them; but students may not be able to integrate and use skills that are learned only by rote and practised only in isolation from the rest of the curriculum.Whether in textbooks or in teacher-led instruction, information is easier to learn to the extent that it is coherent-the sequence of ideas or events makes sense and the relationships among them are apparent. Content is most likely to be organized coherently when it is selected in a principled way, guided by ideas about what students should learn from studying the topic. When making presentations, providing explanations or giving demonstrations, effective teachers project enthusiasm for the content and organize and sequence it so as to maximize its clarity and coherence.

The teacher presents new information with reference to what students already know about the topic; proceeds in small steps sequenced in ways that are easy to follow;

— uses pacing, gestures and other oral communication skills to support comprehension;

— avoids vague or ambiguous language and digressions that disrupt continuity;

— elicits students' responses regularly to stimulate active learning and ensure that each step is mastered before moving to the next;

— finishes with a review of main points, stressing general integrative concepts; and

— follows up with questions or assignments that require students to encode the material in their own words and apply or extend it to new contexts.

If necessary, the teacher also helps students to follow the structure and flow of the content by using outlines or graphic organizers that depict relationships, study guides that call attention to key ideas, or task organizers that help students keep track of the steps involved and the strategies they use to complete these steps. In combination, the principles calling for curricular alignment and for coherent content imply that, to enable students to construct meaningful knowledge that they can access and use in their lives outside school, teachers need to:

(i) retreat from breadth of coverage in order to allow time to develop the most important content in greater depth;

(ii) represent this important content as networks of connected information structured around powerful ideas;

(iii) develop the content with a focus on explaining these important ideas and the connections among them; and

(iv) follow up with authentic learning activities and assessment measures that provide students with opportunities to develop and display learning that reflects the intended outcomes of the instruction.

Besides presenting information and modelling application of skills, effective teachers structure a great deal of content-based discourse. Through participation in such discourse, students construct and communicate content-related understandings. In the process, they abandon native ideas or misconceptions and adopt the more sophisticated and valid ideas embedded in the instructional goals. In the early stages of units when new content is introduced and developed, more time is spent in interactive lessons featuring teacher/student discourse than in independent work on assignments. Thoughtful discourse features sustained examination of a small number of related topics, in which students are invited to develop explanations, make predictions, debate alternative approaches to problems, or otherwise consider the content's implications or applications. The teacher presses students to clarify or justify their assertions, rather than accepting them indiscriminately.

There are three main ways in which teachers help their students to learn. The skills practised to a peak of smoothness and automaticity tend to be retained indefinitely, whereas skills that are mastered only partially tend to deteriorate. Most skills included in school curricula are learned best when practice is distributed across time and embedded within a variety of tasks. Thus, it is important to follow up thorough initial teaching with occasional review activities and with opportunities for students to use what they are learning in a variety of application contexts.

Practice is one of the most important yet least appreciated aspects of learning in classrooms. Little or no practice may be needed for simple behaviours such as pronouncing words, but practice becomes more important as learning becomes complex. Successful practice involves polishing skills that are already established at rudimentary levels in order to make them smoother, more efficient and more automatic, and not trying to establish such skills through trial and error. Instead, most practice should be embedded within application contexts that feature conceptual understanding of knowledge and self-regulated application of skills. Thus, most practice of reading skills is embedded within lessons involving reading and interpreting extended text, most practice of writing skills is embedded within activities calling for authentic writing, and most practice of mathematics skills is embedded within problem-solving applications.

Opportunity to learn in school can be extended through homework assignments that are realistic in length and difficulty given the students' abilities to work independently. To ensure that students know what to do, the teacher can get them started on assignments in class, and then have them finish the work at home. An accountability system should be in place to ensure that students complete their homework assignments, and the work should be reviewed in class the next day. To be useful, practice must involve opportunities not only to apply skills but also to receive timely feedback. Feedback should be informative rather than evaluative, helping students to assess their progress with respect to major goals and to understand and correct errors or misconceptions. At times when teachers are unable to circulate to monitor progress and provide feedback, they should arrange for students working on assignments to get feedback by consulting posted study guides or answer sheets or by asking peers designated to act as tutors or resource persons.

The learning tasks suggests that activities and assignments should be sufficiently varied and interesting to motivate student engagement, sufficiently new or challenging to constitute meaningful learning experiences rather than needless repetition, and yet sufficiently easy to allow students to achieve high rates of success if they invest reasonable time and effort. The effectiveness of assignments is enhanced when teachers first explain the work and go over practice examples with students before releasing them to work independently, and then circulate to monitor progress and provide help when needed. The principle of teaching within the students' zones of proximal development implies that students will need explanation, modelling, coaching and other forms of assistance from their teachers, but also that this teacher structuring and scaffolding will be faded as the students' expertise develops. Eventually, students should become able to use what they are learning autonomously and to regulate their own productive task engagement. Besides being well chosen, activities need to be effectively presented, monitored and followed up if they are to have their full impact. This means preparing students for an activity in advance, providing guidance and feedback during the activity, and leading the class in post-activity reflection afterwards.

In introducing activities, teachers should stress their purposes in ways that will help students to engage in them with clear ideas about the goals to be accomplished. Then they might call students' attention to relevant background knowledge, model strategies for responding to the task or scaffold by providing information about task requirements. If reading is involved, for example, teachers might summarize the main ideas, remind students about strategies for developing and monitoring their comprehension as they read, distribute study guides that call attention to key ideas and structural elements, or provide task organizers that help students to keep track of the steps involved and the strategies that they are using.

Assuming that students have a general understanding of what to do and how to do it, these interventions can be kept brief and confined to minimal and indirect forms of help. If teacher assistance is too direct or extensive, teachers will end up carrying out tasks for students instead of helping them learn to carry out the tasks themselves. Teachers also need to assess performance for completion and accuracy. When performance is poor, they will need to provide re-teaching and follow-up assignments designed to ensure that content is understood and skills are mastered. Most assignments will not have their full effects unless they are followed by reflection or debriefing activities in which the teacher reviews the task with the students, provides general feedback about performance, and reinforces main ideas as they relate to overall goals.

General learning and study skills as well as domain-specific skills are most likely to be learned thoroughly and become accessible for application if they are taught as strategies to be brought to bear purposefully and implemented with metacognitive awareness and self-regulation. This requires comprehensive instruction that includes attention to propositional knowledge, procedural knowledge (how to do it) and conditional knowledge.

Strategy teaching is especially important for less able students who otherwise might not come to understand the value of consciously monitoring, self-regulating and reflecting upon their learning processes. Many students do not develop effective learning and problem-solving strategies on their own but can acquire them through modelling and explicit instruction from their teachers. Poor readers, for example, can be taught reading comprehension strategies such as keeping the purpose of an assignment in mind when reading; activating relevant background knowledge; identifying major points in attending to the outline and flow of content; monitoring understanding by generating and trying to answer questions about the content; or drawing and testing inferences by making interpretations, predictions and conclusions. Instruction should include not only demonstrations of and opportunities to apply the skill itself but also explanations of the purpose of the skill and the occasions on which it would be used. Strategy teaching is likely to be most effective when it includes cognitive modelling: the teacher thinks out loud while modelling use of the strategy.

Cognitive modelling makes overt the otherwise covert thought processes that guide use of the strategy in a variety of contexts. It provides learners with first-person language that they can adapt directly when using the strategy themselves. This eliminates the need for translation that is created when instruction is presented in the impersonal third-person language of explanation or even the second-person language of coaching. In addition to strategies used in particular domains or types of assignments, teachers can model and instruct their students in general study skills and learning strategies such as rehearsal, elaboration, organization, comprehension monitoring, and affect monitoring.

When providing feedback as students work on assignments and when leading subsequent reflection activities, teachers can ask questions or make comments that help students to monitor and reflect on their learning. Such monitoring and reflection should focus not only on the content being learned, but also on the strategies that the students are using to process the content and solve problems. This will help the students to refine their strategies and regulate their learning more systematically.

Co-operative learning promotes affective and social benefits such as increased student interest in and valuing of subject matter, and increases in positive attitudes and social interactions among students who differ in gender, race, ethnicity, achievement levels and other characteristics. Co-operative learning also creates the potential for cognitive and metacognitive benefits by engaging students in discourse that requires them to make their task-related information-processing and problem-solving strategies explicit. Students are likely to show improved achievement outcomes when they engage in certain forms of co-operative learning as an alternative to completing assignments on their own. Traditional approaches to instruction feature whole-class lessons followed by independent seatwork time during which students work alone on assignments.

Co-operative learning approaches retain the whole-class lessons but replace part of the individual seatwork time with opportunities for students to work together in pairs or small groups on follow-up practice and application activities. Co-operative learning can be used with activities ranging from drill and practice to learning facts and concepts, discussion and problem solving. It is perhaps most valuable as a way of engaging students in meaningful learning with authentic tasks in a social setting. Some forms of co-operative learning call for students to help one another achieve individual learning goals, for example by discussing how to respond to assignments, checking work, or providing feedback or tutorial assistance. Other forms of co-operative learning call for students to work together to achieve a group goal by pooling their resources and sharing the work. Co-operative learning models that call for students to work together to produce a group product often feature a division of labour among group participants (e.g. to prepare a biographical report, one group member will assume responsibility for studying the person's early life, another for the person's major accomplishments, another for the person's effects on society, and so on).

Co-operative learning methods are most likely to enhance learning outcomes if they combine group goals with individual accountability. Activities used in co-operative learning formats should be well suited to those formats. Some activities are most naturally carried out by individuals working alone, others by students working in pairs, and still others by small groups of three to six students. Students should receive whatever instruction and scaffolding they may need to prepare them for productive engagement in co-operative learning activities.

During times when students are working in pairs or small groups, the teacher should circulate to monitor progress, make sure that groups are working productively and provide any assistance needed. A well-developed curriculum includes strong and functional assessment components. These assessment components are aligned with the curriculum's goals, and so they are integrated with its content, instructional methods and learning activities, and designed to evaluate progress towards its major intended outcomes.

Comprehensive assessment does not just document students' ability to supply acceptable answers to questions or problems; it also examines the students' reasoning and problem-solving processes. Effective teachers routinely monitor their students' progress in this fashion, using both formal tests or performance evaluations and informal assessments of students' contributions to lessons and work on assignments. Effective teachers use assessment for evaluating students' progress in learning and for planning curriculum improvements, not just for generating grades. Good assessment includes data from many sources besides paper-and-pencil tests, and it addresses the full range of goals or intended outcomes. Standardized, norm-referenced tests might comprise part of the assessment programme. However, standardized tests should ordinarily be supplemented with publisher-supplied curriculum-embedded tests and with teacher-made tests that focus on learning goals that are emphasized in instruction but not in external testing sources. The teacher uses a variety of formal and informal assessment methods to monitor progress towards learning goals.

In addition, learning activities and sources of data other than tests should be used for assessment purposes. Everyday lessons and activities provide opportunities to monitor the progress of the class as a whole and of individual students. and tests can be augmented with performance evaluations such as laboratory tasks and observation checklists, portfolios of student papers or projects, and essays or other assignments that call for higher-order thinking and application.

A broad view of assessment helps to ensure that the assessment component includes authentic activities that provide students with opportunities to synthesize and reflect on what they are learning, think critically and creatively about it, and apply it in problem-solving and decision-making contexts. In general, assessment should be treated as an ongoing and integral part of each instructional unit. Results should be scrutinized to identify learner needs, misunderstandings or misconceptions that may need attention; to suggest potential adjustment in curriculum goals, instructional materials or teaching plans; and to detect weaknesses in the assessment practices themselves.

Teacher effects research indicates that teachers who elicit strong achievement gains accept responsibility for doing so. They believe that their students are capable of learning and that they (the teachers) are capable of and responsible for teaching them successfully. If students do not learn something the first time, they teach it again, and if the regular curriculum materials do not do the job, they find or develop others that will. Teachers' expectations concerning what their students are capable of accomplishing tend to shape both what teachers attempt to elicit from their students and what the students come to expect from themselves. Thus, teachers should form and project expectations that are as positive as they can be while still remaining realistic. It is helpful if teachers set goals for the class and for individuals in terms of floors, not ceilings.

Then they can let group progress rates, rather than limits adopted arbitrarily in advance, determine how far the class can go within the time available. They can keep their expectations for individual students current by monitoring their progress closely and by stressing current performance over past history. At the very least, teachers should expect all their students to progress sufficiently to enable them to perform satisfactorily at the next level. This implies holding all students accountable for participating in lessons and learning activities and for turning in careful and completed work on assignments. It also implies that, in addition to the other elements of good teaching summarized in the preceding principles, struggling students will receive whatever extra time, instruction and encouragement are needed to enable them to meet expectations. When individualizing instruction and giving students feedback, teachers should emphasize continuous progress relative to previous levels of mastery rather than how students compare with their classmates or with standardized test norms.

Instead of merely evaluating relative levels of success, teachers can diagnose learning difficulties and provide feedback accordingly. If students have not understood an explanation or demonstration, teachers can follow through by re-teaching. In general, teachers are likely to be most successful when they think in terms of stretching students' minds by stimulating them and encouraging them to achieve as much as they can, not in terms of 'protecting' them from failure or embarrassment.

Pupil Evaluation

The concept of educational evaluation denotes the process of collecting objectives valid and reliable information about the level of pupils' attainment on different aspects of his personality and reporting the same meaningfully for diagnostic as well as prognostic purposes and for effective use in the improvement of his teaching and learning. The purpose of tests and examinations still remains confined to classify and certify pupils. This is primarily due to equating evaluation with examination and measurement scores. Content examination is thus quite short of the total pupil evaluation. The pupil evaluation involves the processes of:

— collecting objective, valid and reliable information about the desired areas of pupil growth;

— analysing and interpreting the information to make it meaningful for his growth.

— using the information for remedial instruction and

— employing decisions in improving inputs and outputs of education.

The process of pupil evaluation gathering evidence of the behavioural changes brought about as a result of instructional process, judging the adequacy and appropriateness of these changes, and taking suitable decisions about the action to be taken make the curriculum transaction effective. People evaluation depends upon the objectives of learning, methods and materials used for learning and their relationship and implications for pupil growth. The teacher organises suitable teaching-learning activities in order to promote predetermined behavioural changes. The learning experiences so offered in the classroom are directly related with the instructional objectives. A change in these competencies or objectives will also modify the teaching-learning process.

The teaching learning activities are competency-based and not content or textbook based. The content is the means used to assist in selecting and organising suitable learning activities as per needs of the stated competencies or objectives. The extent to which the teaching learning activities result in experiences leading to the realisation of a particular competency or a set of competencies is determined by pupil evaluation outcomes on the one hand and by the learning activities on the other. This integrative nature of evaluation thus demands integrating testing both with teaching and learning. It covers two major aspects:

— analysis and interpretation of results to make it a meaningful evidences and

— analysis and interpretation of results to offer feedback for further improvement of pupils learning.

The first task involves the analysis of results and interpretation of them to give them value and show their worth. For example, a student secures 60 per cent marks in mathematics and 60 per cent in English. As such no values are attached with them. But when we indicate the maximum and average marks secured in the tests as well as prepare merit-lists, the scores of 60 per cent get worth. A pupil's comparative achievements in the two subjects becomes apparent. The result may also be interpreted in terms of the pupil's potentialities, his level of performance *vis-a-vis* his abilities.

The second task involves the analysis of the result and interpretation with respect to the accomplishment of individual competency and the suitability of teaching-learning activities, and also for the appropriateness and adequacy of the evaluation tools used for ascertained evidence. This provides a feedback with regard to attainability of predetermined com-petencies as well as the appropriateness of teaching-learning activities.

Pupil evaluation and measurement are often considered synonymous which is not true. Measurement is the process of collecting data called measures or scores or marks. It provides data but does not attach any value to it.

Evaluation goes beyond, as it analyses the data and interprets it with reference to intended competencies, pupil's capabilities, previous level of attainment, performance of the entire group, etc., in order to make the data meaningful and usable. It judges the value data. In this way, evaluation is measurement plus value judgement. As the aim of education is to promote the all-round developments of each child, it should cover all aspects of pupil growth, i.e., physical, intellectual, emotional and social development. Therefore, all objectives of education should be included for instruction as well as for evaluation. Evaluation is thus comprehensive and objective based, involving pupil assessment in both scholastic and non-scholastic areas of their development.

Assess pupil progress along with the instructional programme so as to make evaluation as part and parcel of the teaching-learning process. Continuous evaluation helps to develop various aspects of pupil growth to their optimum potential. Pupil assessment, when made throughout the year, informs them about their progress at any given stage, makes them regular at studies, helps them maintain punctuality, discipline and better academic achievement as also promotes inculcation of desirable personal and social qualities, and right type of motivation and attitudes for their all round development.

Teachers, through analysis and interpretation of data obtained by the process of evaluation, assess the growth of pupils in terms of attainment of competencies, specially in the context of acquiring the minimum essential levels of learning. Thus, the rate of progress of each individual should be reasonable in the light of their potentialities and the instructional material provided. This also reveals the strengths and weaknesses of pupils, and if required, specific diagnostic tests are administered to know the factors responsible for the shortcomings. Appropriate remedial measures are taken up to overcome these weaknesses. Pupil evaluation is a powerful instrument for improvement of the instructional programme and maintaining proper quality control. On analysis the evidences secured through evaluation, the weak and strong points of the teaching programme as well as the attainability of instructional objectives become apparent. Thus, teachers assess the effecti-veness of their teaching to improve the quality of instruction as also to evolve remedial measures to plug the gaps.

Monitoring and Evaluating Educational Progress

Economic prosperity and social progress depend upon educational reform. This includes extending participation in schooling, broadening the skills base, extending the scope of civic responsibility, building the capacity for responsible civic participation and meeting basic conditions for equity and social justice.

Access to primary education constitutes the greatest concern in all countries. Universal participation in primary education over several years' duration and of good quality is proclaimed and accepted in all of the EFA 2000 Assessments as a necessary condition if countries' social and economic goals are to be achieved and individual human rights recognised. Progress is reported in enrolments in primary education across most regions. But there are too many countries and regions within countries where either there has been little or no progress in the decade or actual decline. Major deficiencies continue in Sub-Saharan Africa, South Asia and in some parts of South America.

Everywhere there are continuing inequalities within countries. So, while the target may be universally 'recognised', it is not being universally acted on with sufficient seriousness of purpose or being achieved. There are countries, however, with different concerns. These in the main are the economically advanced countries, where the goal of universal access and completion of primary education has long since been achieved and there are in place highly developed systems of primary, secondary and tertiary education.

Yet there are unfulfilled targets, qualitative as well as quantitative at all levels, including primary and preschool. Quality is the major concern, and this is leading to new and revised standards for student performance; but there are also grounds for concern in the incidence of non-attendance, school violence, poor motivation and changes in family and community life that militate against effective learning. Japan, a country which has had remarkable success in achieving primary and universal secondary education, a national system of kindergartens and day nurseries and highly favourable staff-student ratios, is not alone in reporting problems of school resistance, bullying, drug addiction and over-reliance on highly competitive examinations and selection procedures. Nationwide parent, teacher and student demonstrations in France testify to mounting anxiety over violence at school.

School failure and attrition rates in secondary education, including very high rates among specific ethnic and socioeconomic groups, and low levels of student motivation are of growing concern in many European countries, North America and Australasia. What, then, is meant by 'universal'. Enrolment targets for perhaps 100% in relatively prosperous parts of countries are sometimes accompanied by targets of, say, 90% or 95% for poorer, more remote areas. In percentage terms the difference is small, but for large population countries, actual numbers are high. In some countries, completion of a 2-3 year programme is seen as a target for poorer, remote rural areas whereas for cities and the more prosperous areas it may be anything from 4 to 9 years. In countries with long-established systems of primary and secondary education, when dropout and irregular school attendance occur along with poor learning outcomes, there is less than universal completion. Social expectations and policy targets in many countries are completion, not just of lower secondary but of upper secondary and/ or vocational training and apprenticeship as well.

The reasons for non-completion of full programmes vary and may be very practical. But in these and other ways, widespread abridgements are occurring in practice to targets of universal access and completion. It is not only the most economically advanced countries that had achieved virtual universal enrolment in primary education by the beginning of the nineties or did so in the course of the decade. Countries of Eastern and Central Europe, the Trans-Caucasus, and in the Caribbean, several countries of Central and South America and Asia have by the year 2000 reached or have within sight the target of universal or near universal participation in primary and at least lower secondary education. Declines have occurred, however, in some countries due in the main to worsening economic conditions or violent disorder as regimes toppled and civil war spread.

Many countries in Sub-Saharan Africa, several Asian states and some very populous countries in South Asia have, for a variety of reasons, made either very little progress or actually regressed. In all of these countries, the need is not always recognised let alone adequately addressed. To draw attention to structural conditions affecting enrolment and participation, the concepts of excluded-included are being used. It is not simply a matter of low rates of enrolment and attendance, but of exclusion, in a positive sense, of the most vulnerable, the most impoverished, the most remotely located, girls, children with disabilities, working children, children suffering the impact of HIV/AIDS. By contrast an inclusive policy, internationally, nationally, regionally and locally, would, by all deliberate means, reach out to the excluded.

Enrolment figures in primary schooling countries need to be read in conjunction with those on length of schooling and completion rates. In India and notwithstanding big improvements over the decade, lack of capacity by schools to retain children has been a serious problem, especially in the upper primary years and for girls. Although in the USA enrolment and school completion rates compare favourably with those in other industrial countries, a substantial minority of students —about one in 20 - drop out of school at the middle and high school levels. The figures are a matter of concern because high school dropouts have lower earnings, experience more unemployment, and are more likely to end up needing public support, going to prison, and becoming pregnant than their peers who have a diploma.

Enrolment data must be treated with considerable caution — some countries have not reported, and others have qualified their returns in various ways. Trend data in particular are very uneven and private provision, whose growth is an important development in several countries, is usually not recorded or only very incompletely. Nevertheless, the global trends have been mapped for the decade and analysed in the Statistical Document and the thematic study on demographic challenges and real, substantial progress has been made in many countries in achieving the enrolment targets.

There is general agreement on the conditions affecting trends and on matters for which concentrated attention will be required in the years ahead. Several countries report either continuing universal participation or major gains. Trends in net enrolment ratios show good gains in most regions and slight gains in others. However they mask considerable variations between and within countries. Also enrolment is not the same as attendance and completion which are highly variable. Enrolment trends must also be seen in light of other demographic movements for example in the number of out of school children in the E9 countries.

The economically advanced and industrialised countries which had achieved universal primary education by the beginning of the decade have in the 90s directed their concerns towards improvements in quality. including the targeting of specific groups whose members perform poorly. When the goal of a fill secondary education and some forms of post school vocational preparation or tertiary education for all has been adopted, policy initiatives in these countries single out risk groups. Of growing concerns are children subject to multiple disadvantage and the socioeconomic groups who are neither at school nor in work. By contrast with these countries grappling with problems of effective secondary schools, primary education represents the only educational opportunity for the vast majority of school age children in the least developed countries.

Good progress, reflecting a decline in the primary school age population and gains made in the 90s will see universal primary education achieved by the year 2010 in several of the world's most populous countries. Many others, however, are still facing the challenge of achieving universal enrolment and completion of as much as 3 or 4 years of primary schooling. The most notable progress has been in East Asia and Oceania and in the Asia-Pacific region overall. Most of these countries have in net as well as gross enrolment ratios moved closer to 100%. Participation rates have improved and the incidence of age appropriate enrolments has increased, reflecting greater internal efficiencies. South Asian enrolment increases, however, have barely kept up with the growth rate in the population of schoolage children, due both to high fertility and survival rates reflecting improved health care and nutrition.

In the East and Southeast Asian sub-region, gender disparity has decreased. It remains marked, though, in some countries in South and West Asia, especially in remote and rural provinces of a few countries. These disparities reflect rapid population growth and the absence of wide-ranging structural reforms. Completion rates have improved in some but not all countries. Out-of-school numbers also remain high, underlining the problem in many countries of continuing population increases. Steady progress in the countries of the Caribbean and South and Central America has resulted in a decline in the number of children out of school. Similar progress has occurred for children in school in the Arab States and some parts of Sub-Saharan Africa.

While enrolment increases are generally either matching or exceeding the population growth rate, it is still a struggle to reduce the out-of-school population.In Sub-Saharan Africa, where there is a disproportionate balance of least developed countries, continuing high population growth rates in combination with other factors make it extremely difficult for many countries to bring about significant reductions in the number of out-of-school children. The positive global trends mask great contrasts between countries and serious internal disparities. A number of factors which are militating against achievement of the Jomtien target temper the optimism that the gross figures generate.

The major world region experiencing the greatest difficulty in making progress, and in some respects has actually regressed, is Sub-Saharan Africa. The dire plight of children who are the casualties of war in several of these countries has been the subject of worldwide publicity. Not so well publicized are the trends which indicate nothing short of a major crisis in the context of Education for All. One third of the population of Sub-Saharan Africa was reported in 1999 by FAO to be under-nourished. In countries that have experienced long wars, vast numbers of people are displaced. In the tropical zone, which covers a large area of Sub-Saharan Africa, life expectancy is much lower than in the temperate zone, a function of the interaction of disease and poverty and short life expectancy is a powerful cause of impoverishment. The bottom ten on the UNDP Human Development Index are all Sub-Saharan African countries. The HIV/AIDS pandemic in this region, according to UN-AIDS figures, far exceeds that of any other region.

Population is increasing at a faster rate than any other region and there are increasing problems of overcrowding in cities and towns. The quality of education, health and other services has declined. Over 40 million primary school age children are not in school; there are very large disparities — gender, urbanrural and others and great contrasts between countries. Yet, in the face of these critical conditions, while most Sub-Saharan African countries have fallen far short of the primary education target (and all the others), and some participation rates have worsened, a few countries have managed to perform well. They include Botswana, Cape Verde, Malawi, Mauritius, and South Africa where primary enrolment rates are 90% or more.

Some countries that started with low enrolment figures have significantly improved over the decade —Malawi, Mozambique and Uganda —others have stabilised high rates—Mauritius, and Seychelles. Some countries have lost ground —Kenya and Zimbabwe, among them; others have remained with very low figures, Liberia and Sierra Leone included. This is not, of course, the whole picture and many different factors have to be taken into account in explaining lack of progress or decline. But a key point is that countries can succeed, with commitment, strategic planning based on realistic goals and leadership, good management and competent personnel. Despite the tremendous difficulties these have been shown to be attainable.

Constraint of Educationals Progress

Economic conditions, ranging from stagnation to inflation to collapse, are widely identified as the major constraint on the supply of schools and teachers, teaching learning materials and structures for monitoring and evaluating progress and pinpointing areas of difficulty. They affect all levels and forms of education but their impact falls unequally, exacerbating problems of provision and access in rural areas, for poorer families and, in some countries, the opportunities for girls and women. Debt remains a major constraint on Caribbean countries in sustaining previous investments in education and in making new ones'. The combination of increasing public debt in some countries and declining disposable income in certain sectors of the population, inhibits the needed mix of public and private financing to drive forward the Jomtien agenda on enrolment and participation. Yet the level of a country's wealth is not always the determinant of school performance.

Countries vary considerably in their levels of investment in education and in the vigour and efficiency with which education targets are pursued. By contrast with countries where there are static or declining levels of investment, major funded reform initiatives have been taken, for example in Brazil, where there have been increases in teacher salaries, a more equitable distribution of funds and a concentration of effort in areas of greatest need.

In the Sub-Saharan region, while in several countries there has been positive per capita economic growth and more robust economic policies are in place, some economies are devastated by civil war, and others suffer the burdens of social unrest or large scale involuntary population movements including refugees from war zones.

The HIV/AIDS pandemic is a human and social tragedy, and also an economic threat. There is overdependence on development assistance to meet basic needs, domestic debt has risen rapidly in some countries, there are large numbers of unemployed youth and adults especially in urban centres and many are inadequately prepared for changing labour markets. Such conditions stand in the way of the increased investment needed to boost primary school enrolments, strengthen retention rates and bring about the needed qualitative improvements. At the same time, they do not provide the right signals for improving efficiency and introducing more innovative ways of using existing resources. There are many conditions affecting countries' achievement of targets for enrolment and participation. The quality of leadership and the mobilisation of the population have been conspicuous in several African countries (but absent in others) and in China and Brazil among the countries where large gains have been made.

The drive to achieve universal enrolment in basic schooling, whether at the primary or secondary stage, usually means a struggle with the last 15 or 20 % composed of cultural, religious and linguistic minorities, remote populations, nomads, pastoralists and migratory agricultural workers, the severely handicapped, street children and some others. Adolescents in economically advanced countries, particularly for some ethnic groups and in poorer parts of cities, have shown great resistance to schooling, creating another potential '15-20%' problem. Mass education means among other things that there is no longer the economic and social status of the former selective systems. Increasing enrolment figures are a function of population increases as much as they reflect an improved capacity to increase participation rates. Africa, for example, continues its upward population trajectory, as does South Asia, while other countries have achieved either a significant slow-down in the rate of increase or a stable population.

Rapid population growth, combined with weak economic conditions, is a major impediment to increased participation and a better quality of schooling. As the Gross Enrolment Rate tables (GER) demonstrate, increased enrolments are not always a source of satisfaction. They may reflect such departures from norms as repeating the grade and overage participation. Enrolments have also been affected by both voluntary and enforced migration—declines in some areas resulting from the devastating effects of natural disasters, war and civil unrest—and increases in others where refugees are concentrated with resulting pressures on what are often already overstretched and inadequate facilities. Cities and towns in many countries are becoming overcrowded as population rates soar and rural emigration increases.

There are both positive and negative effects of the flight to cities , services, for example, are more readily provided in urban than remote rural areas. On the other hand, very rapid urban growth rates, accompanied by unemployment and poverty, linguistic and cultural differences, are a great strain on existing services designed for much smaller numbers in more stable conditions.Generally, and across all of the regions, wherever enrolment and participation levels remain low, the major but not the only factor referred to in explaining failure or inability to meet target enrolment goals set by the governments themselves is the generic concept of poverty.

The weakness of national economies—including inflationary pressures, the increased demands resulting from population growth and the poverty of a large proportion of the population, and accumulated national debt—are major impediments. Unless they are addressed there can be little hope of significant improvements in education. Domestic poverty or hardship, for example, in many countries stand in the way of the increases now sought for in family contributions to schooling. The opportunity cost of child labour is a major factor with poor families. But questions must be asked as to whether governments have devoted a sufficient / rising proportion of their funds to meet the commitments entered into at Jomtien. Some have; others have not. To this issue must be added management of education budgets, including the ways in which national and regional budgets are apportioned to different sectors and the efficient use of resources.

Big improvements in macro and micro policies in a number of countries are required if there is to be an adequate flow of funds to support universal primary education and effective utilisation of resources. Universal provision and access is within the capacity of all countries to deliver. A mix of economic and education reforms, implemented with great determination, can achieve this.

Some countries, prone to cataclysmic events—regular hurricanes and cyclones, large scale flooding, volcanoes, or earthquakes—are under much greater pressure than those where conditions are more or less equable. It has been suggested that climatic changes over recent decades are increasing the incidence of several of these phenomena. Massive floods in Bangladesh and Mozambique and volcanic activity, drought and hurricanes in others not only cause immediate damage and loss of life, but interrupt schooling in countries that may already be under acute pressure to meet growing demand for basic services including primary education. The scale of the refugee problem is an indicator of disruption. Peaking at the all time high of 18 million in 1992, it declined by 1998-but still to a figure of 11.5 million.

The scale of warfare and violence in several countries during the 90s is a bitter blow to the hopes and aspirations at the end of the 80s. A combination, then, of large scale political changes in Central and Eastern Europe, democratisation, and improved economic conditions, especially in parts of Asia, seemed to herald a more peaceful and prosperous decade ahead. However, the all-too familiar patterns of civil war and coups together with changing economic fortunes, especially in countries whose economies depend heavily on commodity exports, has led to stagnation in rates of primary school participation or real decline.

As stated in the regional synthesis report on South and East Africa, 'Restoration of peace and economic growth are essential for the children to be able to go back to school and normal life'. For planning purposes, educational services need to be differentiated—in different parts of countries and for various stages of conflict, from the battlefield itself to the rehabilitation of traumatised children and child soldiers. But not all countries challenged by war appear to have experienced significant declines in enrolment—Rwanda for example.

A very interesting response to what appears to be a growing incidence of disaster and crises in some of the poorest parts of the world is reported in the thematic study on Education in Situations of Emergency and Crisis. Educational crisis strategies are being developed and implemented to reestablish basic education services, reducing the traumatic effects and enabling early return to normality wherever conditions allow this.

The Machel Report on the Impact of Armed Conflict on Children has heightened awareness of the issue and of the need for the rapid provision of emergency education services. The UNICEF report, Education in Emergencies and For Reconstruction, states 'Any emergency education programme must be a development programme and not merely a stopgap measure that will halt when a particular situation is no longer experiencing intense media coverage'.

The roots of the primary school are buried deep in history. It is not just a western invention, but draws its strength and character in part from the great Oriental religions and long established practices for the initiation of children into the social and economic life of traditional societies. Its long and mostly successful history in achieving literate populations and solid bases for continuing learning in many countries helps to explain the continuing worldwide importance and prestige of the primary school. Colonisation, trade and missionary activities have contributed to its place and standing as the key instrumentality of formal learning throughout Africa, Asia, the Pacific, the Americas and Europe.

Educated women tend to have fewer children; when fertility rates decline and conditions are relatively stable, there are better opportunities to provide facilities for child upbringing care and early education and mothers' education. Educated parents also tend to make better use of health care facilities. In general, population decreases favour improved education, health and care of children. But this is not always the case.

The impact of crises such as HIV/AIDS can be completely distorting—of demographic trends and policies for health improvement and education —with serious cost implications, for example for the medical care of teachers and their replacement observers to question whether formal schooling is indeed the way ahead. For them, the school may not be the means to further progress in achieving universal education. This point of view derives not only from inability to meet enrolment targets, but from high rates of dropout and noncompletion, poor performance and dysfunctional overage enrolments.

The use of primary schools for overage students has been necessary, but is increasingly seen to be inappropriate. Interest in nonformal models complementary to primary schools is noted in some countries, and reflects the need to provide basic education for children and particularly women who do not find primary schools suitable for their needs or for whom there are no available schools. It is quite excessive to claim that the formal institution of the primary school as such stands in the way of achieving universal basic education. Yet it is becoming increasingly clear that a variety of means in addition to the conventional pattern of primary schooling is needed in order to attain the Jomtien targets in some countries and regions.

Countries are mobilising additional resources, such as the Quranic schools in Nigeria, which have been effective in lowering illiteracy rates. Although distance education, including the use of telematics and broadcasting has not been shown as the answer to providing expanded opportunities for the primary school age group, their value as ancillaries and for secondary teaching and adult education has been demonstrated. Also, they can be of great value in situations of chronic instability or where educational systems are being rebuilt. Further developments, including cost reduction and a readiness to change some of the formalities and the rigidities of the schooling model, should see a wider use of multimedia and new delivery systems for primary age children. Overall the primary school, however modified and extended, seems set to remain the essential instrument for universal education of younger children and, in many countries, adolescents.

Continuing low participation rates for girls in whole countries and parts of countries (rural areas) and social sectors (low socioeconomic) continued through the decade. They constitute major hurdles to reaching Jomtien targets. In some countries, of growing importance is the low performance of boys —school alienation and dropout, such that although enrolment targets in primary schools are met, those for retention and progress in learning are not. This problem is referred to, for example, in the reports on Brazil and the Caribbean region. Boys' continuation (and performance) throughout secondary schooling is now high on the agenda of industrialised countries in Europe, North America and in Australia and New Zealand. For this reason, some reports draw attention to the need in future to give a new emphasis to the relevance and quality of school as a means of motivating boys to perform well and continue in schools. It is, however, the rate of girls' participation in primary schooling that remains a major obstacle, particularly in rural areas. The marked regional variation in school attendance of 8 year old girls within Cambodia for 1998, illustrates the problem. The areas of low school attendance broadly parallel areas of low population density and low adult female literacy rates. Recognising the need to provide new ways of reaching marginalised groups, nonformal programmes have been launched by governments, local communities and NGOs in India. The programmes are condensed, use curricula and materials similar to those in the formal system, are delivered through parttime teaching including volunteers, at a time and place convenient to learners, and use village and local community facilities. The increased participation of voluntary agencies including NGOs in the 90s is described as 'phenomenal': and there have been big increases in the number of centres, enrolments and investment of financial and human resources. Flexibility and variety in the design and delivery of education are features which, together with qualitative improvement, will continue to be sought. This scheme is not a low cost alternative to primary schools, but a complementary approach to meet special needs.

The gender gap has narrowed globally, but there remain considerable regional variations, and disparities are still particularly pronounced in the Arab States, South Asia and the Sub-Saharan regions. On the other hand, gender gaps in primary school age enrolments are closing in Eastern Asia and Oceania. An average figure for the whole of Sub-Saharan Africa indicates little change in the disproportionate boy- girl ratio over the decade. But there are in this region, as in several others, huge disparities not only between countries but also within them 'as low as 16% girls' enrolment in Mali and 19% in Niger and 100% in South Africa and Malawi. Gender differences in enrolment ratios remain conspicuous in several countries in the South and West Asia Sub-Region (above 30 percentage points in Pakistan). The gender gap in enrolments, retention and survival rates has not substantially decreased. Even in regions like Latin America, where overall gender discrimination is not significant for participation, there are pockets where it occurs, e.g. rural areas and some poorer urban areas. The proportion of girls in the total primary enrolments at the global level has steadily increased; nevertheless the net enrolment rates of girls remain lower than those of boys, notably in Sub-Saharan Africa, the Arab

States and North Africa, and southern and western Asia. Thus in all regions except the most developed countries, gender disparities in primary education enrolment are still large.

It is generally in countries with advanced economies, well developed and stable political and social structures, strong legislation, consistent, longstanding inclusive policies, a well educated teaching force and a highly developed capacity to organise, administer and monitor school systems that primary education has become universal and gained in quality. Even so there are cracks in the edifice which are causing great concern. Notably in depressed urban areas increased levels of bad behaviour and school violence are reported, for example in the USA, Japan and several European countries. Not only in the relatively depressed areas, teachers are experiencing difficulties in maintaining high levels of children's commitment to learning.

Multiple deprivation especially in poorer areas of cities has depressed student attainment levels and aggravated absenteeism. Some countries have initiated special programmes with additional support focused on the most depressed areas: the French ZEPs (Educational Priority Zones) are one of several examples of this concentration of resources. While accurate figures on truancy, low performance and dropout are not available, some estimates suggest that perhaps as much as one tenth to one fifth (or more) of the school age population in some areas, while enrolled, is not effectively participating. In some countries the proportion not completing a full secondary (and hence 'basic') education is considerably higher. A related phenomenon which is equally disturbing is that a high proportion of students completing secondary education do not in fact acquire formal qualifications of value either in the labour market or for further study. They appear in the enrolment statistics, including those for net enrolments, but what the students are actually learning is often of very limited value.It is not simply access and participation rates that matter.

One of the historical reasons for establishing the universal primary and then secondary school was to ensure stability and civic order in emerging democracies. The reform of primary and secondary education has as one of its motives the avoidance of social disintegration in conditions of rapid economic and social change. A major concern at the end of the 20th century in large urban centres and ethnically mixed societies is fostering tolerance and harmony amongst quite diverse groups. It is therefore through the interactions of the two targets—universal participation and the quality of learning processes and outcomes—that the Jomtien agenda is being pursued and needs to be taken further.

Learning Achievements

Individual countries and states within them have their own criteria of learning achievement and have many different ways of assessing and reporting it. There is growing interest in clearer definitions of performance and achievement and in the construction of age-grade norms and other system-wide performance measures. In some countries — the United Kingdom for example —these norms are being used for target setting and in judgements about the quality of performance of schools and teachers. France has in place a comprehensive national system for assessing, reporting on and evaluating students' learning achievements. The Goals 2000 Project in the USA involves leading national and state political figures in setting national goals for primary and secondary education; it has led to national standards in curriculum subjects for assessing student learning outcomes. Standards have also been set for teachers and there is growing interest in defining achievement both for students and teachers according to what they can do, as well as what they know. Several of the countries reporting on this target have given details of major reforms designed to monitor and bring about improvements in student achievement.

The joint UNESCO-UNICEF project, Monitoring Learning Achievement (MLA) which was established in 1992 to monitor learning achievement around the world at the grade 4 level, has stimulated activity in more than 50 countries, and led to specific studies of the quality of children's learning in Africa, the Arab States, Latin America and Kazakhstan. When framework statements on the purposes of education and on curriculum goals in a cross-section of countries are scanned, it quickly becomes evident that quite complex issues for assessing performance, quality and progress arise. These purposes and goals commonly include—in addition to a broad range of subject matter knowledge—competencies, personal qualities, ethical values, social skills, civic responsibility, physical development and health.

Learning achievement is not reducible to scores on cognitive tests. Over-reliance on examinations as a measure of student learning is heavily criticised in some country reports, but is very difficult to change. Long established and widely used assessment measures —sessional examinations of subject content mastery for screening purposes, teacher assessments of pupil performance and progress in specific curriculum topics and learning skills, and standardised pencil and paper tests usually have a strong cognitive bias. This does not suit some students and of itself is insufficient as a measure of learning achievement for any student. In addition to the growing interest in defining minimum standards of cognitive attainment levels by age and grade, countries are also setting goals in terms of competencies and aptitudes which are believed to have a high labour market value and broader sets of life skills including learning readiness and capability. There is often an unresolved tension between these and formal examination and testing requirements.

Cognitive-oriented tests still tend to dominate school assessment, often reflecting heavy emphasis on a narrow range of skills in the practice of teaching. Several countries, China and Japan, for example, have expressed great concern over the grip that tests and examinations have on teachers, students and families. The measured levels of achievement are often very high but thought to be too narrow and to depend unduly on rote learning and memorisation. The national report from China makes the point quite starkly: 'how to cope with examinations obsesses the minds of students, teachers and school leadership'. The goals of basic education are thereby 'seriously distorted'. However to change this situation it is not enough just to reform examinations. New curricula, teaching materials, pedagogical practices and assessment procedures, are required, together with the reform of teacher education. As the author of the national report on China says, 'arduous tasks indeed'. But unless reforms of this nature are undertaken, not only in the examination-dominated countries, the sought for improvement in the nature and quality of learning will not occur. Various proxy measures are used in assessing learning achievement — levels of investment in education, survival and completion rates, gross enrolment ratios, student- teacher ratios, levels of teacher education, and the supply and quality of text books and other materials. On these indicators, there are big problems in many countries. In South Asia and in Sub-Saharan Africa, less than three out of four enrolees reach grade.

In the least developed countries taken together, only half reach this level and many drop out after the first or second grade. Student-staff ratios and levels of teacher education are poor in many countries. Results reported in many of the MLA Study reports raise serious questions about students' learning. While proxy measures and test scores tell only part of the story, together with concerns widely expressed in the reports, they indicate that most countries are still far from achieving what they themselves define as satisfactory learning outcomes.The adoption, at Jomtien, of a target to improve learning achievement is of itself an important contribution to the international movement to focus on learning outcomes and on the quality of learning and teaching processes. As stated in the E9 report, At the end, what matters is whether students are learning what they need and should. To focus on learning, it is necessary to go beyond the formalities of school enrolment and rates of [attendance], and to ascertain whether the students are acquiring knowledge that is useful for a productive and meaningful life. How far, then, have countries been able to demonstrate in the EFA 2000 Assessment what students are learning, the value of that learning, and the progress that has been made in strengthening and improving learning in the decade since Jomtien. The tantalising answer is 'a little and yet a lot'. The reports give a variety of answers to these questions, mainly, however, they are fragmentary and in the form of directions that are being set and illustrative material on assessment policies and practices.

Except for the Monitoring Learning Achievement project which however is concentrated on only one grade level (4th grade primary) — relatively few data have emerged from the EFA 2000 Assessment, either on what students are learning, or on learning outcomes. Nor is there much discourse on the personal and social value of what is being taught and learnt. On the other hand, there is a significant public interest, nationally and internationally, in the processes and results of assessment of student learning.National policy statements for improving educational outcomes are commonplace. National assessment systems are becoming more common especially in economically advanced countries. New curriculum frameworks setting out broad sets of common learnings in Australia, Norway, Sweden, Japan, the Netherlands, the United Kingdom and Canadian provinces among many others have been constructed during the 90s. Many other countries either have in place or are strengthening their national and regional systems to assess what students are learning in school as indicated by the following examples: the National Elementary Achievement Test (NEAT) in the Philippines and the National Primary School Achievement Test (PSAT) in Malaysia; the national assessment of basic education in Brazil (SAEB) (mathematics, language and the main determinants of school achievement and failure); moves towards national standards and state level testing in India; new and additional mechanisms to measure prescribed student learning outcomes at the primary level and minimum competency testing in part of the Caribbean; measurements of children's learning achievements through the Southern African Consortium for the Measurement of the Quality of Education (SACMEQ); and the assessment of basic learning achievements at the grade 4 level in Africa, the Arab States, and Kazakhstan through participation in the UNESCO/ UNICEF MLA project.

Building on the International Educational Achievement (IEA) studies over several decades, is a large scale and very influential study of student achievement in mathematics and science (TIMMS: the Third International Mathematics and Science Study). Further work of this nature, ultimately extending into other curriculum areas, has recently been launched by OECD—PISA (Program for International Science Assessment) which is expected to involve many countries. A general conclusion to be drawn from the results of these and other assessment programs is that there are very large within country differences, often greater than the between-country differences which are the ones that attract most media interest.

The national and international assessment programmes have become a vehicle for training personnel. As a result of the massive publicity they attract through the 'league tables' favoured by journalists and editors, there is also a greatly increased public awareness of the work of educational institutions and teachers. These and other procedures—recently introduced, well-established or still in the planning stage—point to an intention to get a better grip on what students are learning and how well teachers and schools are performing. An issue that has come to the fore in the publicity given to the reports on student learning outcomes is the variability of conditions affecting learning. Initially, these conditions were widely ignored in crude comparisons and rankings. Attention drawn to the contrasts between poorer and richer regions and schools, teacher capabilities, resources for learning, family and community backgrounds and so forth has exploded the myths of equal opportunity and a level playing field without, as yet, subduing the impulse to make glib comparisons.Further analyses of student learning environments and conditions affecting learning is therefore required and to some extent is being undertaken to pinpoint and explain gross outcome differences. Although still in relatively early stages in most countries, this line of inquiry will facilitate policy refinement and the fine tuning of resource allocation and such remedial procedures as may be required.

In the 90s there has been significant improvement in many countries in methods used to determine learning outcomes and the factors that help to explain differences. It is rather surprising, therefore, that so little data on learning outcomes has been provided in the reports. Proxy measures, which are only partly satisfactory, have had to be resorted to in order to gain some insights into learning achievement. Net enrolment rates, years of schooling, teacher-pupil ratios, levels of teachers' education and others are included in the Statistical Document.

But what are students learning and how well are they performing? So little of a systematic kind has been reported in the EFA 2000 Assessments on learning outcomes that achievement of this Jomtien target remains largely unknown. Clearly this is unsatisfactory. For future work both the target itself and ways of ascertaining progress will need careful consideration. There must be a review of the data issue: what kinds of information exist and how might they best be assembled? What further steps are needed to get a grip on what students know and can do? What are the most successful ways of improving learning outcomes?Individual countries often have records of trends in student performance including results in public examinations and test scores, and they might be pieced together to provide single country or within-country profiles. There is no immediate prospect of large scale international studies covering the whole range of student learning or even the full gamut of what are deemed to be core or essential learnings. But there is plenty of scope for countries to improve their own procedures for monitoring and assessing student learnings, for sample and case studies to pinpoint specific issues like urban-rural differences, and for an improved international exchange of experiences. For example, further progress can be made in harmonising the relationship between enrolment and quality of learning and teaching through the national and international efforts of the Latin American Educational Quality Assessment Laboratory (Laboratorio) and the Southern African Consortium for Measuring Educational Quality (SACMEQ).

Several reports do provide brief and indirect assessments of learning outcomes, but there is little encouragement to be drawn from them. The cautious conclusions drawn in the synthesis report of the Asia-Pacific region perhaps best typify the overall situation wherever participation and external conditions are unfavourable: 'Pupil teacher ratios and survival rates are sometimes used as proxies for learning quality. In the present case there is almost no reliable trend data concerning learning achievement that are based on measurement using comparable instruments and procedures. To that extent it may be said that the burden of the evidence suggests that there are, in many countries, problems of quality in the primary cycle.' Many countries note weaknesses in the academic and professional expertise of teachers and the conditions under which they work. Projects in Malawi, Sudan and the Syrian Republic focus on improving the quality of teaching in rural areas; skilled teachers are being redeployed from urban to rural areas in Guinea, higher entry requirements are being set in Egypt and the Libyan Arab Jamarihiya; most countries in Latin America and the Caribbean are moving towards incentives to attract and retain teachers; in Pakistan the Northern Areas Education Project is bringing in additional teachers to meet needs in deprived areas.

Improvements in teacher education are seen as essential for speeding up the pace of reform in China's 1999 Action Scheme for Invigorating Education Towards the 21st Century. These are among many initiatives being taken to improve the quality and supply of teachers. It seems clear that very few countries have in practice set themselves the Jomtien learning target, let alone recorded measurable gains against it. For many countries, the conclusion is inescapable; in the words of the Arab Framework for Action: Quality education is still a privilege for a few. From a global perspective, this means, first, too few countries and, second, that within all countries there are differences, often very big ones, between an education of good quality enjoyed by the minority and a considerably lower and more variable quality of educational experience for the majority. So long as serious inadequacies and inequalities in provision, access and learning opportunities remain, for reasons of both socioeconomic efficiency and equity there should be renewed efforts to establish clear, realistic and relevant targets. Equally, programmes are needed to focus on specified difficulties. Transparent reporting mechanisms should be put in place. Those countries that are setting age/ grade based standards of learning achievement have at least established frameworks for such assessments. When there is universal participation in schooling of medium to long duration and systems of monitoring over time are in place, it will be possible in the next stage of EFA to produce and use internationally comparable data of much greater descriptive and analytic value than exist now. Many countries are not in a position now to produce such data. For them a more immediate task is to define realisable quality targets and ways of achieving them.

Improving Life Skills

The movement to orient both formal and informal education of youth and adults more towards generic learning, broadly defined competencies and 'life skills' has gained in momentum since the 80s. Strongly driven by a mixture of labour market changes and concern over social cohesion, this movement has brought in its train a large number of projects to improve skills and raise motivation. It has influenced national education goals statements, resulting in government-funded programmes, and is prominent in statements and recommendations from business round tables, representatives of industry, trade unions and other NGOs. Likewise, it has featured throughout the 90s in declarations and conferences organised by regional and global bodies.New national qualifications frameworks have been established to: facilitate the recording and the analysis of skills and competences; define appropriate learning experiences and settings; and regulate and interrelate qualifications that attest to competence. Although relatively little is known about the skill level of large segments of the population in many countries, this situation is changing, through surveys, funded research and the use of various proxy measures, including attendance and completion rates especially in vocationally-oriented programmes, and placement on the labour market.

Changes, especially in secondary schools and vocational programmes, together with better health care and welfare services are contributing to improvements in human capital. But youth joblessness, the incidence of low-skilled jobs and mismatches between basic education and training and the labour market continue to cause concern. Major gaps and weaknesses are observable; they are particularly acute in Africa, large parts of Asia and Central and South America but are also apparent in Europe, North America and Australasia. Several international organisations, notably the European Union, the OECD, the ILO, UNESCO, the World Bank and several national agencies have played leading roles in assisting efforts regionally and within countries to define competencies and skills, determine the learning experiences appropriate to them and establish, strengthen and analyse linkages between the labour market and education and training providers. Other international bodies have played similar roles in relation to health, welfare and other behavioural domains. Funded projects are common; but they fall far short of the need and have often proved to make only a moderate impact.

The range of variables in this target area is wide and there is a lack of data on behavioural change. Together with the diversity of agencies and organisations with a degree of responsibility or interest, these factors have meant that the authors of the EFA 2000 Assessment Country Reports found it exceedingly difficult to draw conclusions. The activities relevant to skills development, health, employment and productivity fall outside the scope of any one Ministry and involve the nongovernment sector, communities and enterprises and the media. They are seldom systematically monitored. Too often they consist of a succession of short-term interventions which lack strategic significance. Public funding for out-of-school youth, where available on any scale, comes from a considerable diversity of sources. Governments often lack the incentive as well as the capacity to coordinate activities and produce cohesive policies and strategies.

Skills development and behavioural change in youth are essential for sustainable development but there is a dearth of information on programmes that have been successful in these respects. A better integration of activities, it is often suggested, would bring results but the EFA 2000 Assessments provide scant evidence of changes in this regard. The programme areas that are receiving greatest attention vary by country and regions. In Western Europe, and several other advanced economies, the decade of the 90s has been characterised by a continuing preoccupation with youth and adult unemployment. Numerous programmes have been introduced in schools and vocational training institutions to improve transition from education to working life.

Innovative projects include those based in workplaces and run by private training companies. Guidance and services for labour market placement have been increased and improved. The major objective has been to better equip people for labour market participation. An underlying concern is that unless better results can be achieved, social cohesion is seriously threatened. Programmes, targeted mainly at early school leavers and those whose school performance has been modest, are being extended through the orientation of school curricula to the world of work.

In African countries, formal vocational preparation is high on the policy agenda — but so also are reproductive health and family planning, the fight against AIDS, hygiene and health education and extending primary education, and literacy. Youth unemployment rates are often extremely high and with weak economies and no clear orientation for future labour market growth, programme effectiveness is often questionable. In several South American countries—Bolivia, Colombia and Ecuador among them—curriculum development and assessment are being directed towards skills acquisition in line with international policy trends that favour less attention to the mastery of prespecified content and greater emphasis on active learning, participatory methodologies and—learning how to learn.

Countries in the Asia-Pacific region report mass programmes which aim to improve the skill level of the workforce. Among them are: expanding the capacity of institutions and improving labour market skills in the Malaysian Sixth Plan; improved literacy rates and educational standards in Lao PDR; private and public programmes for Training in Essential Skills in Indonesia; vocational training for targeted groups including the disabled in Cambodia. In the reports of the Trans-Caucasus and Central Asian States and Mongolia, vocational schools and colleges, technical schools and tertiary institutions are seen as the principal vehicles for work-oriented skills training, but in several countries resource flows to education and training institutions have been seriously disrupted.

In some countries, e.g. in Western Europe and Australasia, in addition to the preparatory phase, there is a marked emphasis on skills formation for young unemployed people and on the continuing upgrading and professional development of the work-force. It is most regrettable that, in the regional syntheses, so few data are presented on this important area. Many countries have either not contributed at all or have provided only very sketchy information. The argument that control of the HIV/AIDS pandemic, for example, depends on education is but one of many reasons for paying more attention to behavioural outcomes, difficult as they may be to measure or ascertain. The concept of a 'healthy lifestyle' is behavioural, as is civic responsibility and job capability. The challenge to identify 'behavioural change' is very demanding and indeed thus far seems to be unrealistic on any systematic basis.

There is a great variety of programmes but relatively little evaluation of their effect, e.g. behavioural changes and impact on health, employment and productivity. Research studies on particular groups and settings throw some light and there is a strong conviction internationally among policy analysts that, for example, productivity improvements are highly correlated with advanced levels of skills training, not only in the new technologies, but also with such attributes as team spirit and capabilities in problem-solving.

The EFA 2000 Assessment was intended to be inter-ministerial but it seems that there has been very little input, in many countries, from the relevant ministries other than education. For this as for several other target areas it will be essential in the next phase to again seek closer cooperation across ministries if crosssectoral programmes are to emerge and data be produced on outcomes. Increased acquisition by individuals and families of the knowledge, skills and values required for better living and sound and sustainable development, made available through all education channels including the mass media, other forms of modern and traditional communication, and social action, with effectiveness assessed in terms of behavioural change.

Many countries combined their returns on 'better living' with those on 'life skills'. Partly this is because data are extremely limited on both, but also because there is not a clear differentiation between the two target areas unless life skills were to be taken firmly in the direction of education and training for work, and 'better living' in the direction of overall quality of life and standard of living, health and wellbeing. 'Health', however, was allocated to target area 5 and the concept of behavioural change has relevance alike to the sixth and the fifth target areas.

Basic learning needs were defined at Jomtien and reformulated in the South and East African regional synthesis report prepared for the EFA 2000 Assessment:

— to be able to survive;

— to develop their full capacities to live and work in dignity;

— to participate fully in development;

— to improve the quality of their lives;

— to make informed decisions, and to continue learning.

Declaration, and reformulated in the Sub-Saharan Africa synthesis provides a concise starting point for considering 'better living' and 'sustainable development'. Through the satisfaction of the basic learning needs defined at Jomtien and reformulated in the South and East African regional synthesis report, individuals would both be empowered and assume a responsibility:

— to respect and build upon their collective cultural, linguistic and spiritual heritage;

— to promote the education of others, to further the cause of social justice, to contribute to environmental protection

— to be tolerant toward social, political and religious systems which differ from their own, ensuring that commonly accepted humanistic values and human rights are upheld;

— to work for international peace and solidarity in an interdependent world.

The foregoing sets of needs, qualities, attributes and responsibilities provide a general, highly optimistic backloth to all six target areas. They also cover a large part of the territory occupied by national education goals statements in many parts of the world. But they have a specific reference to the 'better living' theme of the sixth target area. As with the fifth target area it is not possible to produce a trend analysis of the Jomtien decade such that there can be clearcut conclusions about gains made, losses sustained and behavioural changes experienced. For one thing, although there may be widespread agreement on a list of behavioural correlates, their particular interpretation will vary according to cultural and personality differences and value preferences; for another 'better living' is an open ended concept and a creative process whereby individual and collective experience will constantly throw up new dimensions and possibilities.

In recognition of these considerations, countries seemed to find great difficulty in reporting progress, as distinct from the difficulties and obstacles standing in the way of the whole EFA enterprise. Before coming to country statements, however, it is necessary to refer again to those environmental factors, underlying conditions and change forces which, in many parts of the world, bring into question the capacity to achieve or sustain 'better life'. Some parts of the world and some sectors of the community have enjoyed substantial gains in living standards in the nineties.

Community and life-destroying natural disasters, acute civil disorder, economic mismanagement and corruption, rampant disease, substance abuse, malnutrition and hunger, poverty, injustice and inequities are conditions for 'worse living' for large numbers of people. Discriminatory access to education and training, ineffectual literacy programmes, outmoded curricula and assessment practices, chronic underfunding, shortage of equipment and materials, poor teaching and lack of family and community support are not factors that lay the foundation in people's lives for better living or the sustainable development of communities.

The increasing gaps between better off and worse off countries and groups and individuals within countries are an additional force undermining the universalistic principles of distributive justice and ethical relations among people and nations adopted at Jomtien. Unfortunately whole countries and regions have been afflicted in these ways during the 90s. The five Jomtien targets that precede the sixth and the strategies considered appropriate to them, together with the positive action taken during the Jomtien decade, constitute a worldwide programme designed to achieve a better living for hundreds of millions if not billions of people. It scarcely needs arguing that several years of primary schooling of good quality instead of economically forced child labour and premature motherhood is 'better living'.It is, thus, properly the appraisal of the Jomtien movement as a whole and its role in the promotion of education for all and not of the sixth target area in isolation that is required in drawing conclusions about the achievement of 'better life' for all. Perhaps it was this realisation that led so few countries to comment separately and concretely on the sixth target area. Many of them, in drawing lessons from the decade and in formulating ideas for the future, implicitly if not explicitly offered their commentaries on whether or not gains have been made in 'better living'.

'Better living' has connotations of virtue and moral worth, of taking pleasure in and gaining happiness from doing the 'right' things —hence a moral component. For educators and all those concerned with sustainable development there appear to be several inbuilt criteria. These include, for example, efforts in Indonesia, Malaysia and the Philippines to sustain rich cultural heritages, teaching in indigenous languages, using local resources and materials, ensuring that local and diverse communities have an impact on what is taught, and incorporating natural history and culture in the curriculum. In the Latin American sub-regional report, a set of 'better living' themes are listed:

— respect for the dignity of human life, constructing a culture of peace;

— strengthening of democracy and respect for human rights;

— development of a full, affective family and sexual life;

— adoption of healthy lifestyles;

— affirmation of equal rights and respect for ethnic and cultural diversity;

— respect and care for the environment;

— respect for one's own and others' cultural inheritance.

Considering links between schooling and worthwhile pursuits, the authors of the Caribbean synthesis state that children should develop not just competence in but 'a love for reading', and a readiness to see in reading a 'recreational activity' and television as a 'medium for pertinent, focused curriculum information through the ever popular school quiz'. But reading materials and the mass media often have no educative purpose whatsoever. Their uptake and impact for example on levels of violence and anti-social behaviour, raise value questions which few countries or organisations seemed prepared to take up reporting for the EFA 2000 Assessment.

Sustainable development, as the report on Sub-Saharan Africa points out, must start with acknowledgement of the immense diversity of life styles reflecting factors of land form, ecology, settlement patterns, agriculture, extractive and manufacturing industry, trade and transportation and others. 'Sustainable' does not evoke a uniform response or provision: what is a 'better life' for a mountain mining community is not in all respects the same as for city dwellers, desert nomads or intensively cultivated plantation regions, although basic needs and rights may be identical. This suggests a need for considerable flexibility not to say creativity in translating broadly defined education and development targets into relevant, successful action programmes on the ground.

The sixth Jomtien target refers to the mass media and other forms of modern and traditional communication, and social action. Various uses of media in education are referred to in many country reports, for example, distance education in island communities (Tuvalu, Cook Islands, Nauru, Tonga) and in the Latin American sub-regional report. Radio is widely used, and commended as a cost effective medium by the authors of the special study on New Technologies and Cost-Effective Delivery Systems. Very large scale distance education operations have become widespread in parts of Asia, North America and Australia, mainly for adults.

A wider consideration is that use of media for non-formal and informal education opens up a vast territory — not only mass media but also the arts, religion, recreation and sporting activities and community groups. The Fijian report, for example, refers to a campaign by the Ministry of Youth for changing attitudes and motivation, through sports and music programmes for unemployed, rural youth. But the scope and scale of reporting on these and other forms of communication and social action has proved far too great for most countries to be incorporated into the EFA 2000 Assessments.

It is not surprising that there are so few references to these domains, although some countries emphasise the promotion of local and traditional culture through song, dance festivals (Belize), the church (Tonga) and collections of oral literature (Eritrea). The uses of electronic and print media in the formation and education for youth and adults and in improving the quality of life has scarcely featured in the reports. The target as at present worded is too allen-compassing. The overall Jomtien decade gains across all six target dimensions are gains in better living. Improved provision of early childhood education and care is a platform for lifelong learning and personal fulfilment; curricula, learning resources and teaching that are culturally sensitive build on and help sustain cultural heritage and facilitate personal growth; 'survival' and the quality of life are enhanced by improved health education, literacy and sound general and vocational preparation; increased opportunities for more education of good quality help lay the foundations of a better life, and so on.

The gains in access and provision that have been recorded in statistics and discursive reports are gains in better living; the improvements recorded in retention rates, teacher education and training and so forth are gains in sustainable development. Where these gains are not made, 'living' may be no better and is often worse for large numbers of people. 'Better living' cultural and social themes feature in educational goals statements, curriculum designs and nonformal education programmes.If this target direction were to be retained, it should be reformulated to achieve a better focus and enable manageable procedures for monitoring and appraisal. Value issues arising from use of the term 'better living' inevitably arise once the stage of bare subsistence is passed. These will not be easy to accommodate and will require an extensive cross-cultural dialogue.

In the regional report on the countries of Western Europe and North America, 'better living' is captured in the term 'prosperity'. This does not mean just material prosperity 'although economic growth is a byword in the policies of these countries' it refers equally to the uses to which economic growth is put and the criteria for distributing and sharing the benefits of economic growth. In this regard, and beginning in the late 90s, an increase in aid to poorer countries or at least a restoration of the earlier cuts, and debt relief programmes signal renewed attentiveness to the 'better living' needs of large parts of the world. Current 'Jubilee 2000' proposals for debt cancellation and for a focus on social sector expenditures including health and education are most welcome. The thematic study on the work of Donor Agencies underlines the scale of the task to provide conditions for 'better living' for hundreds of millions of people.

Efforts to reduce or control the large scale environmental degradation that have ensued from industrialisation, urbanisation and short sighted agricultural practices and deforestation, are examples of moves to take 'sustainable development' seriously. But that does not mean an end to environmental degradation. Education and health programmes of the right kind have an important role to play in shifting attitudes and improving knowledge and capability. The adverse effects on smaller and poorer countries of globalisation and the lack of balance between multilateral corporation and weak or small national economies means that 'better living' for some countries and groups is being achieved at the expense of others. These forces are not beyond human control and social action.

Several change forces in the wider environment can have positive implications for achieving the EFA targets. Yet few of the reports make any attempt in comments on the sixth Jomtien target to interrelate these wider contextual environmental considerations and educational policy and practice.In education, on a wide front there have to be both targeting and movements. There must be constant referral to the relationships among educational and other policies, practice on the ground and the changing environmental forces.

5

Effective Education: Concerns of the Future

Our context is one of rapid growth in scientific and medical discoveries, technology, including information communications technology (ICT), and the world's population. It is also a context of growing unevenness in such developments in different parts of the world and/or within individual countries. The consequences of this situation include a blurring of boundaries, growing gaps between people, groups and countries and the end of certainty including a diminution of credibility of traditional knowledge and authority of expertise, especially in professions such as education. This context and its consequences are forcing particular issues onto national and international agendas. Foremost among these issues are:

— economic competitiveness and market share;

— sustainability;

— identity within globalisation;

— equity; and,

— the role of public institutions, including for education, in helping make the most of the concomitant challenges.

The society we have, including the identity and cohesion within that society and its understanding and acceptance of other societies, is seen to be largely created in our schools. Schools are one of the few remaining institutions to offer partnerships to families in socialisation and investment through learning. School education helps people make sense of the changes as well as fostering sustainability, including through lifelong learning.

In brief, society's most important investment is increasingly seen to be in the education of its people - we suffer in the absence of good education: we prosper in its presence. In this situation of high expectations of each country's educational provision, those leading schools have an enormous responsibility. It is no wonder that the school improvement movement of the past 20 years has put a great emphasis on the role of leaders.

Not only are school leaders important but also they are generally seen to be taking on more and more roles. Leithwood et al's review of the empirical literature on effective leadership in accountable school contexts identifies 121 school leadership practices. Competency lists for school leader professional development programmes or school leader standards can be just as long. These ever longer lists of practices, competencies or standards prompt a concern that school leaders are not only being pulled in many different directions simultaneously but that they may be being asked to do too much.

Tyack and Cuban point out in their prize-winning book *Tinkering towards Utopia*, that those responsible for schools need to be careful because education can easily shift "from panacea to scapegoat." Despite generally strong local support for their schools, this shift will be fuelled, for example, not only by higher and higher expectations but also by growing international interdependencies and improved communication making global diffusion of 'best practice' increasingly efficient.

The nature of work in post-industrial society is changing significantly and this change affects the role of educational leader. Understanding the role and the nature of preparation for it must be based on recognition of how work is being defined and organised in the 21 st century. Across OECD Member countries, school systems and individual schools are experimenting with new approaches to management that seek to run schools in ways that are right for the 21 st century. In most countries schools are largely or wholly a government responsibility and, as such, the factors shaping government priorities are potentially important influences on the perceived necessity for school reform, the resources available for reform, and the direction of the reforms.

What are the major approaches have governments employed to ensure these reforms are achieved? Three approaches can be identified:

— old public administration (OPA);

— new public management (NPM); and,

— organisational learning (OL).

These three approaches have many similarities with other models including the OECD's scenarios for the future of schooling and Glatter's models of school governance in school education.

The three approaches to school governance are now briefly considered. It is likely that public school systems have elements of each with the emphasis shifting from time to time. However, it will be pointed out that inconsistencies within and between these approaches create its own pressures on schools and their leaders.

Old Public Administration (OPA)

Olsen argues that administrations in Europe "have succeeded in coping with changing environments but they have done so in ways influenced by existing administrative arrangementformal organisational structures have been stable while practices have changed. In what he calls "Old Public Administration" (OPA), administrators, including school leaders, are rule-driven bureaucrats executing and maintaining legal norms with integrity in a neutral way and.with the common good in mind. This perspective emphasizes reliability, consistency, predictability and accountability Some maintain that the role of New Public Administration (NPM), especially those counties forming the European Union, has been modest and that after "some enthusiasm with New Public Management principles, going 'back to basics' and Weberian bureaucracies have been assessed as more attractive. Several reports by OECD/Sigma have advised the CEECs [Central and Eastern European countries] not to copy business methods and NPM reforms in Western Europe. ... It is impossible to simply adopt Anglo-Saxon administrative cultures and such prescriptions are likely to have detrimental and disasterous consequences for the CEECs."

However, taking a wider perspective, there seems little support for OPA. International Futures Programme conference series on 21 st Century Transitions point to four sets of causal forces that could drive transitions worldwide:

— continued diffusion of technological breakthroughs;

— deeper economic interdependence and more intensive competition, from local through global levels;

— greater diversity of social status and identity, both within and between the socio-economic boundaries bequeathed from the 20 th century; and

— ongoing dispersion of power and responsibility."

The last causal force is leading to less hierarchical and less rigid methods for making and implementing decisions in all spheres of human activity. The argument here is, in fact, for less of the bureaucracy that forms the basis of OPA.

New Public Management (NPM)

Despite the fact that some believe OPA continues to be the preferred governance approach for achieving the heightened expectations of schools, it is New Public Management (NPM) that has emerged as the dominant force in many countries. The hallmarks of NPM are:

— a reduction in government's role in service provision;

— downsizing and decentralising the public sector;

— deregulation of the labour market;

— the imposition of the strongest feasible framework of competition and accountability on public sector activity;

— explicit standards and measures of performance, clear definition of targets and indicators of success;

— a greater emphasis on output control - a stress on results, not processes;

— moves to new forms of corporate governance;

— a shift from public funding to private sector provision (the privatisation agenda); and,

— a reduction in the self-regulating powers of the professions.

Under the influence of NPM the restructuring of public schooling has been characterised by:

— decentralisation through school self-management;

— the injection of competition between schools;

— greater demands for financial accountability;

— an increase in consumer control through school governing councils;

— recentalisation of curriculum and assessment control;

— expanding the powers of school principals;

— increasing pressure for outcomes-based assessment;

— the exposure of school performance to public scrutiny;

— the assessment of teachers against employer defined competencies; and,

— tighter regulation of the teaching profession.

Whatever elements of NPM are employed they all have in common a strong dependence on effective school leadership for their successful implementation, albeit what effective leadership means is at least partly different in each case. For example, for the market element effective leadership includes being a good entrepreneur and salesperson, the accountability element requires the principal to have expertise in performance management systems and relating the results to performance-linked pay, and for decentralisation effective leadership includes building a collaborative culture and ensuring that staff and/or the community (and or its representatives) develop sophisticated group problem-solving skills.Given the increasingly pervasive nature of NPM in the education sector of many countries, in what follows its major elements of decentralisation, accountability/market and community involvement and their implications for school leadership are briefly developed.

Decentralisation

The "trend towards decentralisation acknowledges that the dynamic for transformational change in schools must come increasingly from within the school community." However, we find that there are different degrees or models of decentralisation in different countries as well as for different functions. A common approach has been to localise delivery while centralising mandated standards. In "some countries, notably the United Kingdom and the United States, contracting of educational services has become part of a movement to create a clearer division between those who specify services and those who deliver them."

In Korea the focus of educational policy has been shifted from provider-oriented education to consumer and/or learner-oriented education and Austria is aiming to shift from 'administration' to 'service' and to orient management more to outcomes. With such changes the administrative role of the principal "has evolved from the practicing teacher, with added technical and administrative duties, to the full-time manager and developer of human, financial and physical resources."

In the Netherlands, for example, "school directors (principals) are responsible for the quality of their schools" as well as for "all personnel matters including hiring and firing, staff appraisals, and union negotiations ... ." In respect of the curriculum a stable model has not yet emerged.

In Finland, for example, "the movement is towards far greater school autonomy in curriculum matters, while other countries such as the United Kingdom have opted for a centrally defined model, even though presently they are looking for ways of authorising and encouraging local diversity."

In England curriculum decision-making has been divided between central government (content) and schools (pedagogy). In Denmark the notion of principals "as 'instructional leaders' is foreign. Teachers have always been considered 'professional' and autonomous both in their choice of teaching methods, and in their selection of the content of the curriculum (provided they adhered to broad national and local guidelines)."

Increased decentralisation of education systems has posed the issue of the role of local authorities and other intermediate bodies between the central state and the school as well as the role of boards or other bodies directly or indirectly involved in governing schools. The presence of such intermediatory and/or governing bodies result in the need for school leaders to negotiate with multiple powers and stakeholders.

A growing issue is reconciling decentralisation with overall system quality. "At worst, this can create contradictory pressures and tensions. At best, it can establish multiple forms of governance and control, each with its own part in the system." Criticising decentralisation, Leithwood et al point out that evidence of the effects on school leaders of decentralisation is quite extensive and indicates that while assumptions about the role of school leaders in decentralised settings sometimes describes what actually happens in practice, it is often not the whole story.

Decentralisation is associated, as well. with a radically increased emphasis on budgetary considerations, less attention to providing leadership about curriculum and instruction, greatly increased time demands, and the need for more attention to time management.

Accountability

A number of countries are looking at ways of exercising central control over increasingly decentralised and therefore autonomous schools. "Procedures for setting a central curriculum, for inspecting schools or for assessing pupils and publishing results at a school level are all pressures that encourage school managers to conform to a well-defined set of norms." However authors such as Tyack and Cuban believe that it is unfortunate that, "Many policymakers have narrowed.the currency of educational success to one main measure - test scores - and reduced schooling to a means of economic competitiveness, both personal and national."

Leithwood et al argue that an approach dominated by "the establishment of student standards, wide-spread student testing of their achievement and judgements about schools and teachers based on the results ... can have disasterous unintended consequences. For students, such consequences may include, minimising their individual differences, narrowing curriculum to which they are exposed, diverting enormous amounts from instruction to test preparation, and negatively influencing schools' willingness to accept students with weak academic records. ... [The] consequences for teachers, include the creation of incentives for cheating, feelings of shame, guilt and anger, and a sense of dissonance and alienation ... [and] to the atrophy of teachers' instructional repertoires."

Despite these developments, centrally-defined output criteria and local innovation in finding ways of meeting them are not necessarily contradictory; what matters is the degree to which specification of standards becomes so detailed and interventionist that a culture of control rather than autonomy develops.

The use of special programmes with tied resources and the concomitant accountability has become another tool used by central education authorities in ensuring their priorities are given attention in schools. But other bodies such as philanthropic and commercial organisations are also increasingly using this approach.

One outcome is that school leaders need to acquire the new skills of 'grantsmanship' and proposal writing, both for their own school and across schools. Another outcome may be overall school incoherence as it rushes to pick up and be judged on the latest priority programme.

The programme of the school and the performance of principals and teachers may also be regularly scrutinised through personnel assessment or inspectorial visits by central authorities or their delegates.The form of inspection varies by country. For example, in the Netherlands, the Inspectorate in Primary Education conducts formal visits to produce a quality card for each school. The results are published in league tables in national newspapers. In England every school is inspected on a regular cycle by the Office for Standards in Education (OFSTED). The system in Flanders combines school self-evaluation with a complementary external assessment by the inspectorate [including] undertaking a comprehensive analysis of the coherence between national curricular objectives and the schoolwork place. Greece has opted for only school self-evaluation due to its traditional rejection of external inspection.

Case et al's study of the impact of central inspections on three successful schools over a three-year period found that teachers felt professionally compromised, intimidated and stressed by the inspection process and that there were no lasting impacts on what teachers do in the classroom. McNeil traced the effects of imposed stadardisations from the system level into the classroom in three schools that were exemplars for high-quality teaching and learning in urban environments and concluded, "The central message is that educational standardization harms teaching and learning and, over the long term, restratifies education by race and class."

If less engaged teachers means less engaged students then there should be widespread cause for concern. There is evidence that this may be the case. The OECD's PISA found that in 20 out of 28 countries more than one in four 15 year-old students considered school a place where they did not want to go and in almost half the countries the majority of students also agreed or strongly agreed that school was a place in which they felt bored.

It should not be surprising then that an increasing number of countries are rethinking how teaching staff should be assessed. One new approach is the introduction of merit or performance related pay. In UK there is a government initiative to introduce performance management system backed by performance-linkedpay that is the responsibility of the principal.

The emphasis is changing from concern for procedures to concern for results. Teacher unions have strongly opposed such.individualisation of salaries and others have questioned whether a principal can be both an effective 'assessor' and 'assistor'.

Clearly schools need to be open and accountable for what they do. Yet there is a risk that honest self-evaluation essential to improvement can create problems for bodies that are publicly accountable and cannot admit to failure. Three possible ways forward might include developing assessment tools that are appropriate in terms of the goals that schools want to reach, especially non-cognitive outcomes , the use of quality evidence as the basis of policy and practice, and developing a new attitudes to failure, including seeing it as an essential part of learning.

Part of the logic for these developments in accountability is linked to exposing education to the market. In a market people need, it is argued, evidence on which to make their choices. The logic of this argument depends, of course, on the quality of the evidence, which may not always be particularly good.

Community Involvement

Learning is no longer restricted to what goes on within the school walls. It is "now universally accepted in OECD countries that schools must relate well to their surrounding communities if they are to be effective. In societies that have been undergoing profound economic and social restructuring, the school's role needs to be related directly to the changes that are taking place around it."

Decentralisation itself increases the pressure for new forms of governance and partnership including shared decision-making with teachers, parents and members of the community. Principals and others in schools need to "become coalition builders as much as managers of the internal running of schools themselves."

The very terms 'school' and 'community' are no longer as precise as they once were. The schools' functions are being redefined as they become "multi-service establishments, incorporating child care and pre-school as well as formal schooling and recreational services . These added functions have only helped to reinforce the school's long established responsibility for socialisation, morality and citizenship, that is, 'social capital'. This role has, arguably, become even more important as the social capital generated by families, neighbourhoods, communities and other networks tends to shrink in many countries.

Another recent development in NPM, and one linked to decentralisation, accountability and a broadening the 'community' involved in governance, arises from government frustration with established public bureaucracies and their inability to sometimes place the meeting of new challenges above what they may see as their defending territory and/or survival. One approach to this situation sees a requirement for whole-of-government problem solving with a focus on results not procedures.

Organisational Learning (OL)

Another approach for achieving the expectations being placed on schools is OL. This new emphasis may have arisen because research on decentralisation shows that, in itself, it is not enough to transform the way a school is run and that there is a need for school autonomy from within.

Tactical (a series of tactics or quick fixes) or strategic (focus.systematically on particular areas of weakness and what to do about them across the institution)approaches are not seen to be as successful as capacity building. An emphasis on OL may also makes sense: at a time when a basic condition of our lives is hyper complexity and continual learning; where, policy makers are often constrained by the duration of the political cycle as the depth of any reform in education is influenced by the sequence of the electoral process.

In order to meet the heightened, multiple expectations now placed on schools and to have engaged students and teachers, it is argued that schools need to become learning organisations, consciously and continuously pursuing quality improvement. One cannot prejudge what works in a given educational setting. Part of the challenge for schools is to evaluate approaches as they unfold, and to be willing to adapt strategies in the light of their outcomes, as well as applying multiple strategies as appropriate to different contexts. In other words, in developing new learning approaches for students, schools themselves had to be good at learning.

Leaders who form effective management teams have a more pervasive influence than those who rely on their own personal efforts. Skills for school leaders in networking not only within but also across and beyond schools are in demand. But some countries will have further to go in developing this collective, rather than individual teacher, efficacy. For example, Moos reports that the "expectation in England appears to be that the head should bring his/her vision to the school, whereas in Denmark, the head is expected to initiate the dialogue with the teachers in order to build a shared vision together with them.

Within schools that are learning organisations new types of relationship between students, teachers and leaders evolve. The key is to give meaning to the careers of ordinary teachers beyond the context of their individual classroom responsibilities as teachers who feel at least part of the management process will help carry forward change more effectively.

Across countries educators are also trying to engage students more directly in their learning, to make them co-workers with teachers in the learning process rather than just recipients of knowledge because students do things because they are interested rather that because they are told.In Sweden students themselves have an increasing role in decision-making in the belief that they should take on responsibility for their own learning.

Recent research that attempts to operationalise OL in schools has identified a reasonably common set of characteristics. For example, Sackney et al identified engaging in collaborative processes, a willingness to engage in professional learning and growth and to reflect on and experiment with ongoing practices, and ability to align activities with the school's mission. Leithwood et al listed a school's vision, culture, structure, strategies and policy and resources. Marks et al used school structure, participative decision making grounded in teacher empowerment, shared commitment and collaborative activity, knowledge and skills, leadership, and feedback and accountability.

Silins and Mulford found four factors defined OL in schools:

— a trusting and collaborative climate;

— a shared and monitored mission;

— taking initiatives and risks; and,

— ongoing, relevant professional development.

Mulford and others believe that the identifying characteristics of OL tend to group themselves sequentially. At the first stage is a focus on developing common understandings, honesty, and trust through dialogue, sharing, and managing the inevitable conflict involved. These learning processes are then employed to link to the outside, examine current practice critically, and develop shared values as well as a vision for the school. The processes, the content, and shared values are employed to actually make the changes identified, including a commitment and ability to repeat the stages, that is, to continuously learn and improve. These within the organisation characteristics are set within more or less powerful external characteristics such as district policies, especially toward professional development, the student population, and the community.

These stages may be complex, difficult to achieve and, above all, take time. Schools and the systems in which they reside may not have the time, energy, or inclination for understanding, let alone developing, OL. Examination of the list of 121 leadership practices shown to be necessary in dealing with accountability initiatives and compared with five sets of leadership standards from Australia, UK, NZ, and USA would tend to support this position. Practices necessary for OL such as building a collaborative culture, establishing and sustaining a culture of inquiry and reflection and building a culture of teacher leadership are not strongly represented in leadership standards. Other research on school and teacher empowerment and trust paints a similar gloomy picture.

This situation is unfortunate for the little research that has been reported is very supportive of OL as a strategy for successful educational change and improved student outcomes. Recent reviews by some of the most eminent scholars in the field are also supportive. For example, Fullan argues we will "not have a large pool of quality principals until we have a large pool of quality teachers" and that school improvement "depends on principals who can foster the conditions necessary for sustained educational reform in a complex, rapidly changing society."

Inconsistent Demands

In contemporary democracies administrative environments are not ... simple, coherent and imperative.Administration operates in a complex ecology of institutions, actors, goals, rules, interests, powers, principles, values, beliefs and cleavages. Politicians and others are likely to want the administration to serve a variety of changing and not necessarily consistent principles, goals and interests.

Expectations for school leaders have steadily expanded, always adding to and rarely subtracting from a job description that now includes instructional, moral, managerial, participative, and transformational leadership. School leaders must manage educational change at a time when the character and mission of schools is being redefined, must be part of a new understanding about public management that is moving away from a bureaucratic and institution-led approach towards a performance-driven public sector that is more aware of the service it delivers to its users, and are having to find new, effective ways of managing knowledge, in organisations that need themselves to learn continuously.

The contexts faced and the resulting issues have placed particular pressures on schools. In turn, this situation has encouraged changes in the role of school leaders, especially as a result of developments in NPM (decentralisation, accountability and markets, greater community involvement) an/or OL. But these contexts, issues and pressures also result not only in additional but also in competing and often inconsistent demands on school leaders. The worry here is that the cumulative demands and resulting fragmentation and incoherence could undermine the capacity of schools.

The intersection of three demands for change by schools

— to update their content, to become learning organisations and

— to deliver measurable outcomes

— to creates intense and potentially conflicting pressures."

Examples may include those between:

— system level demands, defined centrally and politically, and school level requirements;

— top-down and bottom-up change; managerial and professional/instructional leadership demands;

— assertion of a public right to know and honest self-evaluation that is an essential part of institutional learning;

— competition and collaboration.

We see paradoxes developing, for example, between:

— the radical change that may be needed to create 'real learning' in schools and the need to preserve stable and workable systems for instructing children;

— markets, league tables, choice on the one hand and inclusive schooling, putting the public into public education on the other;

— standards, inspection, compliancy, performativity and innovation, diversity; and,

— looking 'East' for fail-safe schools as the economic underwriter and looking 'West' for critical pedagogy and problem-solving curriculum.

Day et al's recent case study research of 12 English schools that were widely acknowledged for their effective leadership and results identified seven tensions and three dilemmas for principals. These tensions and dilemmas "focus upon their roles not only in maintaining and consolidating what they have already achieved, but also in managing the challenges associated with moving their individual schools forward."

The tensions were leadership versus management, development versus maintenance, internal versus external change, autocracy versus autonomy, personal time versus professional tasks, personal values versus institutional imperatives, and leadership in small versus large schools. The three dilemmas were development versus dismissal, power with or power over and subcontracting versus mediation. Mulford has argued that in order for the school leader to meet global challenges there is a need to achieve a greater balance between constant change and continuity, dependence and independence, individualism and community, and homogeneity and heterogeneity.

Teacher Recruitment, Development and Retention

Research conducted by UK's Institute of Public Policy Research, based on an 8-year long study of 100 companies, concluded that "an employee's satisfaction with their work and a positive view of the organisation, combined with relatively extensive and sophisticated people-management practices, are the most important predictors of the future productivity of companies." The people-management practices referred to here include ones that concentrate on enabling staff to actually enjoy their work rather than feel oppressed by it; ones that encourage questioning and thinking; ones that develop cooperation through investing in social capital and mutual trust within the organisation.

Recent research in England suggests that such conditions may not be a strong feature of schools. A report by the think-tank for the National Union of Teachers in that countr found that younger teachers in particular felt pay prospects and lack of control over the way they taught as a result of government initiatives, were causing them to question their commitment to the profession. Most teachers argued consistently that centrally driven educational reform meant that they experienced change as never-ending barrage of externally imposed, randomly timed and badly managed initiatives that they had little constructive role in helping to shape.

As stress was purported to be a widespread feature of work in teaching in England, Troman studied an opportunity sample of 20 teachers referred to a local authority Occupational Health Unit as experiencing stress. The study found that the intensification of teachers' work was involved in eroding positive staff relationships. Changing trust relations in high modernity (including public distrust of expert systems, professionals) were found to be shaping the social relations of low-trust schooling and impacting negatively on teachers' physical and emotional well being and their collegial professional relations.

School leaders can be a major influence on such school-level factors as well as help buffer against the excesses of the mounting and sometimes contradictory external pressures. As the analytical framework for OECD's 'Attracting, Developing and Retaining Effective Teachers Project' argues, "A skilled and well-supported leadership team in schools can help foster a sense of ownership and purpose in the way that teachers approach their job. ... conferring professional autonomy to teachers will enhance the attractiveness of the profession as a career choice and will improve the quality of the classroom teaching practice."

Spencer makes clear that the "single most powerful recruiter of teachers are schools themselves. People who have had positive experiences in school can prolong that experience by becoming teachers." Once in the profession, intrinsic rewards are consistently rated highest in studies of teacher satisfaction. For example, annual surveys administered to teachers over the past several decades reflect teachers' altruism as one of the most common reasons for entering teaching.

Teachers who work together in a meaningful and purposeful way have also been found to be more likely to remain in the profession because they feel valued and supported in their work. Little is one researcher who has found clear evidence of the positive effect of teacher leadership on teachers' self-efficacy and levels of morale. In contrast, Blasé and Blasé's study of 50 exemplary teachers in U.S.A. and Canada who believed they had experienced significant principal mistreatment found that the adverse effects included early and long-term psychological and emotional problems, physical and physiological problems, damaged schools, and ultimately leaving the job. Unfortunately these researchers also found that workplace abusers often target the bold, best and brightest teachers.

Leadership

In decentralised school settings principals have the autonomy to develop two very different leadership models:

— a more hierarchical and directive model, or

— a more inclusive model which brings teachers in particular, and the local school community into the frame."

Research on decision making in Australian primary and secondary schools found that the more positively teachers viewed the decision making processes in the school the higher the degree of influence and control they perceived to be exerted by education staff groups in the school. Ongoing analysis of this data base shows that where decision making is perceived by teachers in secondary schools as collegial, cooperative and consultative and providing adequate opportunities for participation it will be more likely to lead to positive student perceptions about their school and teachers as well as perceptions about relationships and their own performance than where decision making is more top-down, executive, or does not foster widespread teacher involvement.However, the results also show that while decentralisation may have occurred from the system to school level it had not necessarily occurred within schools and where it had it tended to be about administrative rather than education matters. These results are supported by other research.

Gray points out that in England teachers "note considerably greater changes in areas to do with their schools' management and organisation than in ethos, culture or teaching ... classroom-level 'changes' were far less frequent than school-wide initiatives." From case studies in nine Scottish secondary schools Adler et al also concluded that implementation of devolved school management "has, so far, fallen short of transforming the culture and working patterns of schools but had contributed to a dramatic change in the role and status of headteacher."

Schools "seemed able 'to respond more quickly to changing needs and priorities', but this was mainly in terms of repairs, maintenance and equipment." Teachers will be attracted to, and stay in, the profession if they feel they belong and believe they are contributing to the success of their school and students. Louis and Kruse have shown the important role of school-level leadership in the development of a professional community. Teacher morale, efficacy, conditions of work, and professional autonomy have all been shown to be crucial to the emotional lives of teachers. There is no doubt that teachers themselves prefer principals who are honest, communicative, participatory, collegial informal. supportive and demanding and reasonable in their expectations with a clear vision for the school - principals who work 'with' rather than 'through'."

Day et al conclude that, research findings from diverse countries and different school contexts have revealed the powerful impact of leadership processes related to school effectiveness and improvement. Essentially, schools that are effective and have the capacity to improve are led by headteachers who make a significant and measurable contribution to the effectiveness of their staff.

Research on school leaders in Denmark, Scotland, England and Australia by MacBeath identified a number of characteristics of effective leaders including "Good leaders are in the thick of things, working alongside their colleagues", "respecting teachers' autonomy, protecting them from extraneous demands", and "look ahead, anticipate change and prepare people for it so that it doesn't surprise or disempower them." Durland and Teddlie posit a 'Centrality-Cohesiveness Model of Differentially Effective Schools'. Differentially effective schools can be distinguished by the cohesiveness of the staff and the centrality of the leadership within the school. 'Well-webbed' structures and 'central' leadership where found to be more effective than those based on cliques, or 'stringy' structures, and a perceived lack of leadership.

One of the most congruent findings from studies of effective leadership in schools is that authority to lead need not be located in the person of the leader but can be dispersed within the school in between and among people. There is a growing understanding that leadership is embedded in various organisational contexts within school communities, not centrally vested in a person or an office.

To illustrate, a recent study in USA by McLaughlin and Talbert that examined principals' effects on teachers' community, instructional practices, and careers found no instances of leaders who created extraordinary contexts for teaching by virtue of their own unique visions; nor did the study reveal any common patterns of strong principals' characteristics.

Successful principals turned out to be men and women with varied professional backgrounds who worked in collaboration with teacher leaders and showed respect for the teaching culture. They found various ways to support teachers in getting the job done. "The leadership of these principals was not superhuman;.rather, it grew from a strong and simple commitment to make schools work for their students and to build teachers' determination and capacity to pursue this collective goal." Harris and Muijs argue that, "the real challenge facing most schools is no longer how to improve but more importantly, 'how to sustain improvement?" Further, they argue that, "Sustainability will depend upon the school's internal capacity to maintain and support developmental work ... [and that] sustaining improvement requires the leadership capability of the many rather than the few and that improvements in learning are more likely to be achieved when leadership is instructionally focussed and located closest to the classroom." In other words, Harris and Muijis are supporting the importance of teacher leadership, "a form of collective leadership in which teachers develop expertise by working collaboratively." Research on teacher leadership and improved student outcomes from Australia, Canada, USA supports this position.

Harris and Muijs state that, "one of the main barriers to teacher leadership concern the 'top-down' leadership model that still dominates in many schools. The possibility of teacher leadership in any school will be dependent upon whether the head and the senior management team within the school relinquishes power to teachers and the extent to which teachers accept the influence of colleagues ... heads will therefore need to become 'leaders of leaders' striving to develop a relationship of trust with staff, and encouraging leadership and autonomy throughout the school." To generate and sustain teacher leadership is seen as requiring not only empowerment but also time and opportunities for continuous professional development.

Effective teacher leadership also requires structural change. As Barth has points out: "To capture the potential of teacher leaders, the profession needs to invent, expand, and honour a variety of opportunities for teacher leadership so that there will be more choices than being 'either' a principal or a teacher. The career ladder for teachers has precious few rungs. If more widespread teacher leadership is to be attained in our schools, educators will also have to explore multiple conceptions of the teacher's role: team leader, lead teacher, teacher researcher, master teacher.

There is no more important form of 'school restructuring.' Only when many such roles exist within our profession will the potential to benefit schools that resides in teacher leadership and teachers themselves be realised. In the next decade, 2.2 million new teachers will be needed to staff America's schools. Approximately two-thirds of the entire teaching profession will be replaced. Thus, the coming decade brings with it a profound opportunity to re-create the teaching profession."

A longitudinal study of effective schools in disadvantaged areas in UK found "one thing that is more sharply defined in these eleven schools in the year 2000, compared to 1995, is the wider environment's contribution to the school's success." These contextual factors included local community, government policy, inspection, multiple priority programs, and a push for local identity, such as through the Celtic lands movement.

In discussing the levers of change and improvement in these schools, Maden states that, "It is tempting to dwell solely on the headteacher as a kind of miracle worker, but these heads know that, above all else, securing improvement comes through the hearts and minds of teachers" and that, "It is probable that 'school capacity' is the single most important matter in trying to identify how and why some schools maintain and sustain improvement." As a major part of this 'capacity', "The spelling out of values and core beliefs is important. ... Such values are the school's 'cultural glue', without which individual empowerment and diversity would not be possible."

Mulford and Silins' have recently made clearer the relationships among the variables discussed above. Their Leadership for Organisational Learning and Student Outcomes (LOLSO) research was designed to require four phases of data collection and analysis conducted over four years and allowed for iterative cycles of theory development and testing, using multiple forms of evidence. Included in this design were surveys of 3,500 Year 10 students and 2,500 of their teachers and principals from half the secondary schools in South Australia and all the secondary schools in Tasmania (a total of 96 Australian schools). Two years later the South Australian Year 12 students, teachers and principals were resurveyed.

The LOLSO research demonstrated clearly that the best leadership for organisational learning was a principal skilled in transformational leadership and administratorsand teachers who are actively involved in the core work of the school. What was shown to be especially important was that staffs were actively and collectively participating in the school and that they felt that their contributions were valued.

The transformational school principal was found to focus on:

— *Individual Support* – providing moral support, showing appreciation for the work of individual staff and taking account of their opinions.

— *Culture* – promoting an atmosphere of caring and trust among staff, setting the tone for respectful interaction with students, and demonstrating a willingness to change practices in the light of new understandings.

— *Structure* – establishing a school structure that promotes participative decision making, supporting delegation and distributive leadership, and encouraging teacher decision-making autonomy.

— *Vision and Goals* – working toward whole-staff consensus on school priorities and communicating these to students and staff to establish a strong sense of overall purpose.

— *Performance Expectation* – having high expectations for students and for teachers to be effective and innovative.

— *Intellectual Stimulation* – encouraging staff to reflect on what they are trying to achieve with students and how they are doing it; facilitates opportunities for staff to learn from each other and models continual learning in his or her own practice.

The wording here is important. For example, it is 'working towards whole-staff consensus on school vision' not 'arriving with a vision for others to implement'. Barnett, McCormick, and Conners' study in 12 Australian secondary schools found that having a principal that was too 'inspirational' resulted in a negative association with teacher perceptions of intrinsic motivation for learning in students. These authors conclude that, a visionary/inspirational principal may distract teachers from concentrating on teaching and learning "

OL in the LOLSO study was found to involve a clear sequence of factors and the higher teachers were found to rate the school on these dimensions the more positively teachers' work was perceived in classrooms by their students and the better the student outcomes. The sequential factors were:

— establishing a trusting and collaborative climate;

— followed by having a shared and monitored mission;

— and then taking initiatives and risks;

— within a context of on-going, relevant professional development.

Development

As a result of their more than 10 years experience as principals of alternative high schools in New York city, Mohr and Dichter outline the developmental stages that their school staff went through en route to becoming learning organisations:

— *honeymoon* - sense of community emerges;

— *conflict* - the honeymoon is over;

— *confusion* - what's the role of the leader?;

— *messy* - now things are even less clear;

— *scary* - where are the authority and accountability?;

— *mature* - a learning community is born.

Mitchell and Sackney found that organisational learning in a Canadian primary school involved four processes, three basic assumptions, as well as moving through three distinct phases. Of the four processes, two were cognitive and two affective.

— The cognitive processes of reflection and conversation enabled the teachers to become aware of their practices and of those of their colleagues, to assess the desirability of those practices, and to discover new possibilities.

— The affective processes of affirmation [of each other as professionals] and invitation [into school deliberations] served to create positive working relationships by affirming the professional capabilities of individuals and by valuing the contributions of all staff members.

These four processes were founded upon three basic assumptions that:

— each individual was responsible for the welfare of the group and the success of the school;

— diversity among individuals was recognized, honoured, and valued; and,

— psychological safety would be maintained in group deliberations.

The four processes moved through three phases:

— naming and framing to clarify positions and opinions;

— analysing and integrating especially when new ideas are opened up for possible experimentation; and,

— applying and experimenting.

Indicators of organizational learning were found to emerge differentially at each of the three phases thus implying that these behaviours and processes do not develop overnight, but rather build on one another over time. This developmental nature of organisational learning highlighted for Mitchell and Sackney the importance of the 'naming and framing' and ' analyzing and integrating' phases. The comfort level with organizational learning grew as teachers develop their own understandings about the concept, analyzed their own practices in the light of those understandings, and applied appropriate aspects of what they had learned. Framing is an active process, and teachers need adequate time to talk about and to reflect upon initiatives.

Building from case studies of two urban, public middle schools Achinstein warns that when teachers enact collaborative reforms in the name of 'community', what emerges is often conflict. But conflict is found to be central to an effective community. How teachers manage conflicts, whether they suppress or embrace their differences, may help defines the community borders and ultimately the potential for organisational learning and change.

A related area here is the research on developing partnership in and with a school's community. A number of researchers have conceptualised the process of developing partnerships in and with the community in terms of a lifecycle, moving from a looser structure and more informal relationships in the earlier stages, to a tighter structure and more formalised relationships in the later planning and delivery stages. Kilpatrick et al., identified five stages in this process:

— trigger;

— initiation;

— development;

— maintenance; and,

— sustainability.

This five-stage process is conceived of as cyclical rather than linear, in that the knowledge gained from each stage is then fed back into the partnership development process.

During the initiation stage the seeds of collaborative leadership are sown. At this stage the process is still informal, as potential stakeholders are identified, and community meetings held to build support for the initiative. In the development stage represents a clear shift from informal meetings and gestures of support, to a more formal relationship between partners. During this stage, relationships become more structured, usually through the formation of a management committee, reflecting a greater shift in ownership from individual leaders to the stakeholder group. During the development stage, a good deal of time and attention is given to matters such as the location and structure of partnership meetings, to ensure support for the partnership at both a managerial and operational level

It is at the maintenance stage that stakeholders are able to take the time to critically reflect on the identity of the partnership and its collective efficacy in terms of outcomes, and to celebrate some interim successes. This sense of shared identity is central to the development of community social capital. As noted in Kilpatrick et al., during the final stage, sustainability, school and community renew their vision and goals and scan for opportunities and new problems in relation to the school–community linkage. At this stage there is evidence of ownership of the leadership process by all stakeholders, and clear evidence of a shift from narrow self interests to broader community concerns.

Different leadership roles are needed at different stages of the developing partnership process. For example, in the early stages, leaders need to act as animators, motivators and networkers, gradually being replaced by creators, teachers and conveners. In the mid stages of partnership development, integrators, drivers, and sustainers are needed. The later stages require leaders to act as mentors and as agitators for continued change.

Consistent with the earlier reported in-school research, Kilpatrick et al found that leadership for effective school–community partnerships is a process that gradually transfers leadership from the hands of a small number of individuals at the trigger and initiation stages, to a wider group, representative of community interests, at the development, maintenance and sustainability stages.

There is also a stronger focus on facilitative roles during the earlier stages of the process (trigger and initiation stages) as individuals and groups learn to work together. As the group gradually becomes more comfortable working together, there is a greater focus during the development phase on delivery roles, as procedures are put in place to allow the partnership to meet its objectives.

In the later stages of partnership development the focus of leadership roles tends to move towards the facilitative again, as partnerships begin to explore new initiatives and new ways of involving school and community in community development projects. The dual focus on facilitative and delivery roles supports research by Edwards et al. into the purpose and orientation of partnerships.

As Henton, Melville and Walesh conclude, it seems unlikely one person would be skilled in all roles. Effective leadership through partnerships "is shared by many individuals at various times depending in the situation and the required leadership skills".

Mulford has recently suggested that the factors that make up school principal transformational leadership are sequential with individual support and culture preceding structure, vision and goals and performance expectations which, in turn, precede intellectual stimulation. Understanding concepts such as the developmental nature of OL, community partnerships and leadership can assist in better translating the research into policy and practice. Developmental models, for example, can help us

— understand better the intricacies involved in moving a school, or part of a school, from where it is now to becoming truly a place that attracts and retains teachers and truly effective at learning;

— target appropriate interventions to ensure more effective progression through any developmental stages as well as achieving the ultimate goal of being a place that is attractive for staff and student learning. In targeting interventions recognition will need to be given to the fact that it is a journey and that actions at one stage may be inappropriate, or even counterproductive, at another stage. For example, one of the preliminary but controversial findings from the LOLSO research is that the only hint of a direct relationship between the school principal's leadership and student outcomes, specifically student engagement in school, is a negative one. One interpretation of this finding is that the greater the student engagement in school the less the need for leadership. Another interpretation is that the relationship is curvilinear, that is, beyond some as yet undefined point the principal's attempts to work directly with students rather than indirectly through teachers starts to have negative effects on teacher and student outcomes;

— understand that achieving balanced learning/development may, in fact, mean that a school, leaders and teachers recognise and understand such stages and can take the appropriate action without being 'bowled over' by the change that surrounds them;

— understand that a school will need to be evaluated differently depending on the stage it has reached; and,

— understanding that achieving OL will not be without difficulties and that one of the difficulties is to achieve greater self-determined balances among competing pressures/barriers.

A lack of time and professional isolation are major barrier to collaborative endeavours. Donaldson describes some major attributes of schools that contribute to what he calls a "leadership-resistant architecture" reflected in a "conspiracy of business." There is, according to Donaldson, little time for the school leader to convene people to plan, organize, and follow through.

Contact and the transaction of business often take place 'catch-as-catch-can'. Opinion setting and relationship building in schools he argues are mostly inaccessible and even resistant to the principal's formal attempt to guide and structure the direction of the school. The larger the school, the more complex and impersonal the environment, and the fewer the opportunities a principal is likely to have for individual relationship building or problem solving.

The Leadership for Organisational Learning and Student Outcomes (LOLSO) study

The LOLSO study find that the leadership that makes a difference is both position based (principal) and distributive (administrative team and teachers). But both are only indirectly related to student outcomes. This result is consistent with other reviews of research in the area as well as a recent OECD report, which concludes that, "The relationship between strong leadership and good student results is not a direct one. Good leadership helps foster the kind of school climate in which learning flourishes, rather than directly inspiring students to achieve."

Organisational learning (OL), or a collective teacher efficacy, is the important intervening variable between leadership and teacher work and then student outcomes. That is, leadership contributes to OL, which in turn influences what happens in the core business of the school - the teaching and learning. It influences the way students perceive teachers organise and conduct their instruction, and their educational interactions with, and expectations for, their students. Pupils' positive perceptions of teachers' work directly promote participation in school, academic self-concept and engagement with school. Pupil participation is directly and pupil engagement indirectly (through retention) related to academic achievement.

LOLSO also found that whether the principal was male or female and the teachers' years in education, age and gender were not factors promoting leadership or OL. The lack of gender differences is consistent with recent research based on a survey of the key values all women and a sample of the same number of men principals in England and Wales.

However, school size does make a difference: the larger metropolitan schools of over 900 students did not provide the environment most conducive for principal transformational and teacher distributive leadership or for student participation, although having a larger school was positively related to students' academic self-concept. The results add weight to the research extolling advantages of smaller schools.

This issue has been recognised in some parts of USA with large schools now dividing themselves into smaller units in order to provide the web of support necessary for student and teacher involvement with the school and improved learning outcomes. Another important contextual factor was found to be the socio-economic status (SES) of the school. SES had its expected positive relationship with student academic achievement, retention and academic self-concept.

Although such findings need to be placed in the context of the results of OECD's PISA study which demonstrated that poor performance in school does not automatically follow from a disadvantaged socio-economic background of students. Interestingly, the LOLSO study found that SES had a negative relationship with student perceptions of teachers' work. On the other hand, the students' home educational environment had a stronger relationship than SES to students' academic self-concept but also a strong positive relationship with students' participation in school and students' perceptions of teachers' work.

Having a community focus in a school (teachers perceive the school as having productive relations with the community and that schools' administrators are sensitive to and work actively with it) was found to be another outcome of both transformational principal leadership and distributive administrative team and teacher leadership. However, no link was found between having a community focus and either OL or improved student outcomes. Some may find the lack of a direct link between a school having a community focus and either organisational learning or student outcomes to be potentially problematic.

On the basis of the results, if a choice had to be made between working with and being sensitive to the community and improving home educational environments, the latter will have more direct and immediate 'payoff' for student outcomes. The success of the English Excellence in Cities education mentors program is a case in point. Of course, having a strong community focus may be important for other reasons including in the development of social capital in the community, especially in poor inner city and rural communities.

It is worth noting the perhaps controversial finding that students' academic self-concept was not related to their academic achievement. Even though we, along with others found that academic self-concept did not link to other student outcomes, including academic achievement, it does not follow that academic self-concept is not an important student outcome. For example, pupil self-concept has been shown to be related to later life successes such as employment and earnings.

The Australian LOLSO results and implications are also consistent with other contemporary research in the area. For example, in their chapter bringing together the lessons from a book of international research on leadership for change and school reform, Riley and Louis focus on leadership that is more than role-based, that is leadership as an organic activity involving the formation of a network of values-driven relationships. Integral to the success of such dispersed leadership are both pupil and teacher voice.

Also at the international level, an OECD nine country study on innovative initiatives in school management concludes that, "Changes designed with little involvement of those destined to use them are rarely effective ... In that sense every teacher is a school leader ... . It is striking ... how frequently team-working is cited as a key ingredient to the success of new approached to school management." The study points out that, "In such learning organisations, individuals and teams become reflective practitioners and are able to review their own situations and deal with problems or challenges as they arise." "A transformation in the way that students learn ... requires students, teachers and managers each to develop greater autonomy, rather than be told what to do by a higher authority." The study continues, "putting all one's hopes in the powers of a charismatic principal has rarely produced a long-term solution to a school's problems, and has sometimes proven counter-productive." In brief the study concludes that, "...it is impossible to detach the improvement of the ways in which students learn within schools from the ways in which schools themselves develop as learning organisations."

Many of PISA' and LOLSO's results are also consistent. On average PISA found that those students who liked school perform better than those who do not. The aspect of student engagement found to be most closely associated with reading performance was their ability to control the learning process, that is, figuring out what they need to learn, work out as they go what concepts they have not understood, look for additional information when they do not understand, check whether they remember what they have learned, and make sure they have remembered the most important things. While there was no single factor that explained why some schools or countries had better results, school policies and practices that tend to be associated with success in reading (taking account of other observed school and home background factors) can be summarized as follows:

— student use of school resources (library, computers, laboratories);

— university qualified teachers; student:

— staff ratio from 10:1 to 25:1;

— school policy and practice (as reported by principals) regarding teacher expectations of student performance, teacher morale and commitment and school (not teacher) autonomy; and,

— classroom practice (as perceived by students) involving positive teacher-student relations, good disciplinary climate and, to a lesser extent, emphasis on academic performance and high demands on students (including homework).

The Australian Council for Educational Research's longitudinal surveys of Australian youth has also stressed the important of student engagement with school. They found that a high engagement at the school level even moderates the negative effects of SES and indigenous status. In brief, they conclude that it does matter which school a student attends. Provision for, and encouraging students to participate in, a broad range of school activities leads to a student's closer connectedness to the school community as well as flow on effects to more academic parts of the curriculum.

In USA Goddard et al, Heck and Sweetland and Hoy have found close links between school environments and improved student learning. Goddard et al found that "collective teacher efficacy is a significant predictor of student achievement and is greater in magnitude than any one of the demographic controls. These researchers conclude, a one unit increase in collective teacher efficacy is associated with an increase of more than 40% of a standard deviation in student achievement. Heck found that not only was higher SES directly related to greater student improvement and larger schools produced smaller student gains, but also that schools where the head teacher leadership was rated as more supportive and directed towards instructional excellence and school improvement and the school climate was seen in positive terms "produced greater-than-expected improvements in student learning over time."

Sweetland and Hoy in a study of 86 middle schools that teacher empowerment was related to higher levels of teacher self-report as well as student proficiency tests (in reading and mathematics) of effectiveness "... a school climate that is open, collegial, professional, and focused on student achievement provides the atmosphere for productive teacher empowerment in teaching and learning decisions ... [but the link to student achievement in through] a collective efficacy among teachers."

After 15 years studying school reform, the Consortium for Research in Education comprising researchers from five of USA's leading universities have a relatively straightforward 'theory of action' about what it takes to make better schools:

— clear and ambitious goals;

— a strong focus on instructional practice;

— extensive investment in continuing professional development;

— strong curricula and in leadership at the system and school levels; and,

— accountability including incentives to provide positive reinforcements where improvement is occurring.

Also in the USA, Elmore details five principles that lay the foundation for a model of distributive leadership focused on large-scale improvement in schools:

— the purpose of leadership is the improvement of instructional practice and performance;

— instructional improvement requires continuous individual and collective learning;

— learning requires modelling;

— the roles and activities of leadership flow from the expertise required for learning and improvement, not from the formal dictates of the institution; and,

— the exercise of authority requires reciprocity of accountability and capacity.

In UK detailed case study research following up on 11 effective schools in disadvantaged areas some five years after the initial investigation has found that the levers of change and improvement included:

— distributive leadership;

— organisational learning

— pupil participation and engagement

Earley et al found that the main themes from case studies of ten exceptionally well led UK schools were headteachers as:

— problem-solvers and 'solution-driven;

— highly visible during the working day; having developed strong senior leadership teams;.

— regarding middle managers as 'the experts';

— strongly emphasising continuing professional development;

— mediators of change, negotiating it effectively, and adapting it to fit existing values and ethos; and,

— having strong and involved governing bodies, or at least chairs of governing bodies.

In Hong Kong, Cheung and Cheng found that self-management at the school, work-group and teacher levels were statistically associated with enhanced performance of a school. More recently, Cheung and Cheng's follow up case studies in three 'outlier' primary schools from of their original sample of 63 found that:

— the school that was low in school, work-group and teacher self-management had poor performance, that is, low student academic achievement, low teacher perception of the school's productivity, adaptability and flexibility, and low teacher job commitment, challenge and meaning;

— the school low in school but high in work-group and teacher self-management produced enhanced performance in student' academic achievement;

— the school high in all three levels of self-management produced enhanced performance in student academic achievement, organisational effectiveness and individual teacher job attitudes.

Wylie and Mitchell are involved with ongoing research into ten 'ordinary' New Zealand primary schools, which have gained a reputation for the improvements they have made in recent years in the context of major system decentralisation. They identify six principles that underlie the activities, relationships and processes, which allowed these schools to develop over time. These six principles centred on the creation of community:

— which could recognise itself positively;

— put in the effort required for change;

— which participated in stimulating professional development;

— that found their own way but with a single-minded focus on student learning, through critique and development of classroom teaching;

— but benefited from having open doors to government, community, professional developers, professional organisations, and so on; and,

— with strong leadership.

While strong leadership was not found to be confined to principals, Wylie and Mitchell elaborate: "Principals had an iron determination as well as being good communicators, with a love of their school and its students, and sound educational knowledge. They were also incurable learners. ... They provided good models for their staff and most encouraged others in their school to take on leadership roles."

Having examined the important links between leadership and teacher recruitment, development and retention and leadership and student outcomes, this paper now shifts its focus to the recruitment and development of school leaders themselves.

Recruitment of School Leaders

Studies of school leader supply and demand did not commence in earnest until the late 1980s and concerns over a potential shortage did not become apparent until the mid-1990s. By the turn of the century the media attention to the issue had grown. This attention was particularly obvious in countries such as US and UK. A Web search by the author for this paper using 'school principal shortage' turned up 140,000 items, the highest ranked of which were from these two countries.

The problem can be understood in at least three different ways. The first is that there is a growing shortage, the second is one of declining candidate quality and the third is the mobility rate of leaders from one position to the next. There is much more written about the first than the second or third issues. Is there a shortage? A number of recent publications from different countries say that the answer is a clear 'yes'. "Some countries, particularly United States and Flanders, find it difficult to attract suitable candidates for what is seen as an increasingly onerous job."

Grady et al's study of a sample of all Australian government school principals found that regardless of location, type, size or level of school, gender, or age, ninety two percent of Australian principals expected to retire or resign from the principalship more than five years before they 'have to'.

More recently, schools in all systems, states and territories in Australia have reported far fewer applicants for the job as principal. In a study of 1,400 primary and secondary school teachers, principals and deputy principals in Australian state of Victoria in 2000 found that 88 per cent had no intention of becoming principals. Any shortage may be made to appear worst where there are high mobility rates. For example, Galvin and Sheppard found that in the U.S.A, state of Utah the mobility rate of school administrators from one position to the next was almost as high as the attrition rate.

Williams has found that in Ontario, Canada, close to 75 per cent of principals and over 40 per cent of vice principals expect to retire by the year 2007. The high level of vice principal retirements raised the issue of the quality or depth of the future applicant pool for principal positions. James and Whiting found that in England and Wales fewer than half the deputy principals were actively seeking or regarded themselves potential aspirants for the principalship.

Respondents in a more recent large English study of those in leadership positions "were of the view that recruitment and retention of school leaders is likely to become increasingly problematic." Four out of ten deputy/assistant principals in this study stated that they had no plans to become a principal and four in ten principals were considering early retirement. In South Africa, Pounder and Merrill found that only 30 per cent of qualified potential candidates expressed intentions to pursue a high school principal position in the next five years.

Reasons for the shortage of school leaders

The reasons for decline in interest in school leadership include:

— job-related stress from the pressure of long hours, budget cuts, overcrowding and shortage of qualified teachers;

— time fragmentation - the way time, space, and communication patterns are structured often results in administrators having virtually no time for reflection or talk with trusted colleagues about concerns and fears - a leader can easily be isolated and many have to bear the burden of leadership alone;

— an unsupportive external environment including the growing pressure of high-stakes testing and accountability - a set of local, state, and federal mandates, many of which are seen by school leaders as unfounded;

— social problems that schools are assuming in trying to instruct students - the harsh realities from the outside, such as poverty, inadequate health care, and unemployment;

— the pressures of unrelenting change which are not necessarily to education's advantage;.

— the perception that education has become a economic/ political football in which the principalship is not valued;

— family and personal life;

— inadequate remuneration for the increased responsibility and workload;

— a lack of feedback on their performance; and,

— a selection process that can be too complex and intrusive.

Ackerman & Maslin-Ostrowski argue that today in USA, schools and school leaders are caught in a strong riptide. School leaders and those aspiring to leadership persistently cite job-related stress and time fragmentation, the growing pressure of high-stakes testing and accountability, and the social problems that schools are assuming in trying to instruct students as major factors influencing their standing.

External forces and demands infiltrate schools and can have a powerful influence on the career of an administrator.

A school leader today, for example, "is apt to be experiencing the pressure of budget cuts; overcrowding; shortage of qualified teachers; and a set of local, state, and federal mandates, many of which are unfunded. Harsh realities from the outside, such as poverty, inadequate health care, and unemployment, create enormous challenges for a leader inside a school.

The culture and norms found within schools can also present unique challenges for the leader. As Ackerman & Maslin-Astrowski explain, "The ground-floor conditions - including the way time, space, and communication patterns are structured – are integral parts of the messy world of school leadership. An administrator has virtually no time for reflection or talk with trusted colleagues about concerns and fears a leader can easily be isolated and many have to bear the burden of leadership alone.

A great deal of data have been gathered on Australian school principals and their professional and personal background, formal education, employment history and work experience, professional development, retirement or resignation intentions, and descriptions of their actual and ideal school and principalship.

The major reasons for the finding that most principals intended to retire more than five years before they had to related to pressure of the job (41%), schools being asked to do too much (30%), and to do other things, take up new challenges and/or let others have a go (23%). After answering eleven pages in the rest of the Questionnaire, many of the respondents took the opportunity to add further comments on the page provided.

The strongest themes running through these additional comments were summarised under the following three broad groupings.

— The pressures of unrelenting change which are not necessarily to education's advantage e.g., it is a never ending story of change and upheaval which isn't benefiting anyone, especially the children and many dedicated teachers are becoming cynical and tired - this is sad;

— the increasing, multiple and sometimes conflicting expectations which result in an excessive workload for the Principal filled with growing tension, stress and, increasingly, burnout e.g.,administrivia and the paper warfare preclude my involvement with staff, instructional leadership, teaching, and children"; and,

— the perception that Education has become a economic/ political football in which the Principalship is not valued e.g., in the Ministry's eyes we are administrators first and teachers second yet parents tend to see the opposite. Currently we are over used, taken advantage of and disposed of all too easily, and the government want to reduce power and resources to schools and then blame schools if it doesn't work.

Williams study of close to 1000 incumbent principals and vice principals in Ontario, Canada, also found that virtually all of their major dissatifiers were related to policy initiatives taken by the government and implemented, often poorly, by local district boards. Major dissatifiers included the inadequacy of time to plan for provincially mandated change, the number of curriculum changes mandated, inadequacy of time to work with students, heavy workloads, and the increasing non-student reporting requirements.

A unique aspect of the Williams study was an investigation of the reasons given by a group of identified excellent potential principals, who had decided not to pursue a career in school administration. The majority of determinants were related to role definition, selection and leadership development and concerns over the climate.surrounding public education. Of particular concern was "the group's perception that principals could not function as meaningful agents of change. They perceived that the province had centralised so much power over educational matters and imposed so many changes in such a short period of time while simultaneously cutting resources that principals could have little in school impact.

More recently in Australia, D'Arbon et al's study of why teachers would not apply for principalship in Catholic schools in the state of New South Wales found that the highest ranking disincentive to be the impact the job would have on the person's family and personal life. The second highest ranked factor was an unsupportive external environment. Their study also confirmed results from other studies that teachers are content with their current role, do not see adequate remuneration for the increase in responsibility and workload and perceive that the selection process is too complex and intrusive.

Lacey found teachers in the state of Victoria were found to be steering clear of the principalship because of the perception that the job is too stressful, demanding and unrewarding. Stress and long work hours were seen as the key turn-offs. The James and Whiting study in England and

Wales identified six factors that had influenced the career decisions of deputies not to seek principalship: role overload, contentment with current job, negative impact on the individual's family, self-doubt, concerns over public accountability, and external factors such as inadequate funding for schools and the scale and pace of bureaucratic initiatives.

Leaders in schools in Earley et al's recent study in England said they were de-motivated by the bureaucracy and excessive paperwork and also by the constant change in the education system. Baker notes that "England's schools are emerging from the wringer of accountability testing just as American schools are being fed into it" and that lessons to be learnt from the English experience include the need to "guard against pushing accountability so far that it tips over into excessive central control and hamstrings teachers." Baker points out that in "countries where accountability measures have undermined teachers' autonomy, there is now a recruitment crisis."

In USA, Cooley and Shen found that current principals and those aspiring to the role believed that: the principal's salary is not commensurate with the level of responsibilities that the job holds; the demands of the role have a negative impact on a person's home life; prospective applicants are only interested in particular principal positions, such as those that are close to their current residence and those where there is a positive relationships between board, administration and teachers.

Observational studies of the work actually undertaken by school principals confirm their hectic life. These studies have shown the brevity, variety and fragmentation in their work activity. This situation led to principals facing uncertainty, ambiguity, superficiality, constant pressure, and a lack of feedback on their performance.

Recent research by Cranston et al in Australia and New Zealand on what principals really do has found that they work long hours, feel increasing pressure, identify increased variety, diversity, conflict, and some overload in the demands of their role. At the same time the majority of them are satisfied in their role as a principal, especially where their actual role aligns with what they actually would like the role to be like and with what the systems expects of them.

Cranston et al found that principals wanted more of a leadership and less of a management role, "that is one that engages them in a major way on operational matters related to students and staff." Also in New Zealand, Brooking et al found primary school principal recruitment was hampered by the perception of a separation of the principal as a manager from the body of teachers as employees within the school.

Added reasons for a decline in interest in school leadership include:

— an increasing pool of "Generation X" teachers who do not see teaching, let alone leadership, as a life-long career. Traditional notions of any career may no longer be as stable as they have been - for example, the attrition rate in the first five years after graduation for teachers in both England and USA is reported to be 50 per cent.

— the lack of promotional opportunities in, or the 'low ceiling' nature of, a career in teaching. As a way to overcome this problem, Brooker and Mulford have proposed a promotion model where all posts of responsibility in schools become contractual.

— principals value highly their teaching experience for success as a principal yet increasingly school leaders are 'forced' out of the classroom.

— the older age profile of principals - in England and Australia two thirds are aged 46 or older - combined with the fact that early retirement/resignation from the principalship has been made easier and is an almost universal intention. Boyland reports that older teachers are much more vulnerable to career threatening psychological illnesses such as anxiety and depression. This situation was found to be particularly acute for men over 45. In a study of 266 schools in UK 71% of long-term absences for men over 45 were caused by stress compared to 58% for the same age group of women. The average difference between compulsory retirement age and intended retirement/resignation in an Australia-wide study was found to be 5.5 years.

— the overwhelming majority of leadership positions are held by particular groups in society - for example in England from White ethnic origin and female in primary schools and male in secondary schools. In USA, where 55 percent of the student population are African American or Hispanic, "Women, who make up more than 70 percent of the teaching force, now comprise 35 percent of the nation's principals. ... white males who comprise less than 25 percent of the teaching force - and are the least credentialed educators - comprise nearly 50 percent of the nation's principals and over 80 percent of the nation's superintendents and central office directors!"

— failure to recruit or seriously consider qualified licensed female candidates. Brooking , for example, found that in New Zealand primary schools, as a result of the conservative, patriarchal attitudes of the Boards of Trustee employers, the majority of principals are male. Women principals were found to be largely ghettoised into the least desirable, small, low status, difficult schools which are often in low socio-economic or isolated rural areas.

— most of those wanting to become principals, or to move on to another principalship, prefer to go to a school that is not in a 'challenging situation'. Type of school may be important in better understanding the attractiveness of school leadership. Those in higher socio-economic schools were found by Wylie to spend more time on work relating to the school's roll, reputation and buildings and grounds whereas those in low socio-economic schools were doing more pastoral care work and working more with outside agencies.

— the temptation to hire non-educators, despite the evidence from alternative certification programmes for teachers showing they are not as successful and are twice as likely to leave the profession as traditionally trained teachers. Despite this long list of reasons for the shortage of school leaders, research has found that principals and their deputies were the most satisfied educators. This satisfaction was especially likely where the actual role aligns with what the leader actually would like the role to be and with what the system expects of them. It has also been found that teachers placed in a leadership role were more likely to aspire to become principals, because experience debunked the myths about the job.

In sum, there is evidence of growing shortages of school leaders and a suggestion, but little evidence, of a declining quality of candidates for school leadership positions.

The reasons for this shortage could be grouped under the societal, system and school influences.

At the societal level these influences include:

— societal problems (poverty, inadequate health care, unemployment);

— unrelenting change;

— increasing and sometimes conflicting expectations; and,

— a feeling that education is an economic and political football in which those in schools are not valued.

At the system level these pressures include:

—mandates and accountability (such as curriculum and/or priority programmes, high stakes testing, performance management;

— bureaucracy (especially excessive paper work, the increase in intermediatory bodies and new approaches such as whole-of government);

— poor employer/professional educator relations;

— declining authority to act;

— budget cuts;

— overcrowding;

— teacher shortages; and,

— teaching as a low-ceiling career.

At the school level these influences include:

— competition;

— long hours;

— an emphasis on administration rather than leadership;

— involvement in education of community; and,

— a 'conspiracy of busyness, that is the way time, space and communication patterns are structured.

These influences result in the job of school leader being seen by potential candidates as too demanding, conflictual, stressful, deskilling, lonely, isolated, separated from teaching, lacking support, unrewarding, and only for particular groups in society. Although it is interesting to note that evidence suggests that the issue of rewards is see differently by potential candidates and the school leaders themselves - with leaders believing it is a rewarding job. Clearly existing school leaders have not got this message of job fulfilment across to those who would follow them.

The result of these influences and perceptions of the role of school leader has been a shortage and possible declining candidate quality except perhaps for schools in non-challenging circumstances. There has also been the temptation to use non-educators, even though research shows this 'solution' not to have been a success. It may be that a daunting standards-driven school leadership training regime and/or a lack of support from the system may also be having a negative impact on school leader recruitment.

Professional Development

A research study surveying new principals in Europe found that 65 per cent had received no formal or structured preparation for the job. In Canada, Hickcox reports that current training is sporadic and uncoordinated for both new principals and incumbent principals, and certification is voluntary and often not achieved. In contrast, a review of developments in principal training programmes in England, Australia, Hong Kong, and Sweden led Caldwell et al to conclude "there remains an underlying concern that the role of the headteacher is essentially unfeasible, that that this, more than the limitations in training and development, is the fundamental reason for the shortage in the number and quality of applicants.

There are signs that the professional development of school leaders is receiving greater attention in some countries. This interest should not be surprising given both the investment societies are now making in education and the importance governments and systems are placing on schools and the leadership of those schools. This renewed interest may also be fanned by shortages of school leaders and possible links between quality professional development and recruitment and retention.

Despite the need for, and renewed interest in, the professional development of school leaders, it remains a massive and complex topic. Much is already published and there is a resurgence of interest in the area.

First, let us turn to some of the research findings and/or issues in respect of the proposed stages and dimensions in the provision of school leader professional development.

Career stages

Consistent with the concept of lifelong learning, and assuming school leadership involves a career, the stages in a school leader's career are receiving growing attention. For example, implicit in the data collected in Earley at al's recent study establishing the current state of school leadership in England "is a call for a coherent school leadership professional development framework which begins shortly after qualification as a teacher and continues through and beyond headship."

Sweden has a long standing four step approach to principal training: recruitment for those wanting to become principals; introduction for those newly appointed; a national programme after about two years in the job; and, continuation which comprise mainly university courses.

The Hong Kong continuing professional development framework for school principals has separate programmes for aspiring, newly appointed and serving principals. In an evolving context where traditional notions of career are no longer as stable as they have been, there is an urgent need to pay particular attention in a coherent and systematic manner to a period of induction as an important and distinct learning phase in a school leaders life and work.

For example, in USA "New Leaders for New Schools" is a public-private partnership dedicated to recruiting and training inner-city principals. Principals-to-be get seven weeks of tuition-free training in educational leadership, a one-year paid 'residency' under the tutelage of a master principal, and, once in change of their own schools, two years of intensive professional development. Transition from one career stage to another, for example from teacher to head of a subject department or school principal, also brings its own difficulties and issues Two of the most used techniques for such transitions are internships and mentoring.

The literature on internships suggests program variety based on characteristics such as duration, type of experience and balance of outside/inside influence. Yearlong experiences tend to be recommended for teachers aspiring to school leadership but a shorter time for experienced leaders, such as those who have been a deputy. The socialisation inherent in the internship is seen as a dynamic evolving process by which the intern and the intern/mentor relationship changes and develops. The stages in this socialisation include: formal initial contact; apprehensive, cautious minimal; comfortable settling in; more confident, sharing efficacy; and, independence. How interns develop is partly a result of the role that various agents play in the process, as well as the contents and methods used by these agents.

One of the strongest agents of influence in an internship programme is the mentor. They not only typically assign or negotiate the intern's responsibilities, clarifies concerns, answers questions, checks perceptions, and acquaints them with the school culture but also protect them from mistakes that may harm their careers, sponsor them into new career opportunities, and expose them to new experiences.

There are two categories of content identified in the literature that are useful in evaluating and understanding the internship experience: technical and cultural. The technical is instrumental and involves acquiring and appropriately using the knowledge and skills of the role. Cultural or moral learning includes the sentiments, beliefs, standards of practice, and value orientation of the role. Methods to learn the technical side of the role can vary from trial and error and bombardment to more structured and gradual exposure to the techniques.

A typical method involves scaffolding in which interns observe, talk through, reflect, and do. What they 'do' usually evolves from technical, short-term tasks to more basic issues of developing a collective vision and building a senior leadership team. In terms of cultural learning, interns learn the sentiments, norms and values of the role by observing and interacting with the supervisor or mentor about what is acceptable, important, requires attention, and problematic as well as issues to do with the artefacts (keys, office), rituals (social distance between teachers and leaders), rites (intern selection), and ceremonies (how introduced to staff) of the job.

Mentoring has a long history and is currently undergoing a resurgence of interest in education. What are its functions, processes, mentors, and benefits and pitfalls? Three functions of mentoring are professional, career and psychosocial development. The professional development function refers to helping others learn the knowledge, skills, behaviours and values of the leader's role. The career development function includes issues of career satisfaction, awareness and advancement (for example by helping establish networks). The psychosocial development function focuses on personal and social well-being, as well as role expectations, conflict and clarification/identity.

Several primary processes are inherent in mentoring. The first and most basic is personal relationship. The second is active guidance, teaching and challenge. The third involves the management and implementation of a planned curriculum, especially one that involves the active collaboration of others in the school. These processes of personal relationship and active guidance involve an intentionality that is critical to the success of mentoring.

Other mentoring processes include teaching/coaching, reflective mentoring, and sponsorship. When informing is necessary, adult learners respond more to demonstration and modelling approaches but in general they respond best to learning-by doing. Mentors also need to be challenged to try new roles, responsibilities and even the mentor's strategies and choices.

Mentors need to know when to intervene and when to allow learning from mistakes to occur. They also need to be reflective and encourage open and honest reflection with their mentees. Keeping journals, shadowing, storytelling, and visioning can all help in this process. Sponsorship involves not only nominating mentees for desirable positions but also creating opportunities to allow the mentee's skills to be seen by others. It also involves actively introducing interns to those in the education system who can help advance their career. Mentor selection is a critical part of any mentoring program.

At least four characteristics should be considered in mentor selection: successful and well-regarded school leaders who have strong character reputations, commitment to mentoring and their own development as a mentor, commitment to being learners themselves, and time to mentor. Matching mentees with the right mentor is often difficult but is thought to work best when both choice and developmental needs are balanced. Not only should the selection and matching be intentional processes, but also the preparation of mentors should be planned and emphasised. Mentor training should cover the content (the purpose and nature of the scheme), methods (teaching/coaching, reflecting. sponsoring), and assessment of mentoring.

The benefits of mentoring for the mentees can be summarised as: exposure to new ideas and creativity; visibility with key personnel; protection from damaging situations; opportunities for challenging and risk-taking activities; increased confidence and competence; improved reflection. But because mentoring is an active, reciprocal learning process, mentoring has benefits for mentors as well. These include: learning new skills; opportunity to critically evaluate their own processes; renew interest in teaching; increase own career networks; increase their importance to the larger education system; long-lasting friendships/supporters.

Pitfalls of mentoring include: mentors may have their own agendas that do not include the best interests of the mentee; mentee dependence on the mentor; mentors trying to clone mentees in their own image; an overly cosy and comfortable relationship that results in a support of instrumental and conservative views and a perpetuation of the status quo.

What is clear in techniques such as the internship and mentoring is that emphasis is put on the links between leadership style and the culture of the organisation: a movement away from the notion of leadership as transactional to the notion of leadership as transformational having the potential to alter the cultural context in which people work. Inevitably, there seems to be a preoccupation with 'transactional' models in systems where strong central control has been retained, while in those systems where decentralisation has been most evident, considerable interest in 'transformational' models has emerged.

Dimension in the Professional Development

Three dimensions of professional development of school leaders are proposed for attention. These dimensions are content/design, delivery mode and measures of success. First, the content of school leader professional development depends in part heavily on how the role of school leader is conceived - teacher, administrator, and/or transformational manager of learning organisations.

Gronn argues that "compared with the [past] processes of managerial and leadership professionalisation ..., the [more recent] idea of customised leader formation represents a substantial, paradigmatic break with precedent. Under ascriptive- and meritocratic-based systems the relations between providers and beneficiaries operated, for the most part, in the interests of the suppliers of the requisite knowledge, skill and values. With customisation, however, the reverse situation prevails and provider-beneficiary relations are increasingly subject to the discipline of the market. And the market for future leaders tends to be demand-driven. The assurances sought by market beneficiaries under customisation arrangements (typically, the employers of prospective educational leaders) are that their recruits will be suitably, rather than simply naturally, or even formally, fitted as previously."

Gronn points out that, while the precise institutional nature of customised leader formation is still taking shape around the world, three core elements are distinguishable. These are: national or system-wide standards of effective leadership, coupled with accredited diagnostic assessment of the performance potential of individuals against those standards, and a likely increased reliance on commercially contracted search agencies as the most risk-averse means of guaranteeing the selection of school leader recruits in conformity with desired sets of standards.

Hipp and Huffman's research in USA on professional learning communities, schools that continuously inquire and seek to improve teaching and learning, has also found that, "Beyond doubt, the preparation of school administrators is key." In contrast to Gronn's description of what is happening in the customisation of school leader professional development, these researchers argue that, "Educational administration programs need to prepare potential school leaders to move beyond issues of management, and provide practical experiences that focus on relationships and learning outcomes. . . . Specifically, leadership preparation programs must guide potential leaders in the following: establishing collaborative decision-making, developing a shared vision, aligning the energies of diverse groups of people, supporting the interdependency of individuals in the organisation, and providing opportunities for shared learning among staff."

In fact, in the current literature on continuing professional development three broad conceptualisations are readily identifiable. These conceptualisations are knowledge for, in and of practice. They can be seen as a continuum, at one end of the spectrum teachers/leaders are cast in the role of implementers of knowledge generated by experts and formulated by policy elites that they bring back to their schools and put into practice in their daily routines. In response to this extreme there is acknowledgement of teacher/

leader craft knowledge that cannot be ignored if school cultures are to be transformed in significant ways. A third way takes issue with both these perspectives and suggests teacher/leader knowledge is both local and public simultaneously and while professional learning is context specific wider social forces shape it significantly also.

There is increasing importance placed in the content of professional development of school leaders on values. Caldwell , for example, identifies a set of six values that underpin what he calls a new sense of the public good - access, equity, choice, growth, efficiency, and harmony. Begley argues that acquiring administrative sophistication is a function of understanding the influence of personal values on organisational and social practices. Partly as a result of working with groups of school administrators in Canada, Barbados, Sweden, Australia, and Russia, Begley identifies four.motivational bases of values and seven sources of values and value conflicts.

Second, a wide variety of delivery modes of school leader professional development can be identified, including:

— who (university, employer, union, some partnership) - in England recent research has shown that, "School leaders look chiefly to their peers, both within and outside the school, for ideas and inspiration";

— where (on-site, elsewhere, distance, some combination);

— how (course involving lecture, tutorial, problem-based learning, some combination, mentorship, apprenticeship and whether offered full time, part time, in flexible mode); and,

— when (at times most conducive to participants. schools. employer and/or to maximise the transfer of learning)

Mulford pointed out that in respect of the 'how' question. while experiential approaches may be more effective for certain training outcomes, they also tend to involve greater levels of self-disclosure and risk for trainers and trainees alike. They also move the locus of 'control' within training away from the trainer. Further, Mulford reminds us that training strategies need to be considered in light of the characteristics of the learner and the context or setting in which training takes place, as well as the desired learning outcomes. This implies that a balance will always be needed. but moreover that this balance needs to be re-calibrated for particular learning groups within a given programme structure, rather than simply between different programmes with different target groups or objectives.

Clearly, this has very significant messages for the training of trainers – an issue that has received much less attention than programme content or methods in the countries that we have reviewed. Third, and finally, measures of the success of school leader professional development are not widely or readily available. Such measures might include:

— feedback from participants, course designers and course providers on the relevance of content. quality of delivery mode and usefulness of the measurements of success:

— feedback from multiple sources (participants, employers. colleagues, staff, students) on the success, or otherwise, of the school leader after the professional development and/or in a subsequent stage in their career, especially in different types of schools and communities; and.

— measurements of any links between school leader professional development and both teacher and school leader recruitment, development and retention - professional development needs to be of a nature that it acts to attract, support and professionally develop rather than repel, interrogate and blame school leaders.

One specific area that has received growing attention in measuring the success of school leader professional development links standards and performance management. This area clearly develops out of the New Public Management form of educational governance. Leithwood et al compared five sets of standards for educational leadership development from USA, Australia, UK and New Zealand. They found that all five sets had in common an emphasis on financial management including hiring appropriate staff, being a role model, establishing professional development as an ongoing school-wide activity, monitoring and evaluating teacher and pupil progress, using test score to guide curriculum and instruction, wide consultation, parent and community involvement and effective communication to all stakeholders, and valuing diversity.

Missing from the lists were teacher leadership, balancing the full range of duties expected of the school leader, teacher stress and morale, endorsing new programmes in order to aid implementation, consequences of high-stakes testing, marketing, working effectively with school councils, outreach or entrepreneurial functions, and acknowledgement of the political, social and organisational features of the contexts in which leaders work.

Gronn describes the development of school leadership standards in the UK and USA and then identifies a number of serious concerns with this approach. These concerns include their links with.business, the presumed causal connection between heads' actions and learning outcomes on which the entire standards edifice rests, the possibility that they erode significantly the previous voluntarist tradition of diverse and plural forms of professional preparation, and potentially reduce the degree of differentiation amongst the pool of prospective heads for appointment to diverse school communities, and that a daunting standards-driven headship training regime may have a negative impact on headship recruitment.

Mongan and Ingvarson have examined the Australian state of Victoria's principal performance management system and found it wanting in several important respects. In particular they found no attempt to link performance management with improved educational outcomes for students, school improvement or improved quality of management in schools. As a result of reviewing the professional development of principals in UK, New Zealand and Australia, Dempster concludes that the use of standards and competency frameworks for school leaders is in its early stages and that there is little research evidence about the impact and effects of these frameworks.

However, he points to criticism of some of their limitations as including that they are more likely to "concentrate on role definitions acceptable to employers than on professional self-development in fields of interest to individuals working in atypical contexts", fragment professional performance, separate performance from circumstances in which it occurs, and implies a degree of precision difficult to realize in professional settings. In his own country, Australia, he sees system imperatives "being met at the expense of both principals' autonomy and their engagement with the moral and ethical values associated with the profession." Barber has gone as far as to claim that in countries where accountability measures, such as performance management, have undermined teachers' autonomy, there is a recruitment crisis.

These three dimensions in the professional development of school leaders (content, delivery mode and measurement of success) can be found in recent reviews of the area. Ribbins, for example, argues for an approach to school leader professional development which:

— is centrally concerned with improving the quality of schooling and the achievement of pupils;

— is systematic, comprehensive and of high quality;

— makes available continuing opportunities for every career phase;

— has a concern for practical skills but also for a more philosophical approach;

— involves a range of providers;

— provides core training, but supports development opportunities that mean more than this; and,

— is based on the best available evidence and fosters the research that generates this.

Another example is provided by Bredeson who proposes a set of design principles for expanding and legitimising learning opportunities for those in schools. Using the metaphor of architecture and building on empirical research and exemplary practice Bredeson identifies six design themes:

— professional development is about learning, including teachers and principals being part of its design;

— professional expertise is a journey, not a credential;

— opportunities for professional learning are unbounded;

— student learning, professional development and organisational mission are intimately related; and,

— professional development is about people, not programs and activities.

The proposed stages and dimensions can also be found in two major cross-country studies of the professional development of school leaders. It is to these two studies that we now turn before concluding the paper with some possible implications arising from the material presented.

Some recent cross-country research findings on the professional development of school leaders

Huber and West have provided an overview of established school leadership development believed to represent current best practice from ten different countries. Their analysis is based on eight programme dimensions - aims, content, methods, pattern (such as number of days and the time span needed), status (compulsory or voluntary and relevance for career prospects), and the costs and who bears them. The authors classify the programmes they studied in two ways. The first classification involved the degree of centralisation against two axes, one relating to the level of central control over the education system as a whole, the other relating to the level of central government involvement in the design, delivery and accreditation of programmes. What they find is that in predominantly centralised systems (such as France, Germany, Hong Kong, and Singapore) there are predominantly centralised arrangements for the development of school leaders. Programmes are standardised, closely monitored, mostly mandatory and governments maintain close involvement in the quality assurance process. At the other extreme are New Zealand and the Netherlands. Here, there is considerable autonomy at school level, with local rather than national determination of school objectives and plans.

There is also a thriving local economy providing a range of training programmes and opportunities. The remaining examples are places where there are varying but significant levels of autonomy at school level, but where the general pattern and approach is substantially subsidised. Huber and West make the point that these examples show us how two major preoccupations of politicians can be accommodated; on the one hand school level decision-making and strong local involvement in the direction of schools, on the other, some guarantee that the government is ensuring a supply of suitably trained and experienced candidates will be available to manage the stock of schools. They believe more countries will be moving into this quadrant of the matrix in the coming years.

The second of Huber and West's classifications involves the emphasis given to experience and course-based elements in school leader professional development learning opportunities. They note that the examples fall into three groupings with the emphasis changing from the programme in France, which is heavily experiential to the programme in Hong Kong, which is substantially course- based.

The first group which is centred around experiential methods has adopted development programmes that feature some form of 'internship. The third group, in contrast to the first, tends to rely on traditional, course-based learning, trusting individual programme members to make the link from the course and, perhaps from the workshop, to their workplace, from general 'theory' to their particular practice. The middle group offers a balanced or 'mixed-economy' – showing some emphasis on practical work and applications, but most often within the trainees' own school situations, and with the support of a mentor. At the same time, these programmes seem to offer a strong 'traditional' core of training sessions that are course based.

Huber and West conclude by stating that there are important advantages arising from those programmes that seek to supplement activities in the training room with tasks in the school- centred around experiential methods mixed model centred around courses.

Their research prompted Huber and West to offer eight generalisations about current trends in school leadership preparation:

— increasing attention is being paid to the identification of specific programme aims and objectives – a move from the general to the particular in planning;

— emphasis within training is shifting from maintenance functions onto activities that promote school improvement and explicitly seek to raise standards of achievement;

— increasing emphasis being given to the development of the individual trainee, personal development rather than training for a role, with much greater interest in individual values and how these values act upon the culture within the school;

— growing interest educational or instructional leadership;

— movement away from unconnected 'single issue' or 'single shot' training events towards a more carefully planned and coherent programmes typically offered over a sustained period of at several points in the school leader's career;

— the emergence of new partnership arrangements that have been formed to design, to implement, to monitor and evaluate school leader development programmes - typically, the partners will include representatives from the employing organisations, from educationalists in the university sector and, increasingly, from professional associations that represent school leaders themselves;

— a needed drawing together of theory and practice; and

— emerging convergence of curriculum content onto teaching and learning issues and the personal and interpersonal skills of leadership.

Dempster also uses two intersecting continua to define four orientations to professional development: system reconstruction or reproduction and a focus on people or system.

— An emphasis on system reproduction and the system results in a 'system maintenance' orientation towards professional development. Under this orientation educational leader professional development is likely to be competency-based, linked to central authority policies and priorities and focussed on authorities, responsibilities and accountabilities.

— A focus on system reconstruction and the system results in a 'system restructuring' orientation. Professional development here would assist a school leader develop values and attitudes consistent with the system, make changes in the structure and function of their school in system-determined directions, work towards system-nominated change outcomes within set budgets, and in gathering and using system-stipulated performance data.

— The combination of a system reproduction and a focus on people results in a 'professional sustenance' orientation. School leader professional development here would be based on issues arising from 'on-the-job', be linked to the leader's personal definition of professional identity and be consonant with ethical professional independence.

— The final combination of system reconstruction and a focus on people results in a 'professional transformation' orientation. Professional development for the school leader under this orientation would undertake constructive social, system and organisational critique, question taken-for-granted understandings, analyse and reshape personal and collective professional knowledge, and reconstruct schooling and school leadership in alternative ways.

Dempster's own involvement in professional development for school principal projects spanning four countries led him to state that system focused orientations dominated and that there "is little evidence that 'the other side of the coin', the people side is receiving similar attention." He concludes that, "principals' professional development requires a fine balance between learning what the system requires of individual leaders and what practising professionals requires of themselves and their colleagues ... [but that] achieving this balance is not easy when the demands of day-to-day administration coupled with loyalty to employers draws principals learning towards system initiatives, priorities and policies and the certainty of effective routines."

Educational Concerns for the Future

There has been a great deal of progress worldwide over the past half century towards implementation of the right to education in terms of access to education, it nevertheless remains that the vision that came to be embodied in Article 26 of the Universal Declaration of Human Rights was not just a quantitative one. It was also a qualitative one concerning the purposes and hence contents of education. For those who drew up and adopted the Declaration, education should aim to foster the best elements in the human spirit while promoting respect for human rights and fundamental freedoms generally.

Quite early in the drafting of Article 26, therefore, the question of education's purposes and contents, and the related question of parental choice, emerged as central to the task of formulating a complete conception of the right to education. Paragraphs (2) and (3) of Article 26 were the result:

(2) Education shall be directed to the full development of the human personality and to the strengthening of respect for human rights and fundamental freedoms. It shall promote understanding, tolerance and friendship among all nations, racial or religious groups, and shall further the activities of the United Nations for the maintenance of peace.

(3) Parents have a prior right to choose the kind of education that shall be given to their children.

It is not easy to assess progress in regard to the implementation of these principles. Yet, the original rationale for propounding them surely remains as valid today as half a century ago. Although international tensions have abated since the end of the Cold War, there still remains everywhere the challenge to develop a veritable 'Culture of Peace'. The persistence of racial, ethnic and religious antagonisms in different parts of the world, and their degeneration into violence and armed conflict, even genocide, in certain cases in recent years, bear ample witness.

International concern for the purposes and contents of education has increased over the past decade, as societies in every region of the world struggle to cope with unprecedented political, economic, social and cultural challenges. Already at the beginning of the 1990s it was recognized that if young people learn little from their education – especially their basic education – then the purposeful nature of education itself is in question: Whether or not expanded educational opportunities will translate into meaningful development – for an individual or for society – depends ultimately on whether people actually learn as a result of those opportunities, i.e., whether they incorporate useful knowledge, reasoning ability, skills, and values. The focus of basic education must, therefore, be on actual learning acquisition and outcome, rather than exclusively upon enrolment, continued participation in organized programmes and completion of certification requirements. Yet, demands for education to contribute towards the solution of problems in diverse fields of global concern have multiplied. Increasingly it is realized that the consolidation of peace is inextricably linked to the prospects of achieving sustainable development and the eradication of poverty, and that effective education is a prerequisite for achieving these goals.

Education for Peace, Human Rights and Democracy

In the early decades following the proclamation of the Universal Declaration of Human Rights, the international context was not favourable to the exchange of views and experience among countries concerning the purposes and contents of education, at least in the areas specifically mentioned by the Declaration.

The Cold War was at its height and many peoples were struggling to free themselves from colonialism. Peace and human rights were contested subjects, foci of discord as much as of harmony between nations. At the national level, the emphasis of educational policies in probably the majority of countries was primarily quantitative rather than qualitative: expansion of access to education at all levels and adjustment of educational structures, contents and methods mainly with a view to facilitating this. International discussion and debate concerning the contents of education focused primarily on their updating and modernization, and related improvements in teaching methods. The themes treated at the annual International Conferences on Public Education during this period are indicative: in the twenty years following the adoption of the Universal Declaration of Human Rights, the purposes of education spelled out in Article 26 were the main focus of discussion and debate just twice.

The first international treaty specifically concerning education that was adopted after the proclamation of the

Universal Declaration of Human Rights – the Convention against Discrimination in Education – utilized exactly the same wording as Article 26 of the Declaration in its statement of the purposes of education.

In 1974, an international Recommendation specifically concerning the purposes and contents of education was adopted, with a focus on education for international understanding, cooperation and peace and education relating to human rights and fundamental freedoms. Its contents were drawn in part from an earlier recommendation on education for international understanding adopted by the International Conference on Public Education in 1968 .

The 1974 Recommendation was to be influential, serving in many countries as a basic reference source for national policies aiming to strengthen the 'international' dimension in the contents of education. In certain respects it was ahead of its time, notably in its emphasis on the need for education to stimulate an 'awareness of the increasing global interdependence between peoples and nations'. When this Recommendation was reviewed by the International Conference on Education twenty years later, agreement was reached that it should be supplemented by an up-to-date Declaration and Integrated Framework of Action on Education for Peace, Human Rights and Democracy.

The use of the term 'democracy' was an innovation compared to the 1974 Recommendation, which had referred to 'human rights and fundamental freedoms', but it had been evoked in the Universal Declaration of Human Rights itself (in Article 29) and in the Preamble of UNESCO's Constitution, and had been utilized a year earlier in the

Declaration adopted by the International Congress on Education for Human Rights and Democracy (Montreal, 1993), and again a few months later in the Declaration adopted by the World Conference on Human Rights (Vienna, 1993):

> States should strive to eradicate illiteracy and should direct education towards the full development of the human personality and to the strengthening of respect for human rights and fundamental freedoms. The World Conference on Human Rights calls on all States and institutions to include human rights, humanitarian law, democracy and rule of law as subjects in the curricula of all learning institutions in formal and nonformal settings (Vienna Declaration and Programme of Action, para. 79).

Following up on the Montreal and Vienna Declarations, the General Assembly of the United Nations in 1994 proclaimed the ten-year period beginning 1 January 1995 as 'United Nations Decade for Human Rights Education', while also proclaiming 1995 as 'United Nations Year for Tolerance'.

In 1995, the General Conference of UNESCO adopted the Declaration of Principles on Tolerance, Article 1 of which explains that

> Tolerance is respect, acceptance and appreciation of the rich diversity of our world's cultures, our forms of expression and ways of being human. It is fostered by knowledge, openness, communication, and freedom of thought, conscience and belief. Tolerance is harmony in difference. It is not only a moral duty, it is also a political and legal requirement. Tolerance, the virtue that makes peace possible, contributes to the replacement of the culture of war by a culture of peace.

In 1999, the General Assembly of the United Nations adopted the Declaration on a Culture of Peace, Article 4 of which proclaims that 'Education at all levels is one of the principal means to build a culture of peace. In this context, human rights education is of particular importance'.

Looking back over the whole period from 1948 onwards, the international community's vision of education's purposes, as reflected in internationally agreed normative texts relating to 'the strengthening of respect for human rights and fundamental freedoms', the promotion of 'understanding, tolerance and friendship among all nations, racial or religious groups', and furthering 'the activities of the United Nations for the maintenance of peace', has expanded into a much more comprehensive, stated commitment to the principles originally proclaimed in paragraph 2 of Article 26 of the Universal Declaration of Human Rights than could have been foreseen in 1948.

Yet, as much as the treaties, Recommendations and Declarations themselves, if not more so, it has been the surge of practical activities over the past decade in so many countries at the grassroots level, in individual schools and educational institutions, that has given meaning to this commitment. Two areas of activity in particular may be mentioned: civic education and teaching/learning materials in the fields of history, geography and social studies.

Civic education, or 'education for citizenship' as it is sometimes known, has acquired particular significance in countries that have recently adopted democratic political systems, but it has also drawn concern in countries where such systems have long been established and where signs have appeared of low voter turnout, declining participation in the political process, and incidents of aggressive behaviour towards ethnic and cultural minorities.

A large-scale international comparative study of civic education in twenty-four (mainly industrial) countries, currently being carried out by the International Association for the

Evaluation of Educational Achievement (IEA), promises to provide much useful information on the variety of national experiences in this area.

International cooperation in developing appropriate teaching and learning materials to further the ideals embodied in the Charter of the United Nations and the Universal Declaration of Human Rights is still a relatively modest aspect of international cooperation in the field of education generally.

Throughout the period of the Cold War, from the late 1940s until the late 1980s, it was kept alive mainly by UNESCO, by means of publications, workshops, symposia and other activities designed to facilitate the exchange of views and experience among educators in different countries.

In cooperation with the United Nations Centre for Human Rights, the first International Congress on the Teaching of Human Rights was organized in Vienna in 1978, and a second such Congress in Malta in 1987. Among the Organization's best-known activities, the Associated Schools Project, launched in 1953 with 33 secondary schools (in 15 countries) aiming to experiment in new methods of teaching pupils about foreign countries and peoples, human rights and the activities of the United Nations, has since grown into a worldwide network of over 6,000 schools in 163 countries.

The activities of the Associated Schools today are focused on four main themes: global challenges and the role of the United Nations system; human rights; knowledge of other countries, respect for different cultures and the world heritage; and the environment.

A more recently established network is the UNESCO International Textbook Research Network, which was started in 1992 in cooperation with the Georg-Eckert-Institut für internationale Schulbuchforschung, Brunswick, Germany. This network, focusing mainly on textbook development and revision in the fields of history, geography and social studies, now extends to over 300 experts in 51 countries located in all regions of the world.

The guiding principles of the network are drawn from the 1974 Recommendation and the Declaration on Education for Peace, Human Rights and Democracy. Concern for the revision of history textbooks has been particularly marked in the past decade in the countries of Eastern Europe and the former USSR. 'Disarming history' was the theme of the recent International Conference on Combating Stereotypes and Prejudice in History Textbooks of SouthEast Europe, organized by UNESCO in Visby, Sweden, in September 1999.

In response to the strong interest in the Asia and Pacific region in values education, the Asia-Pacific Network for International and Values Education (APNIEVE) was set up in 1995 to promote and develop intercountry cooperation among individuals and institutions working in this area, through the organization of seminars and workshops, the exchange of information and personnel and the implementation of joint projects including research, teacher training, curriculum development, and preparation of teaching materials.

Education for Development

The second major theme or focus of the international community's vision of education's purposes that has emerged in the years since the Universal Declaration of Human Rights was proclaimed has been 'development'. Sometimes the emphasis has been on the individual's development, as in the Convention on the Rights of the Child.

At other times the emphasis has been on society's development, or on a particular aspect of it, as in the Programme of Action adopted by the United Nations Conference on Environment and Development. The two aspects of development – individual and social – have in recent years come to be recognized more clearly as interdependent.

The individual's development is stressed in Article 26 ('full development of the human personality'), but the individual is placed firmly in society ('respect for human rights and fundamental freedoms', etc.). An old idea in one form or another in most philosophies of education, the principle that 'Education shall be directed to the full development of the human personality' was adopted almost without debate when Article 26 was drawn up. There only was some brief discussion of whether terms like 'physical', 'intellectual', 'spiritual' and 'moral' should be added to 'personality', but in the interest of keeping the Declaration as concise as possible they were left out.

The idea of 'free and full development of the human personality' was central to the vision of society that inspired the Declaration. In fact, at one stage during the process of drawing up the Declaration, a proposal was actually made to include an Article containing the wording: 'The object of society is to enable all men to develop, fully and in security, their physical, mental and moral personality, without some being sacrificed for the sake of others'.

Elements of this proposal were retained in the final version of the Declaration in both Article 26 and Article 29 (the only Article which mentions 'duties'): in the former case where 'the full development of the human personality' is declared to be a goal to which education shall be directed, and in the latter case where it is declared that 'Everyone has duties to the community in which alone the free and full development of the human personality is possible'.

In this perspective, education that is directed to 'the full development of the human personality and to the strengthening of respect for human rights and fundamental freedoms' can be clearly seen to be an education that is directed to the development of a certain kind of society, indeed, arguably one that provides opportunities, among other things, for 'education for all throughout life'. The development of society in general terms is evoked in the Preamble of the Declaration, in a passage quoted from the Preamble of the Charter of the United Nations that refers to the 'peoples of the United Nations' being 'determined to promote social progress and better standards of life in larger freedom . . .'.

In the first internationally agreed normative text relating to the purposes of education that was adopted after the Declaration was proclaimed, the Declaration of the Rights of the Child (1959), the emphasis was mainly on the individual's development:

> The child is entitled to receive education, which shall be free and compulsory, at least in the elementary stages. He shall be given an education which will promote his general culture, and enable him, on a basis of equal opportunity, to develop his abilities, his individual judgement, and his sense of moral and social responsibility, and to become a useful member of society.
>
> The best interests of the child shall be the guiding principle of those responsible for his education and guidance; that

> responsibility lies in the first place with his parents.
>
> The child shall have full opportunity for play and recreation, which should be directed to the same purposes as education; society and the public authorities shall endeavour to promote the enjoyment of this right
>
> (Declaration of the Rights of the Child, General Assembly Resolution 1386 (XIV) of 20 November 1959 Principle 7, New York, United Nations, 1959).

This emphasis is retained in the Convention on the Rights of the Child (1989).

The Convention against Discrimination in Education, which was adopted the year after the Declaration on the Rights of the Child, retained the original wording of the Universal Declaration of Human Rights in referring to the purposes of education.

The next major internationally agreed normative text relating to the purposes of education, the International Covenant on Economic, Social and Cultural Rights, basically retained the original wording of the Universal Declaration in referring to these purposes but added some extra wording ('sense of its dignity', 'participate effectively in a free society', 'ethnic'). Elsewhere, the Covenant acknowledged a direct link between education and 'economic, social and cultural development', although it associated this link, as was conventional in those days, mainly with technical and vocational training. Thus, paragraph 2 of Article 6 concerning the right to work states:

> The steps to be taken by a State Party to the present Covenant to achieve the full realization of this right shall include technical and vocational guidance and training programmes, policies and techniques to achieve steady economic, social and cultural development and full and productive employment under conditions safeguarding fundamental political and economic freedoms to the individual.

In the 1950s and early 1960s when the Covenant was being drawn up, there was a good deal of faith in many countries in linking education to 'manpower planning', but the idea that education generally is a critical factor in economic growth and development was less often emphasized in national development policies than it is today. In many countries, public expenditure on education was largely regarded as a form of 'consumption' that economic growth made possible rather than as something that could promote such growth; the 'knowledge economy' of today was not foreseen.

In a broader perspective, international consensus on the role of education in 'development'—whether economic, social or cultural – was hostage to the alternative visions of 'development' that prevailed on the two sides of the Cold War. By the 1980s, however, appreciation of the role of 'human capital' had become firmly established in international thinking about economic development, while at the same time, as the Cold War waned, a more humanistic view of development in general also gained ground.

Echoing the Universal Declaration of Human Rights, the Declaration on the Right to Development adopted by the General Assembly of the United Nations in 1986 proclaimed the 'human person [to be] the central subject of development'. Translation of this principle into an internationally agreed Programme of Action designed 'to put people at the centre of development' was achieved a decade later . Since then, even the notions of 'human capital' and 'human resource development' have been questioned, as it comes to be realized that people are not merely 'resources for further production'.

In the comprehensive vision of 'development' that has emerged out of the many international declarations and programmes of action adopted over the past decade, education is increasingly called upon to contribute towards the solution of problems in diverse fields of global concern ranging from poverty to population growth, health (HIV/AIDS, drug abuse) and the environment, although resources for international cooperation in education appear to have recently levelled off.

Educational choice

With consensus now having been reached in the international community that 'peace and development are closely interrelated and mutually supportive', 'education for peace, human rights and democracy' and 'education for development' can be seen as ultimately directed towards the same end: a world 'in which alone the free and full development of the human personality is possible', in effect a world which recognizes 'the inherent dignity and equal and inalienable rights of all members of the human family'. Yet this is a world of learning 'choices' as much as one of learning 'needs', whether these are considered from the standpoint of the individual or that of society.

Recognizing the scope that exists for different approaches in pursuing the agreed purposes, and fearing to accord too much power to the State vis-à-vis the family, those who drew up and adopted the Universal Declaration of Human Rights added the third paragraph: 'Parents have a prior right to choose the kind of education that shall be given to their children'.

Implementation of this principle has not always been easy. In practice, the issue has been less often the principle itself, even though it is still not everywhere recognized. than the question of whether (or to what extent) the State should support different kinds of education for particular groups, especially ethnic, religious or linguistic minorities. Other difficulties, notably those relating to differences in school quality within state school systems, were evoked in the World Education Report 1993.

The first international treaty to include provisions concerning parental choice and the rights of minorities in education was the Convention against Discrimination in Education, which still remains the most comprehensive treatment of the matter in any international treaty. A mostly similar wording in respect to parental choice was adopted later in the International Covenant on Economic, Social and Cultural Rights; 'minorities' are not specifically mentioned, but could be understood to be covered by the reference in Article 13(4) to 'the liberty of individuals and bodies to establish and direct educational institutions', a wording that was adopted again later by the Convention on the Rights of the Child (1989).

The International Covenant on Civil and Political Rights, included in its Article 18 (concerning 'the right to freedom of thought, conscience and religion') a paragraph similar to that of both the UNESCO Convention and the International Covenant on Economic, Social and Cultural Rights, on 'the liberty of parents and, when applicable, legal guardians to ensure the religious and moral education of their children in conformity with their own convictions', and its Article 27 refers specifically to 'minorities', though not to their education. A similar wording, except for the use of the term 'a child' instead of 'persons' and the addition of 'or who is indigenous' after 'minorities', was adopted in Article 30 of the Convention on the Rights of the Child (1959).

In the period since the Convention against Discrimination in Education and the International Covenants were adopted, the main international normative instrument relating to the education of minorities has been the Declaration on the Rights of Persons belonging to National or Ethnic, Religious and Linguistic Minorities, adopted by the General Assembly of the United Nations in 1992. Paragraphs 3 and 4 of Article 4 of this Declaration concern education:

3. States should take appropriate measures so that, wherever possible, persons belonging to minorities may have adequate opportunities to learn their mother tongue or to have instruction in their mother tongue.

4. States should, where appropriate, take measures in the field of education, in order to encourage knowledge of the history, traditions, language and culture of the minorities existing within their territory. Persons belonging to minorities should have adequate opportunities to gain knowledge of the society as a whole.

Paragraph 3 puts a more positive stress on action by the State in regard to teaching and learning in the mother tongue than is given by the more neutral formulation of the Convention against Discrimination in Education. Paragraph 4 also contrasts with the UNESCO Convention by pointing in effect to the need for the community to understand or at least have 'knowledge of' its own minorities, besides the need for 'persons belonging to minorities . . . to gain knowledge of the society as a whole'.

In these respects, the 1992 Declaration amounts to a call for States not only to recognize, in the purposes and contents of their education, the cultural diversity of the population whom the education is intended to serve, but also to promote through education a harmonious appreciation of that diversity. The International Commission on Education for the Twenty-first Century, in a memorable phrase ('Learning to live together'), later called for much the same thing. From this standpoint at least, the fears of unleashing excessive State power over the purposes and contents of education, which originally inspired the third paragraph of Article 26 of the Universal Declaration of Human Rights, would seem not to have been borne out.

Index

Accountability 112
Authentic learning strategies 139

Basic learning needs 2

Collective bargaining rights 126
Commercial skills 3
Compulsory education 26
Cultural minorities 296

Decentralisation 222
Democratization 111

Educational infrastructures 114
Educational policies 111
Educational technology programs, 142
Elementary education 2
Entrepreneurial functions 283

Face-to-face training, 142
Financial management 138
Formal education system 121
Functional literacy 2
Fundamental education 1
Fundamental freedoms 291

Inconsistent Demands 232
Information and Communication Technologies (ICTs) 129
Instructional practices, 240
Intellectual Stimulation 244
Intentional processes, 277
International Bureau of Education (IBE) 122
International consensus 8
International Council for Educational Development 32
International Society for Technology in Education 133

Leadership 237
Leadership for Organisational Learning and Student 242
Lifelong educational system 36
Lifelong learning 5

Mass Education 5
Meritocratic-based systems 279

New Public Administration (NPM) 218, 219
Non-governmental organizations 40
Noninstructional purposes 138
Noninstructional tasks 133

Office for Standards in Education (OFSTED) 226

Old Public Administration" (OPA) 219
Organisational Learning (OL) 218, 229, 252
Organizational learning 246

Pedagogical application 138
Peer-to-peer sharing 132
Popular Education 5
Professional development programmes 217

Quality professional development 273

Socio-Economic Status (SES) 253

Teacher professional development 131
Teacher training approaches 142
Technical and Vocational Education (TVE) 59
Technological skills 134
Technology-based activities 134
Technology-enhanced learning, 140
Time-consuming activities 135

United Nations Children's Fund (UNICEF) 32

Web-based instruction 130